Caroline Keen holds a PhD from the School of Oriental and African Studies (SOAS), University of London. She is the author of *Princely India and the British: Political Development and the Operation of Empire* (I.B.Tauris).

'This is an exciting story and it is well told by a confident and engaging author. The Manipur incident, though small scale, is important, because it shows that it was impossible to work out a "one size fits all" pattern for the government of India in dealing with the Native States, that is, those not under direct Government of India rule. In its dealings with Manipur, the government got it wrong on all counts – it was a classic British fudge of ignoring the man nearest to the situation, Frank Grimwood, and getting boxed into a corner from which there was no retreat. Grippingly told, this is a valuable addition to the story of colonial India.'

– Rosie Llewellyn-Jones, author of *The Last King in India*

AN IMPERIAL CRISIS IN BRITISH INDIA

The Manipur Uprising of 1891

CAROLINE KEEN

BLOOMSBURY
NEW DELHI • LONDON • OXFORD • NEW YORK • SYDNEY

BLOOMSBURY INDIA
Bloomsbury Publishing India Pvt. Ltd
Second Floor, Building No. 4
DDA Complex LSC, Pocket C – 6 & 7
Vasant Kunj, New Delhi 110070
www.bloomsbury.com

BLOOMSBURY, Bloomsbury Academic India and the Diana logo are trademarks of Bloomsbury Publishing Plc

First published in India 2020
First published in 2015 by
I.B.Tauris & Co. Ltd
London. New York
www.ibtauris.com

British Library Cataloguing-in-Publication Data
A catalogue record for this book is available from the British Library.

Library of Congress Cataloging-in-Publication Data
A catalog record for this book is available from the Library of Congress

ISBN: 978-93-90358-29-8
10 9 8 7 6 5 4 3 2 1

For sale in the Indian subcontinent only

Exclusively distributed in the Indian subcontinent by
Manohar Publishers & Distributors
4753/23, Ansari Road
Darya Ganj, New Delhi 110002
Tel.: 23284848, 23289100
Email: sales@manoharbooks.com, manoharbooks@gmail.com

Typeset in Garamond Three by OKS Prepress Services, Chennai,India

Digitally Printed and bound in India by Replika Press Pvt. Ltd.

CONTENTS

LIST OF ILLUSTRATIONS

LIST OF MAPS

FAMILY TREE: DESCENDANTS OF GARIB NIWAZ

APPENDIX V. DESCENDANTS OF GARIB NIWAZ
(main lines only)

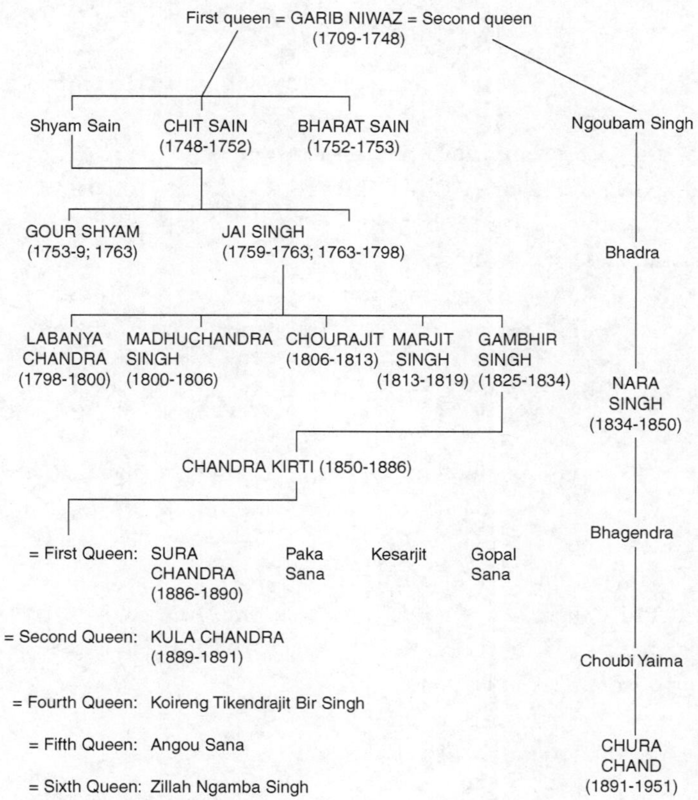

DRAMATIS PERSONAE

The Palace

Angao Senna, prince of Manipur

Bhairabijit Singh, Pucca Senna, prince of Manipur and commander of the horse

Chandra Kirtee Singh, maharaja of Manipur 1850–86

Chura Chand, maharaja of Manipur 1891–1941

Gopal Senna, prince of Manipur and Dooloroi Hengeba or commander of the doolies

Jatra Singh, keeper of the maharaja's stores

Kesarjit Singh, prince of Manipur and Samoo Hengeba or commander of the elephants

Kula Chandra Singh, Jubraj or crown prince; known later as regent

Mia Major, army commander

Nilamani Singh, Ayapurel or officer in charge of the maharaja's escort

Samoo Singh, the Luang Ningthou, high-ranking official and member of the Top Guard

Sur Chandra, maharaja of Manipur 1886–90

Thangal General, formerly army chief and minister of state

Tikendrajit Bir Singh, alias Koireng, prince of Manipur and Senapati, or commander in chief

Usurba, guard attached to Quinton's party

Zillah Singh, youngest prince of Manipur

The Residency

Frank St Clair Grimwood, political agent in Manipur 1888–91
Ethel St Clair Grimwood, wife of Frank
Col. James Johnstone, political agent in Manipur 1877–86
Lt. W. H. Simpson, 43rd Gurkha Light Infantry, visiting detachment at Langthobal
Rassik Lal Kundu, head clerk to Political Agency

The Chief Commissioners' Escort

Capt. T. S. Boileau, 44th Gurkha Rifles (GR)
Lt. L. W. Brackenbury, 44th GR
Capt. G. H. Butcher, 42nd GR
Surgeon J. T. Calvert, medical officer 42nd GR
Lt. J. B. Chatterton, 42nd GR
W. Cossins, assistant secretary to chief commissioner of Assam
Capt. J. W. Cowley, 43rd GR, commanding detachment from Cachar
Durga Dutt, *jemadar* 44th GR
Gunna Ram, bugler 44th GR
Lt. P. R. Gurdon, assistant commissioner of Assam
Lt. E. J. Lugard, 42nd GR
J. W. Quinton, chief commissioner of Assam
Col. C. McDowall Skene, 42nd GR commanding escort
Lt. C. S. Williams, 43rd GR, in Cowley's detachment
Signaller C. S. Williams, telegraph officer
Lt. Albert Woods, assistant commissioner of Assam

Field Force

Birbal Nagarkoti, *jemadar* of 43rd Gurkha Rifles in charge of Langthobal detachment
Brig.-Gen. H. Collett, commanding officer of Assam District and commander of the Manipur field force (Kohima column)
Capt. F. M. Drury, commanding reconnaissance party, 4th Gurkha Rifles

Brig.-Gen. T. Graham, commanding officer of Myingyan District of Burma and commander of the Tammu column

Lt. C. J. W. Grant, 12th Burma Rifles, stationed at Tammu

Major H. St John Maxwell, deputy commissioner in Cachar and president of the court for trial of senior Manipuri officers; political agent in Manipur 1891–3, 1895–6, 1899–1902 and 1904–5

Lt.-Col. St John F. Michell, in Cachar column and president of the court for trial of princes

Lt.-Col. R. H. Rennick, commander of Cachar column

Major R. K. Ridgeway, 44th GR in Kohima column and member of court for trial of princes

Others

Viscount Cross, secretary of state for India

A. W. Davis, assistant political officer in Kohima and member of court for trial of princes

Capt. du Moulin, correspondent of *The Allahabad Pioneer*

Col. H. M. Evans, 43rd Gurkha Rifles, and president of military Court of Enquiry

The Marquess of Lansdowne, viceroy of India

Mano Mohun Ghose, advocate of the High Court in Calcutta

W. B. Melville, superintendent of the Telegraph Department in Assam

J. O'Brien, telegraph officer

Sir Frederick Roberts, commander in chief in India

MANIPUR UPRISING TIME LINE

May 1886:

Maharaja Chandra Kirtee Singh dies; succeeded by his son, Sur Chandra Singh.

Mid-1888:

Frank St Clair Grimwood first promoted to political agent in Manipur.

September 1890:

Abdication of Maharaja Sur Chandra Singh.

22 March 1891:

Chief Commissioner's party arrives in Manipur. First *durbar* postponed.

23 March:

Second *durbar* postponed.

24 March:

4:45am: Brackenbury proceeds to north gate of fort.

5am: Butcher and Simpson depart with assault party to Senapati's residence.

8am: Simpson reports Brackenbury party surrounded.

9am: Chatterton takes main gate of fort.

10am: Skene's detachment joins Butcher's assault party.

10:30am: Calvert reaches Senapati's temple.

12pm: Skene returns to residency. Counter-attack on residency from Naga village.
4:30pm: Butcher's party and Skene's detachment return from Senapati's residence.
4:45pm: Simpson and Calvert return with wounded to camp; Chatterton ordered to retire from main gate.
5pm: Repositioning of enemy; incessant rifle fire on residency until 8pm.
8pm: Ceasefire sounded; wounded moved into residency cellar.
9:30pm: Chief Commissioner and party proceed to main gate of fort.
11:30pm: Chief Commissioner and party enter fort.

25 March:
2am: Survivors leave residency.
Jemadar Birbal Nagarkoti leaves Langthobal for Tammu.
Melville and O'Brien attacked at Myangkhang by Nagas.

26 March:
8am: Survivors reach main Cachar road, and at noon meet up with Cowley.

27 March:
Signaller Williams captured between Sengmai and Kohima.

28 March:
5:30am: Grant leaves Tammu for Manipur.

31 March:
Grant reaches Thobal.

3–5 April:
Negotiations between Grant, Williams and Manipuri commanders.

7 April:
Williams released from jail.

9 April:
Grant ordered to retire.

10 April:
Grant meets up with Presgrave.

25 April:
Grant and Nagarkoti wounded outside Palel.

27 April:
Three columns reach Manipur.

30 April:
Funeral of murdered officers.

7 May:
Thangal General surrenders.

9 May:
Regent arrested.

23 May:
Senapati arrested.

1–2nd October:
Gurkha Rifles leave for India.

November:
Mountain battery leave for Burma; 44th Gurkha Rifles leave for Shillong.

9 March 1892:
Expeditionary arrangements cease at Manipur.

29 April 1892:
Installation of Chura Chand as raja.

ACKNOWLEDGEMENTS

As I was sifting though India Office records some years ago in search of nineteenth-century material on the Indian princely states, the hair-raising accounts of news unfolding in the small north-eastern state of Manipur in 1891 succeeded frequently in luring me away from pedestrian governmental reports. I was determined to return at a later stage to explore more deeply what was obviously a remarkable story of the violent uprising which occurred against the backdrop of a beautiful, remote corner of India in the spring of 1891, and this book is the result of research undertaken between 2004 and 2009. Since Manipur and the events of 1891 were largely unknown territory in England, I was to a great extent working in a vacuum; however I owe a huge amount to the help of Professor John Parratt who, with his wife, Saroj, wrote an excellent book in 1991 to commemorate the centenary of the Manipur revolt, and is a fund of knowledge on the state and its history. Miles Taylor's help in spurring me on to publication has yet again been invaluable, and I am most grateful to Rosie Llewellyn-Jones for ploughing through the manuscript, to Neil Faulkner for his comments and to Richard Mead and Lieutenant Colonel Moirangthem Ranjit Singh for their expert advice on military matters. The staff of Asian and African Studies in the British Library were, as always, unfailingly helpful. Azmina Siddique of

I.B.Tauris has been a great support in dealing with pre-publication issues and I am grateful to Ian Macdonald for such painstaking copy-editing. Finally, my thanks go to my husband, Nigel, and my sons, Dominic and Thomas, for their interest and encouragement throughout the gestation of the book.

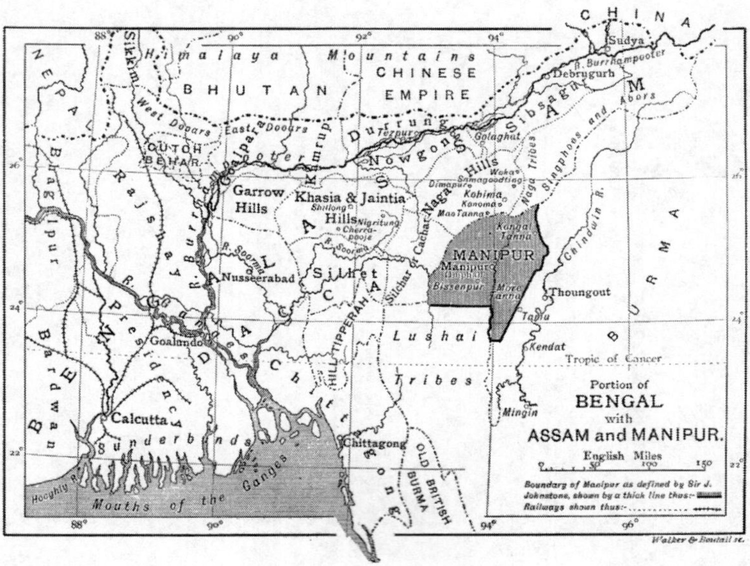

Map 1 Map of Manipur and the Naga Hills, James Johnstone, 1896 (Pictures from History).

INTRODUCTION

At the end of the nineteenth century, two-fifths of the Indian subcontinent consisted of states governed by hereditary princes of varying rank who recognised British sovereignty. Attached to these rulers in an advisory capacity were a minimal number of British officers in the Indian Political Service. When matters ran smoothly, in accordance with the well-defined terms of treaties drawn up between the British and individual princes, indirect rule proved a cheap and fairly undemanding system of imperial control. Nevertheless, the Indian princes proved to be a constant thorn in the flesh of the British. Not on the whole an acutely painful problem, but a niggling irritation for which, due to the complexity of Indian royalty and the relationship between ruler and ruled, it was hard to find a lasting solution.

In the half century up to 1857, the majority of princes had been placed firmly under the British thumb, many defeated in battle and their states swallowed up into the territory of an expanding British India. However the events of the Indian Mutiny were to change this dynamic. The loyalty of the reigning princes during the revolt demonstrated clearly the potential of the Indian states as a political force in support of British rule, counterbalancing anti-imperialist elements. Although gross princely misrule was never tolerated after 1857, the British were forced to walk a tightrope of diplomacy as far as the Indian states were concerned until Independence in 1947. The tentacles of the Political Department of the Government of India might squeeze the princes tighter from time to time, and viceroys differed in their approach to individual rulers, but there was a constant awareness of the need to maintain the bulk of royal support for the British cause.

However government officials were always highly sensitive to any development or incident within princely territory which might injure its prestige or infringe its rights. Not surprisingly, the task of attempting to formulate a single policy with which to deal with the vagaries of over 600 individual states proved an impossibility. When faced with a crisis the Government of India frequently vacillated, acting too little and too late in its attempts to avoid rocking the princely boat while maintaining a tough imperialist stance. The story of the uprising of exceptional violence and intense anti-British feeling which occurred in the small north-eastern state of Manipur in 1891 illustrates clearly this lack of decisiveness.

The Manipur revolt was a unique event in princely Indian history in the latter half of the nineteenth century, and proved during that time to be the greatest single military challenge to British rule after the Indian Mutiny. Although there were extreme cases of misgovernment within states, which warranted royal depositions – as in the cases of the Gaekwar of Baroda in 1875 and the Maharaja of Jhalawar in 1896 – such disciplinary action by the Government of India was by and large accepted by the local population and provoked no violent response. In Manipur, where no such misgovernment was evident, the armed rebellion which followed British intervention in royal affairs was without precedent at the height of the Raj, and disastrous consequences followed the ill-considered British use of intimidation and the cavalier underestimation of fierce native loyalty to princely rule.

This account of the Manipur revolt is told almost entirely by those who were involved in the events of 1891 and their repercussions. As with all historical accounts, there are many sides to the same story, portraying the fortitude and flaws which formed an essential part of the fabric of empire.

CHAPTER 1

THE ROAD TO MANIPUR

At the end of the nineteenth century, the British official heading for the first time towards a posting in the north-east of India would have undoubtedly been lulled into a false sense of security. Calcutta, the port of disembarkation, was a city which at first sight left no doubt as to the power and ability of the British Raj. Having negotiated the bizarre currents and numerous sandbanks of the Hoogly River, from all accounts the view was most imposing. The Strand in the foreground bristled with masts of ships from every corner of the world, with a background of substantial white buildings, their windows enlivened by bright green sun shutters. The city extended for several miles along the banks of the river and contained a large number of remarkably fine edifices, notably Government House, the residence of the Viceroy of India, the Cathedral, the High Court, the Medical College, Post Office and Museum. A prominent feature of Calcutta was the Maidan, a large grassy area lying between the city and the river. In this space stood Fort William, the largest and most important British fortress in India, covering a space of about 2 square miles. On the land side the Maidan was bounded by Chowringee Road, the site of many of the most opulent houses in Calcutta. East of Chowringee Road were streets consisting chiefly of European residences, and to the north of Government House lay the business quarter of the city, with handsome shops, large hotels, and palatial banks and business houses of every description. The principal thoroughfares of the city were broad, well kept and watered. However beyond these, and largely out of sight of new arrivals, were filthy, badly drained alleys and the large and densely populated native city with its crowded lanes and busy markets.[1]

Despite the impressive proportions of the city, for the British traveller passing through Calcutta there was only one reasonable hotel, the Great Eastern, the lower section of which was fitted up as a huge store in which last-minute purchases could be made before departing up-country. A journey to Upper Assam from any part of India was a considerable undertaking in the latter part of the nineteenth century. The simplest route was to leave Calcutta at night by train in order to strike the Brahmaputra at Goalundo early next morning to board a steamer which visited three main ports of call: Gauhati, 200 miles upriver, in order to disembark for Shillong; Nigriting, a further 150 miles, to disembark for Kohima in the Naga Hills and the princely state of Manipur; and yet another 100 miles to Dibrugarh, further up the valley. Until 1891, Shillong and Dibrugarh were the British military stations of Assam. Travelling by the Eastern Bengal Railway from Calcutta to Goalundo was easily accomplished in eight or nine hours, however the line was so badly laid, the rattle of the trains passing over the shaky wooden bridges so painful, and the cars so stuffy that a journey on this line was not a happy experience. The first-class carriages were fitted with sleeping bunks in double tiers, as in a cabin on board ship, but the constant vibration made sleep an impossibility. The stretch of country was flat and uninteresting, although at night bizarrely illuminated by a multitude of fireflies.

Goalundo consisted of a collection of small huts erected on the banks at the meeting of the Ganges and Brahmaputra rivers. It was the terminus of the railway and, as the tea planter and seasoned traveller George M. Barker observed upon arrival at the benighted place, 'the confines of the whole civilised world'.[2] The inhabitants of the town were frequently flooded out, a somewhat depressing situation to which they had become reconciled, and twice in the course of the year were forced to move house, according to the dry or rainy season when the river fell or rose to a significant degree. Under these variable conditions there was little point in constructing a house of any substance; for half the year it would be uninhabitable. Even during the dry season the width of the river at Goalundo was considerable, with a huge volume of water flowing at a rapid rate.

An army of natives surrounded the railway station, acting as porters to transport luggage from train to steamer. From contemporary illustrations, a river steamer was a bizarre-looking contraption: a 'huge black and white mass of floating wood and iron work'[3] which looked disturbingly top heavy. All river steamers were constructed with paddles in order to draw as little water as possible and each towed one or two tenders, lashed to her sides by wire cables to carry cargoes of goods from Calcutta on the journey upriver and tea and jute on the way down. The forward upper saloon deck of the steamer, reserved for first-class passengers, was comfortably arranged with cabins and a dining saloon, and the rear part of the upper deck was set aside for servants or other native passengers. A thick roof, consisting of either corrugated iron or bamboo covered in thatch, ran the whole length of the upper deck for protection against sun or bad weather. Cargo, coal, stores, cookhouse, and pens for sheep and fowls to be used on the journeys were accommodated on the lower deck, an area which was rarely visited by the occupants of the upper deck due to the general squalor.

Between Goalundo and the first port of call on the river, Dhubri, the scenery was by all accounts exceedingly tedious. Little broke the line of the long low-lying banks of sand that bordered the Brahmaputra. Every now and again there was a small area of vegetation to enhance the view, and around these oases a few wooden huts had been constructed and occupied by fishermen. This stage of the journey took between four and five days, and 'for intense monotony could only be equalled to an expedition into the great Sahara'.[4] However it was not unusual for excitement of a somewhat unpleasant nature to be caused by a sandstorm if there was a strong wind. Visible from three or four miles away, and approaching at a great rate, a cloud of whirling sand would penetrate every orifice – even creeping under the lid of a tightly shut case. Above Dubri the scenery rapidly improved. The banks were no longer of grey sand but green grass, and the magnificent peaks of the snow-clad Himalayas formed a spectacular background to the vast expanse of level territory lying between the river and the first outlying spur of hills.

During the cold season dense fog frequently hung close over the surface of the river, giving an uneasy sense of foreboding and adding greatly to the problems of the already challenging navigation. Sometimes the fog was so heavy that the steamer could not continue on her way until noon. To add to the delays, on a dark night it was impossible to make progress. Even with bright moonlight to illuminate the channel the risk was extremely great, and usually each evening at sundown the anchor was dropped and the vessel made comfortable for the night. At the first sign of daylight the anchor was heaved up, 'amidst a fearful din caused by escaping steam, rattling cables, and yelling Lascars'[5] and the voyage continued.

The chief difficulty in navigating the Brahmaputra arose from the shifting nature of its bed. Month by month there were changes; huge banks of sand in the centre of the river were submerged and disappeared, only to reappear in a new locality. This process occurred rapidly, and a channel that was navigable one day could in two or three days' time become quite impassable. To deal with such an unknown quantity the river was divided into various sections, each of which had to furnish a supply of pilots for the steamer service. A pilot's life was hardly one of undiluted pleasure. Frequently kept waiting on the banks of the river for two or three days at a time when the steamer was late, exposed to all kinds of weather and uncertain of when he might see his home again, he inevitably faced the perils of the treacherous currents when he leapt for the shore at the end of his duty. In addition, if the hapless man through bad piloting ran the vessel aground, he was subject to the rage of a captain who failed to see the humour of being stuck high and dry on a sandbank tenanted by alligators and turtles, sometimes for days if the river was falling after the rains.

Gauhati was the most important station of Assam and the nearest point of disembarkation for Shillong, the hill station famous for the regiment quartered there and the headquarters of the Chief Commissioner. In the garden of the rest house at Gauhati, which stood on a small hill overlooking the river, were several old guns, relics of the Burmese occupation of Assam from 1817 to 1826. Many of the hills in the area were studded with tea bushes, and the bright green of the leaves covered the hills in regular lines like those of a chessboard. There was a large bazaar and a number of temples built of red brick, with imposing carved figures in relief and curiously shaped gods carved out of the solid rock face. After the city the flat country, with its unvarying monotony, again intervened between the Himalayas on one side and the Naga Hills on the other. Steaming upriver from Gauhati the succeeding stations up to Nigriting were similar, but on a considerably smaller scale. The most attractive was deemed to be Tezpore with its accumulation of carefully cut stone scattered about the town, apparently 'beautiful relics of an ancient temple whose foundation-stone was never destined to be laid'.[6]

It was a march of several days' duration from Nigriting via Kohima to the city of Manipur, roughly 200 miles from the Brahmaputra. About a third of the way, and well known to British soldiers who regularly traversed this route, was Dimapur, a deserted city whose ruins lay buried in dense forest. In the vicinity were a number of huge tanks of clear water, the largest of which was at least half a mile long and a quarter of a mile wide. According to legend, a past ruler of Dimapur had ordered that upon his death his body and jewels should be enclosed in a golden boat and sunk in the largest lake. The boat was secured by a strong chain to the bank, which proved too great a temptation for some of the inhabitants, who procured half a dozen elephants and a crowd of men to try to pull it out. The boat emerged a little and then suddenly slipped back, drowning both men and elephants. Rumour had it that Dimapur had been wiped out by invading hordes in the middle of the sixteenth century, and it is quite possible that treasure was indeed hidden in the lake as this was a favourite way of hiding valuables in India. One of the old gateways of the city was still standing, although much damaged by trees growing out of it, and inside the perimeter were rows of curious collapsed pillars, both round and square and intricately carved with lotus flowers, peacocks, tigers and elephants.[7]

Due to its magnificent scenery, the road between the city of Kohima, the capital of Nagaland (by the end of the nineteenth century absorbed into British India), and the state of Manipur was one of the favourite routes for British personnel travelling in the area. Some of the hills were as high as 9,000 feet and yet three days' journey beyond Kohima the road was almost level, winding in and out of narrow valleys. Forests of oak covered the area and in the cold weather the trees lost their foliage, giving the hillsides a ghostly aspect; however on crossing the last ridge from the north the tree jungle disappeared, giving way to hills covered in grass. The valley of Manipur seen at the end of the rainy season was a vast expanse of flat land bordered by hills and mostly covered with water, through which rice crops were growing vigorously. In the dry season it looked very different, with brown dried-up areas in the place of green grass jungle. To the south was the large Logtak Lake, some 7 miles long and up to 2 miles wide, and far away to the north-east the glittering roofs of the temples of Manipur, the capital city of the state, were visible.

The state lay between latitude 24° and 26° north, and longitude 93° and 95° east. In 1891 it was bounded on the west by the British districts

Figure 1.1 The Irang river on the Cachar Road from Manipur (The Alkazi Collection of Photography).

of Cachar and the Naga Hills Agency; to the north by the Naga Hills Agency and primitive Naga tribes;[8] to the east by the Kubo Valley, a portion of Upper Burma; and to the south by a collection of hostile Kuki tribal lands.[9] The total area of the Manipur state was over 8,000 square miles, of which the valley portion comprised only 650 square miles. The valley was in the centre of the large mountainous tracts of Assam, Cachar, Burma and Chittagong and its height was about 2,570 feet above sea level. As a result Manipur contained within its borders a climate which varied from tropical to freezing. Several rivers from the north and west (the Imphal, Irbil and Thobal) flowed past the Logtak Lake where they joined the Kortak, which emerged from the lake, and formed the Namkathe. They were all fordable at any time of the year, but only navigable by dug-out canoes and only within the limits of the valley. The rivers in the hills flowed through deep-cut gorges which were crossed by cane suspension bridges[10] or pontoon bridges formed of large bundles of bamboo. All the rivers were liable to sudden floods and difficult to cross after heavy rain.[11]

The principal features of Manipur were rice fields, swamps, small muddy rivers, bamboo clumps, barren low hills and villages similar to those of East Bengal. It seemed likely that at some stage the entire flat area had been a lake, as the water in the valley was only 2 or 3 feet below the surface of the ground. As the lake dried up the hill people had come down to cultivate the fertile land and gradually settled on it, intermarried, and as a result produced a mixture of the surrounding tribes. The soil of the valley was principally black loam which, according to a nineteenth-century British soldier stationed in the state, 'repays the slightest and rudest cultivation a thousandfold'.[12] The numerous dykes and water ditches throughout the country were full of small fish and a variety of water shrimp, which formed, with rice and milk, the staple diet of the Manipuris and apparently were often eaten rotten out of preference. The hill ranges lying between Cachar in the west and Manipur were densely covered by tree jungle, including India-rubber, oak, ash and bamboo, and on certain slopes teak and fir. In addition the tea plant, wild apricot, plum, apple, pear and peach flourished, together with rhododendrons and wild azaleas of several kinds in the forests, as well as many species of brilliant orchids and, in some areas, an abundance of tree ferns. The mineral resources of the country were very poor, but iron, copper, salt and lime were found in small quantities.

The Manipuris lived in villages placed in long lines on both banks of a river, or on the edge of *jheels*, and each family had some water immediately adjoining its compound. Every house stood in about an acre of its own well-planted land, which was surrounded by a brick wall. The better houses were constructed of wood and bamboo, and the poorer ones built entirely of bamboo. The walls were usually of reed plastered with mud and cow dung. All were thatched with grass, and faced to the east, in which direction a large open veranda was situated where all household work was carried out except cooking, which was performed inside. On the south side of the veranda was the seat of honour, upon which a mat or cloth was laid for the exclusive use of the head of the family. It was generally held by British officers that the people of Manipur were not particularly sanitary in their habits. When heavy rain fell their gardens were flooded, and a fair share of the accumulated filth washed into the drinking-water tanks, the result being frequent epidemics of cholera. Foreigners appeared to suffer much from bronchial afflictions, doubtless owing to the waterlogged soil, however it was generally agreed that if sanitary laws were properly observed the valley might be a most healthy place and the population would rapidly increase.

A British military intelligence report of 1891 described the origin of the Manipuris as obscure. Although they claimed to be of Hindu origin, it was possible that they were the descendants of a Tartar colony which emigrated from the north-west border of China in the thirteenth and fourteenth centuries. The report stated that:

> The general facial characteristics of the Manipuris are of the Mongolian type, but there is a great diversity of feature among them, some them shewing a regularity approaching the Aryan type . . . very good-looking and fair. The Manipuris are decidedly a muscular race, having good chests and well-formed limbs. They are generally spare in habit of body, and fat people are rare . . . The religion of the country is ostensibly Hinduism,[13] but this is apparently of recent introduction, or, according to the pundits, a revival. All the Manipuris are 'Baishnabs' or followers of Vishnu.[14]

At the end of the nineteenth century the valley still possessed a few sacred groves, which were isolated patches of forest left, according to aboriginal custom, for the wood spirits. Colonel James Johnstone, Political Agent in Manipur from 1877 to 1886,[15] a man with a great knowledge of Eastern languages and customs whose aim it was to better the lot of the inhabitants of the state, considered Manipuris to be a 'fine stalwart race' with 'stable and industrious qualities' which in his opinion the neighbouring Burmese did not possess. The occupants of the valley or plain were the Meeteis, the majority ethnic group of Manipur. Fed by additions from the various hill tribes surrounding the valley, the resulting homogenous people possessed great activity and energy, were good-humoured even under extreme difficulties and were never obviously aware of fatigue, even on a long and trying march.[16]

Dues to the state were met by forced labour known as *lalup*, under which every male Manipuri unless exempt by the sovereign was liable to ten days' labour every 30 days. Such labour consisted of personal service at court, cultivation of the maharaja's fields attached to each village and, for the Naga tribesmen, the collection of rubber and tea seed, the latter being the monopoly of the maharaja and his principal source of revenue. Needless to say the burden of *lalup* fell upon the poor, and the rich succeeded entirely in escaping it. When sickness occurred, the *lalup* member had either to carry out his duties or purchase a substitute, and his family was often impoverished as a result. The military capability of the state also depended upon the system, and every Manipuri capable of bearing arms was called out from time to time to go through ten days' training. A small standing army of about 3,000 men was kept up, with about 1,800 soldiers continually on duty along the frontier posts. The remaining 1,200 formed the maharaja's bodyguard, of which 1,000 were infantry armed with Enfield rifles, 'arrayed in old red castoff British tunics with blue dhotis and pagris, drilled and disciplined in English fashion'. The rest were artillerymen and lancers, less efficient than the infantry and 'rather a laughable sight in their big flap Manipuri saddles, mounted on little 11 hand ponies. Many foals trotting after their mothers in the ranks.' Members of the standing army did not receive pay, but were granted land which was cultivated for them through the *lalup* system.[17]

Although the state was declared to be 'wretchedly poor as regards revenue', it appeared to be 'very prosperous as regards the condition of its people'.[18] Destitution and begging were unknown, although a cruel system of slavery existed. Only under very special circumstances was it possible for those persons indentured to the ruling maharaja of Manipur to be released, and upon each of his marriages the ruler passed on several slaves to his new wife's family. Favourite ministers and others would also be rewarded with a number of slaves, and lesser individuals were able to possess slaves by purchase. If a man were fined in a court of justice and unable to pay his fine, he could be sold to an individual willing to settle the amount. Parents under great hardship sold their children, and any children born of those slaves became the property of their master. A husband would often sell his wife and children and, marrying another woman, 'commence life afresh'. On repayment of the purchase money this class of slaves could regain its freedom, but with no means to accumulate money 'except a nugget fall from the skies' this was hardly an option.[19]

However despite the adversities, in Johnstone's view Manipur required very little to make it 'a model native state of a unique type, and its people the happiest of the happy'.[20]

CHAPTER 2

MANIPUR IN THE NINETEENTH CENTURY

The first relations between the British and the Manipuris dated from 1762, when Governor Verelst of the Bengal Presidency entered into a treaty with the ruler of Manipur. Little came of this treaty and practically the British connection with the state dated from 1823, after Manipur had been invaded by the Burmese in 1819 and its people driven out or carried off into slavery in Burma. The three royal princes, Marjit, Chaurjit and Gambhir Singh, were forced to flee to Cachar, where they stayed until 1824 when war broke out between the British Government and the Burmese. Assistance in arms and money was given by the British to Gambhir Singh in order to enable him to recover the state. Manipur at this time contained only the miserable remnants of a thriving population of at least 400,000 – possibly 600,000 – that had existed before the Burmese invasion, and Gambhir Singh's task was to encourage exiles to return and to attempt to rebuild the prosperity of his little kingdom. He was a wise and strong, if severe, ruler and, although owing his throne greatly to his own efforts, he continued to hold a deep feeling of gratitude to the British Government, promptly obeying its orders and doing his utmost to instil in his officers the same sense of loyalty. A force of 2,000 men was formed, thereafter called the Manipur Levy, consisting of cavalry, infantry and artillery drilled by two English officers, which was to prove of immense value in its ability to move without the paraphernalia of a regular army. Gambhir Singh died of cholera in 1834 on the day that the Kubo Valley, previously an area of Burmese territory which had been occupied by the Manipuri ruler, was restored by the British to the Burmese in an effort to end a number of long-running disputes. This event created a great deal of ill feeling between the ruling power and the royal family.[1]

In 1835 the officers of the Levy were withdrawn, and a political agent appointed to reside in Manipur. However, although Manipur was a protected state and undoubtedly looked upon by the India Office as dependent, so little emphasis was placed on its dependence that the Manipuris regarded themselves as free agents and 'with the haughtiness common to all races of Mongolian origin, considered themselves as doing the British Government an honour by condescending to permit that Government's political agent to reside at the Manipur Court'.[2] For much of the latter part of the nineteenth century the political agent had no access to the maharaja other than at *durbars* arranged at the ruler's pleasure, and the position of political agent was more that of an ambassador than a friendly advisor sent by an imperial authority to maintain cordial relations. The idea was perpetuated that Manipur was an independent state, the existence of which had in the past depended upon British assistance and was guaranteed by the British in order to serve as a buffer between British India and Burma.

Following the death of her husband, Gambhir Singh, the queen dowager in 1844 made a failed attempt to poison the regent of Manipur, Nar Singh, who had been the late Maharaja's minister, and the principal members of the royal family were exiled including her son, Chandra Kirtee Singh. Nar Singh then seized the throne and ruled until his death in 1850. His weak brother, Debendra Singh, succeeded to the *gadi*, but ruled for only three months. Chandra Kirtee Singh, with the help of Nar Singh's remaining three brothers, was able to oust Debendra Singh, and in 1851 the British Government guaranteed the throne to him and to his descendants upon his pledge to follow the advice of the political agent in matters of government. In turn the British promised to prevent, by force of arms if necessary, any attempts by rival princes to dislodge him. After 1851 many attempts were made on the part of members of the Manipur royal family to usurp the ruler, but all were defeated. However although the resolution to support him was firmly upheld, it was unfortunate that on no occasion did the Government of India make a sustained attempt to improve Chandra Kirtee Singh's system of administration.[3]

Despite his shortcomings in government, Chandra Kirtee Singh was considered by James Johnstone to be 'far the ablest man in his dominions, and a strong and capable ruler'.[4] The Maharaja possessed a vast fund of information, which he acquired by constant questioning, and had a great enthusiasm for mechanical arts of all kinds. English scientific works were explained to him and his research extended to the anatomy of the human body, of which he had a good knowledge. He owned a large collection of European artefacts, and glass was manufactured in his workshops. For such a powerful man his rule was mild in comparison to that of his predecessors, and like Gambhir Singh he recognised the degree to which his prosperity depended on his loyalty to the British Government. At the same time, he was acutely aware of his rights, and earnestly desired to preserve his country intact and to give the British no excuse for annexation.

When Johnstone arrived in Manipur in 1877, the location was deemed by one of the secretaries in the Indian Government to be 'the Cinderella among political agencies' due to the loneliness, the 'surrounding savages' and the ill-feeling caused by the British restoration to Burma of the Kubo Valley over the heads of the Manipuris.[5] However despite its remoteness and small size, the site of the state in a sensitive defensive position between Assam and Upper Burma gave it the right to its own British political agent, in contrast to the numerous small states in India overseen by a roving agent whose annual winter tour allowed only a matter of days with each. In recognition of this close tie, loyal support was given by the Maharaja to the British in the Naga War of 1879.[6] A force furnished by the Maharaja and led by Colonel Johnstone raised the siege of Kohima by the Nagas and prevented a major catastrophe. At this time, the Manipur Political Agency was placed directly under the control of the Assam administration and the Maharaja was presented with two mountain guns and 1,000 stand-of-arms. A party of 22 men was sent from Kohima under a European non-commissioned officer to instruct the Manipuris in the working of the guns, and in 1884 the Maharaja requested 60,000 rounds of ball cartridge to enable the troops to be put through a regular course of musketry. He again gave great assistance to the British on the outbreak of the Burmese War in 1885, for which he received a further two seven-pounder guns. Chandra Kirtee Singh died in May 1886 after a reign of 35 years and was succeeded by his son, Sur Chandra Singh, a young man then aged 33.

According to James Johnstone, at that time an able political agent supported by the government should have stepped in to make much-needed reforms and to 'introduce a more modern spirit in keeping with the times', however the opportunity was missed. Sur Chandra was 'a good, amiable man, with plenty of ability, but very weak ... the Government of India seems never to have realised that excessive care and caution were necessary'. Despite the fact that the Foreign Department of the government had a lengthy and extensive knowledge of Manipur, in Johnstone's view a suitable man was never found to take the Maharaja in hand. The posting may not have required 'the very highest class of intellect, but it certainly did require a rather rare combination of qualities, together with one indispensable to make a good officer, namely, a real love for the work, the country, and the people'.[7] With the presence of a regiment of native infantry at Langthobal, 4 miles from the capital, to uphold British authority, the prestige of the Government of India within the state should have increased in the latter part of the 1880s. However the opposite appeared to be the case. On one occasion sepoys of the political agent's escort were hustled and beaten by some Manipuris at a public festival, and on another the man carrying the government mail bag between the capital and Langthobal was stopped and robbed.[8]

To add to the instability, primogeniture did not exist in Manipur and since Chandra Kirtee had six wives, all of whom had produced sons, there was much opportunity for palace intrigue. The situation was further complicated by a decree given by Chandra Kirtee before his death that the succession should not pass directly to Sur Chandra's son, but first to his own sons born of the junior queens. The British agreed to guarantee only the immediate succession of Sur Chandra.

Following three failed attempts to gain possession of the *gadi* by parties outside the royal family, matters were quieter during the second half of the 1880s until a case of brutal flogging by the son of the fourth wife of Chandra Kirtee, who held the position of Senapati, or Commander in Chief of Manipur, and was prone to violent outbursts. In this case the objects of the Prince's attack were two slaves belonging to his half-brother, Bhairabijit Singh, more commonly known as Pucca Senna. It was alleged that, because the slaves refused to give up two ponies to the Senapati, they were

> held down by their arms and legs and were beaten across the small of the back until both fainted. Some water was poured over their faces, and when this had partially revived them they were again beaten until one of them appeared to be lifeless. The two men were then placed on a *macharn* over a fire and partially roasted. All this took place in the presence of the Senapati who was sitting looking on and giving instructions.[9]

Mr I. A. J. Primrose, the current Political Agent, reported when they were brought to the residency[10] hospital, 'I have never seen a more sickening sight than the state of those poor men. Their backs were raw, the wounds extending to both flanks. One man lay in an insensible state. His recovery is doubtful as his liver and kidneys have both been injured.'[11]

This incident caused Sur Chandra to state his intention of banishing the Senapati from the state. By great misfortune at the same time, according to Johnstone, an 'uncultured' British sergeant in the state shot a cow, 'the sacred animal of the Hindoos, an outrage far exceeding any that our imagination can paint'. The Maharaja flatly refused to punish his brother while such a heinous crime as cow killing was allowed to pass unnoticed by the British. The cavalier approach by the British in turning a blind eye to the strength of native feeling in 'a state so full of prejudice and suspicion as Manipur'[12] was to have its repercussions. It is possible that had justice been meted out to the British soldier concerned, the Manipur uprising might have been avoided. As it happened the Senapati was permitted to stay in the state, and towards the end of the decade it became evident that the Maharaja's brother was assuming greater power in Manipur.

CHAPTER 3

CAST OF CHARACTERS

Despite the signs of a changing balance of power within the royal family, in September 1890 Maharaja Sur Chandra was apparently firmly seated on the *gadi* of Manipur. Two years earlier Frank St Clair Grimwood, a junior officer in the Political Service, had to his great pleasure been offered the post of Political Agent in the state. Frank, born in 1853, was the third son of Jeffrey Grimwood, a magistrate belonging to the Essex landed gentry, and had been educated at Winchester and Oxford. He held a Postmastership (scholarship) at Merton College from 1872 to 1874 and took a Third Class in Finals in 1875, a result which was not necessarily an accurate assessment of his academic ability. At this date the undergraduate membership of Merton was largely drawn from major public schools, and for such students there was often no great incentive or need to take a good degree; indeed, fewer than half of Merton students studied for an Honours degree, the majority settling for a Pass.[1] Frank appeared in a photograph of the Merton College Eight in 1874, but there is little evidence of his other social activities. Following a period as a barrister at Lincoln's Inn, he had qualified for the Bengal Civil Service by examination in 1884 and arrived in India two years later.

After a short time in Bengal he was transferred to Assam, and appointed to a junior posting in Sylhet before his promotion to Political Agent in Manipur in 1888. Early in his career Frank had played a memorable game of polo with three royal princes on the Manipur ground, said to be worthy of that at Hurlingham, and was elated at the prospect of repeating the exercise on a regular basis.[2] High on the list of information solicited on the application form of a man to be posted to a

Figure 3.1 Frank St Clair Grimwood from a photograph by Vandyk, reproduced in *My Three Years in Manipur*.

princely state were queries about the applicant's popularity, horsemanship and sporting ability – and it appears that book-learning and related skills were not highly thought of by those who administered the selection process. There was probably something to be said for the government's argument that political work required more than intellectual agility, in that a political officer who surrounded himself with files was unlikely to make headway. To win the confidence of the rulers in question, personal contact was essential and it is possible that Frank, in placing emphasis upon the physical rather than the mental aspects of his work, may have been less able to deal perceptively and diplomatically with the extraordinary circumstances which arose in Manipur during his posting.

Frank and Ethel, his newly married wife of 21, journeyed from the town of Cachar, 126 miles to the west of the Manipur capital. Cachar itself was not a particularly large station, although it housed more Europeans than most Assamese districts due to the regiment quartered alongside the usual civil authorities. The district had a large population of tea planters and, as a result of the constant flow of visitors, maintained a relentless social life. The march to Manipur was, however, to prove anything but enjoyable, and Ethel's descriptions of weathering torrential rain, gnats and horseflies, and the traversing of rivers via a series of bamboo suspension bridges 'swinging violently . . . a great height from the water, which you can see between the chinks of the matting as you walk across',[3] reveal her to be a woman of remarkable courage and resilience. The Grimwoods were accompanied by servants, coolies and elephants, and an escort of Manipuri sepoys – supposedly 30 altogether, although Ethel never saw more than 12: 'When marching they had counted themselves over twice by running on ahead directly they had presented arms, and going through the same performance round the corner.'[4]

Ethel recalled her first view of the 'white walls of the maharaja's palace, and the golden-roofed temple of his favourite god', as well as 'the blue waters of the Logtak Lake, studded with islands, each one a small mountain in itself. Villages buried in their own groves of bamboo and plantain trees dotted the plain, and between each village there were tracts of rice-fields and other cultivation. The whole valley looked rich and well cared for.'[5] The Grimwoods were met by ten elephants and a guard of 50 sepoys under the command of a high officer of state, Colonel Samoo Singh, a 'hideous old gentleman'.[6] Seven miles from Manipur a further presentation took place with four members of the royal family who had constructed a small hut, 'nicely matted and arranged with chairs', and arms were presented with 'much blowing of trumpets'. To add to their somewhat dishevelled appearance after the rigours of the journey, a rat had eaten a large hole in Frank's hat and all the fingers from Ethel's right-hand glove. This meeting was to be the couple's first introduction to the Senapati, or Commander in Chief of Manipur, who struck them as 'very good-natured-looking' with 'a pleasing countenance'. However, as Ethel declared later, 'little did we foresee the terrible influence he was destined to bear on our future!'[7]

Ethel, a slim, handsome woman, was born of an Anglo-Indian family[8] in Muttra in West Bengal where her father, Charles Moore, a member of the Indian Civil Service, was a judge. Prior to her arrival in Manipur

Figure 3.2 Ethel St Clair Grimwood from a photograph by Vandyk, reproduced in *My Three Years in Manipur*.

Ethel had already pictured herself as mistress of a residency, 'of possessing servants in scarlet and gold, with "V.R." on their buttons, and a guard-of-honour'. She was in no way disappointed, declaring that 'My first impressions of our house and surroundings on this occasion were of the most favourable description ... and at the end of the lawn was the flagstaff of my dreams and the ensign of Old England waving proudly in the breeze'.[9] The Manipur residency, to play a major role in the 1891 uprising, had been designed and built by James Johnstone in 1880 and was adjacent to the royal palace in the capital, separated from it by a wide moat in which the annual boat races were held.[10] The building was constructed in the half-timbered style of old English houses, modified to suit the climate but raised on a 6-foot high solid brick foundation and approached on four sides by flights of masonry steps. The lower storey contained roomy cellars and was shot-proof in the event of the residency being subjected to crossfire from contending parties during periods of unrest in the city.[11]

The large compound, about 16 acres in area, was surrounded by a ditch and a mud wall varying from three feet to six feet in height, quite capable of being defended if necessary. The main entrance was through the quarter-guard of the permanent escort of the residency, a building which housed the telegraph office and the treasury. To the right of this were the hospital and school; to the left, the quarters of the sepoys. A long tree-lined carriage drive led up to the house with a stretch of grassland on both sides dotted with deodars and flowering shrubs, and a tennis court in the centre on the right. A hedge of roses divided the outer grounds from a well-planted flower garden surrounding the house, at the end of which was a small lake with an island frequented by wild duck. There was a track around the compound to exercise ponies and just beyond the western wall were compounds with native houses, surrounded by hedges of trees and bamboos. The residency was a spacious building with a handsome 24-foot-square *durbar* room for receptions. There were fine dining and drawing rooms, and airy, comfortable bedrooms with fireplaces. The house was surrounded by a veranda, strewn with rugs and skins, and the porch was covered by a spectacular purple bougainvillea.[12]

Fortunately for Ethel the red-coated servants existed in abundance, together with two Gurkha orderlies. Even in Johnstone's day the native residency staff had been impressive: a head clerk; doctor; secretary; and Manipuri, Burmese and Kuki interpreters as well as six orderlies or 'lictors'. Acting as private servants there were three Naga girls, a cook and assistant, and under the assistant four young Nagas learning their trade. Finally a bearer and, below him, two or three more Nagas, not to mention washermen, grooms, gardeners, and water carriers.[13] Ethel and Frank had nine gardeners, or *malis*, who were Nagas belonging to one of the villages which lay behind the residency ground. The Nagas, not noted for overdressing, insisted on working stark naked which appeared to leave Ethel quite unfazed. Having given the *malis* various undergarments which they used determinedly for other purposes, she declared with feeling, 'After this I gave up trying to inculcate decency into the mind of the untutored savage.'[14]

Two days after the Grimwoods' arrival in Manipur a *durbar* was arranged to meet the Maharaja, which turned out to be 'a very imposing function indeed'. Ethel further recounted that:

> Red cloth was spread all over the veranda and on the front steps, and our whole escort of sixty Ghoorkas was drawn up on the front lawn. The Maharaja arrived with a grand flourish of trumpets, attended by all his brothers, and accompanied also by a large following of Sepoys, slaves and ministers of state, each of the latter with his own retinue.[15]

Frank went to the outer gate of the residency to meet the Maharaja, where he shook hands with all the princes and returned with the ruler into the house and the *durbar* room. The entire *durbar*, being only a 'complimentary ceremony' did not last longer than ten minutes, but before he left the Maharaja expressed a wish to see Ethel, who reported that 'They all stared at me very solemnly, as though I were a curious sort of animal, and shortly afterwards they took their departure.'[16]

Despite this unpromising start, during their first term of office Frank and Ethel became extraordinarily intimate with the royal family, no doubt flattered by the attention they both received from the palace. Had Frank received a sufficient grounding in the Political Service he would have discovered that this was a state of affairs much frowned upon by the Government of India, which deliberately transferred political officers frequently on the grounds that too long an exposure to the problems and personalities of one state or region could encourage an unhealthy spirit of partisanship. However for the British couple the company was particularly welcome as, with the exception of the Gurkha regiment stationed at Langthobal,[17] four miles away from the residency, the Manipur posting was exceedingly lonely and other Europeans non-existent. Frank played polo with the princes, and he and Ethel were often included in duck, deer, and occasionally tiger shoots. The palace entourage visited the residency quite informally. The eldest daughter of the Maharaja was 15 and came regularly to see Ethel and Frank with nine or ten girls of the same age, of whom more than half were royal and all most curious to see Ethel's clothes and dining implements. Unfortunately the girls' habit of decorating themselves with flowers to be photographed by Frank and their participation in water parties on the residency lake were to cause some scandal at a later date. English photographs were of great appeal – as, to the male members of the royal family, was Frank's collection of guns. Ironically in the light of the subsequent use to which his own weapons were used, the Maharaja on one occasion arranged a field day for the Grimwoods when two of his mountain guns were brought out with different types of shell, fired by the Senapati himself with remarkable accuracy.

According to Ethel, Maharaja Sur Chandra was

> a short, fat, ugly little man, with a face something between that of a Burmese and Chinaman – rather fairer than the Bengal natives, but much scarred with small-pox. He was dressed very simply in white – a white coat with gold buttons, and very fine white muslin Dhotee. He had a large white turban on his head, in which was a spray of yellow orchids. Gray woollen stockings covered his legs, fastened at the knee with blue elastic garters with very fine brass buckles and his feet were encased in very large roughly-made laced boots, of which he seemed supremely proud.[18]

Like his father he could speak Hindustani, as well as local dialects, but little English. As has been stated, James Johnstone during his term of office considered him 'an amiable young man', but 'of a weak character, although possessing some ability'.[19] Despite his shortcomings Sur Chandra was a devout Hindu and appears to have taken seriously the daily tasks required of him as ruler, listing these in writing to the Chief Commissioner of Assam in 1890:

> Since my accession to the gadi I have daily performed all the duties appertaining and attaching to my position. In the morning I generally received the reports of the fort sentries and guards and matters relating to the jail administration. Immediately after noon I sat to hear representations, complaints and petitions of my subjects. In the afternoon I generally sat with the Jubraj [Crown Prince] and the Ministers to hear and pass orders on important State matters . . . I have never neglected the duties of the State. I have kept my dominions in profound peace and have never at any

> time been the cause myself, or through my subjects, of anxiety to the Indian Government.[20]

Johnstone later expressed his regret at the British lack of support for Sur Chandra: 'Backed up and influenced by an honest and capable Political Agent he would probably have made an excellent ruler. And had we done our duty by him, he might now be at the head of a flourishing little state, instead of having died an exile in Calcutta'.[21]

The Maharaja's eldest half-brother Kula Chandra, son of the second rani, bore a resemblance to the ruler but was stouter and uglier, 'so pronounced in his obesity that with some difficulty he can waddle a few yards'.[22] He was about 35 years old, 5 feet 8 inches tall with a dark complexion, small moustache and, according to the correspondent of the Allahabad newspaper, *The Pioneer*, 'a very villainous cast of countenance, rather Chinese; very small pig's eyes, with a slight squint'.[23] Johnstone described him as an ignorant, uncouth boor, who knew no language but his own, was quite unfitted for any responsible work and took little part in public affairs.[24]

The son of the fourth rani, Tikendrajit Bir Singh, was the Senapati, or Commander in Chief of Manipur, about 32 and taller than the Regent, with a small moustache and 'a lighter skin than most natives ... nice eyes and a pleasant smile, but his expression was rather spoilt by his front teeth, which were very much broken'.[25] Less flatteringly, a British telegraph officer added to this picture, describing him as of 'Middling height, light complexion, black eyes, very flashy in dress, eats beetles[26] all day [sic], has a looking glass in front of him all day, admiring himself every 5 or 10 minutes, slight moustache.'[27] However a Gurkha officer provided the best clue to the Prince's character, portraying a face with 'an air of resolution. The deep pitted frown that scars his forehead and the thin set lips show his determined but fiery temper.'[28]

In Johnstone's view the Prince was a depraved sadist who even during the reign of his father, Maharaja Chandra Kirtee, had on several occasions attempted to flog Manipuri subjects to death for relatively insignificant offences[29] and had been threatened with permanent banishment from Manipur by his half-brother, Maharaja Sur Chandra, for attempting to burn two slaves alive. In words that may well have influenced the view of the Government of India when dealing later with the crisis in Manipur, the Political Agent described Tikendrajit

Figure 3.3 Prince Tikendrajit Bir Singh (Pictures from History).

as 'a bad character, cruel, coarse, and low minded. From early childhood he was given to foul language and was absolutely dangerous when he grew up.'[30]

In total contrast to Johnstone's view, Ethel was most taken with the Senapati, seeing him as 'manly and generous to a fault' and 'more broad-minded' than the royal family in general.[31] Supposedly the proud possessor of nine wives, he was also from all accounts a remarkable sportsman, a magnificent rider and reportedly the strongest man in the country: 'he could lift very heavy weights and throw long distances, and to see him send the ball skimming half across the ground with one hit was a very pretty sight'.[32] Undoubtedly swayed by his sartorial elegance, Ethel reported that the Prince sported the most dashing attire for polo, 'a green velvet zouave[33] jacket edged with gold buttons, and a salmon-pink Dhotee, with white leather leggings and a pink silk turban', and admired his long hair which was twisted up into a knot at the back of his neck.[34]

Sur Chandra's full brother, Bhairabijit Singh, was Pucca Senna, or Commander of the Horse, and was much disliked by the local populace. He was said to be both extremely bad-tempered and jealous, and considered lazy by the Grimwoods despite his prowess as a champion polo player. Pucca Senna visited the residency on a daily basis, ostensibly to learn English but, it was suspected, more probably to ingratiate himself with the Political Agent. Much business was concluded during the lessons, 'The Political Agent finding it a great relief to quietly mention matters to the Pucca Senna, and get them done without having to talk over a lot of betal [sic] eating bigotted Ministers in open Durbar.'[35]

Of the remaining princes, Kesarjit Singh, Samoo Hengeba, was the officer in charge of the maharaja's elephants, numbering about 60. It was his duty to organise all arrangements in connection with the creatures, and on grand occasions, when the maharaja rode on an elephant, Samoo Hengeba[36] acted as *mahout*. His brother Gopal Senna, Dooloroi Hengeba, was in charge of the maharaja's *doolies*.[37] This mode of travelling was confined to the rich, and was considered a mark of great dignity. Those who could indulge in such luxury had to obtain special permission to use *doolies*, although the privilege was occasionally conferred upon ministers of state by the maharaja as a mark of recognition for their services. The Maharaja 'seldom travelled in any other style, as he was a very stout, apoplectic kind of personage, and it suited him better to be carried than to ride or go on an elephant. His *dooly* was a very magnificent affair, made of wood, with gilt hangings all round it and a gilt top, which could be put over it in wet weather'.[38]

Prince Angao Senna was in charge of the road between Burma and Manipur. He was supposed to travel up and down it to check the state of repair, but it was doubtful whether this in fact ever happened. In his mid-20s, Ethel remembered him as always with 'a large piece of betel-nut in his mouth' and inordinately fond of gambling on the outcome of pigeon fights until the State ceased to pay his debts.[39] Angao Senna was tall and fairly stout, with a darkish complexion and small moustache. Finally, there was Zillah Singh, a boy of about 17, 'a slight, graceful creature' with a fair complexion who rode a tiny pony and 'never troubled himself with too many garments'. His turban fell off frequently and his long black hair streamed in the wind as he raced about the polo ground.[40]

One of the highest-ranking ministers in the state and a member of the Durbar, or 'Top Guard' (the supreme ruling council)[41] was Thangal General, who was to play a major part in the 1891 revolt. The illegitimate son of a Manipuri, the general's Naga blood was a great hindrance to his acceptance in a Hindu state. However, according to the account of a British officer, his 'skill, diplomacy and early recognised genius overcame the difficulties of his birth and led to his rising to the position of Prime Minister in the land, and of being adopted into the Hindu faith, given the sacred thread and being permitted to marry into the highest Khettri family in Manipur'.[42] He was a remarkable man with a chequered history. His uncle had saved the life of Maharaja Gambhir Singh, Sur Chandra's grandfather, when the ruler's older brother had attempted to murder all his relations. Having been introduced to court at an early age, Thangal General was one of the 'props' of the throne when Gambhir Singh assumed power, and loyally supported the ruler until his death. Following the failed attempt by Gambhir Singh's widow to gain control for her infant son, Chandra Kirtee Singh, Thangal had accompanied the rani into exile and had carefully supervised the boy's childhood and youth. When in 1850 the young Maharaja returned to Manipur to assert his rights, Thangal accompanied him and greatly contributed to his success. In Johnstone's opinion, although 'a very devoted and patriotic Manipuri, [he] was extremely partial to Europeans' and, recognising the power of the British Government, 'nothing would have induced him to join in any plot against our rule in India'.[43] Despite his ignorance of English, he was able to point out any village in the state on an English map. He had developed this facility through studying geography in great depth to protect the borders of Manipur from British survey officers, who were suspected by the Manipuris of conniving to place as much territory as possible under British control.

Born around 1817, Thangal General was taller than the average Manipuri and remarkably active for his age. According to Ethel, the general had 'a fine old face, much lined and wrinkled with age and the cares of state which had fallen upon him when he was quite a young man'. She added,

> He had piercing black eyes, shaggy overhanging white eyebrows, and white hair. His nose was long and slightly hooked, and his mouth was finely cut and very determined. He was fond of bright colours, and I never remember seeing him in anything but a delicate pink silk dhotee, a dark coat made from a first-rate English pattern, and a pink turban, and when the orchids were in bloom, he seldom appeared without some gorgeous-hued specimen in the top of his turban.

To Ethel he resembled an eagle with his 'keen, rugged expression and deep-set, glowing eyes'.[44]

In keeping with this analogy he was credited with more bloodshed than any other man in the kingdom. If a village had misbehaved, raided another or refused to pay revenue, Thangal would

> travel out to that village and wipe it off the face of the earth. Men, women, and children were cut down without the slightest compunction. Few escaped, and these travelled away and joined other villages; but every house and barn and shed was burnt, pigs and fowls destroyed, and ruin and devastation reigned where prosperity and plenty had held sway before.[45]

Nevertheless he had his virtues: he was very enterprising, and fond of building bridges and improving the roads in and around the capital. Like the Senapati he was a keen soldier, and in his youth had been a first-rate shot. He was a devoted follower of Sur Chandra Singh, and, according to Johnstone, detested the violent and unscrupulous nature of the Senapati, 'whose evil influence he always feared would wreck Manipur'.[46] This probably made the latter recall him to public life to keep his eye on him. Thangal was by force of circumstance, however unwillingly, obliged to act as a loyal subject of his own de facto chief and to participate in the palace coup of 1890.

CHAPTER 4

THE ABDICATION OF SUR CHANDRA SINGH

In December 1888 after only ten months' residence in Manipur, Frank and Ethel Grimwood were informed that they were to be posted to Jorhat in the Assam Valley. This development suggested that Frank was less experienced than most of his predecessors in the Manipur posting; it appeared that a number of senior men were returning to India after furlough who needed to be provided with districts ahead of the junior officers. Frank's successor, a Mr Heath, for whom the lack of European company in Manipur was a great penance, viewed his new situation with much dread – a feeling that proved to be quite justified. The following April, the Grimwoods received a telegram informing them that Heath had died of dysentery and that the Manipur job would again belong to Frank. Ethel found to her surprise that she was somewhat less eager than her husband to return to the state, declaring later that maybe 'a warning of all that was yet to come filled me with some unknown presentiment of evil'.[1] Heath's 'sudden, sad death' seemed to haunt her, and the misfortune which seemed to befall British personnel in Manipur was all too evident:

> Poor Mr. Heath was buried in our own garden, quite close to the house – so close, in fact, that I could see his grave from my bedroom window. There had been two graves there before – one was Major Trotter's, who was once political agent in Manipur, and

> died there from wounds which he had received fighting, in Burmah [sic]; the other was that of a young Lieutenant Beavor, who had also died at the Residency of fever ... I longed to get my husband to give up a place so associated with gloomy incidents, and take some other district in the province.[2]

Matters were quiet in Manipur until September 1890, although rumours of petty differences between the princes – and in particular between Pucca Senna and his more powerful brother, the Senapati – reached the Grimwoods from time to time. If one brother visited the residency frequently, the other objected strongly and refused to attend himself for some time. The brothers were also rivals in love. Both wished to marry a girl deemed to be the most beautiful female in Manipur, the daughter of a wealthy goldsmith who was a prominent member of the maharaja's council. The girl was 'taller ... than the average Manipuri, about sixteen years of age, and very fair, with quantities of long black hair. She was always very well dressed, and had a great many gold bracelets on her arms, and some necklaces of pure gold which weighed an enormous amount.'[3] At a *nautch*[4] held one night at the residency she appeared as chief dancer; all the princes were observers, and the two rivals sat on either side of Ethel. The Senapati was 'all cheerfulness and good-humour' throughout the proceedings, but 'the Pucca Senna was very gloomy and morose'.[5] Shortly afterwards it emerged that a violent quarrel had ensued in which the Maharaja had taken the side of Pucca Senna, and the Senapati had sworn never to speak to the latter again – an oath which he kept resolutely. The eight brothers split up into two factions: the Maharaja Sur Chandra, Pucca Senna, Samoo Hengeba and Dooloroi Hengeba, sons of the first wife of Chandra Kirtee, formed one group; Kula Chandra, the Senapati, Angao Senna and Zillah Singh joined together in another.

Further dissent was caused in the palace by the creation of the new job of judicial general for Pucca Senna, although the main functions of adjudicating in all civil and criminal cases belonged traditionally to the Jubraj, Kula Chandra, 'who could not be but annoyed with the Maharaja for his artfully keeping himself in the background while Pecca Sing obtained his object'. Following this affront, an irreversible royal rift was eventually caused by the relatively minor matter of the constant friction between the young Zillah Singh and Pucca Senna. Pucca Senna succeeded in persuading the Maharaja to forbid Zillah Singh to sit in the Durbar, at the same time depriving him of some small offices of state which he usually performed and the traditional 'honour and distinction' of having the bugle sounded when he went out or moved around the palace. Already 'subjected to insult on various occasions, and made to suffer in silence', the youngest prince lost no time in enlisting the help of his powerful brother and ally, the Senapati.[6]

At the same time Pucca Senna lied to the Maharaja, alleging that Angao Senna was the ringleader of a revolt against him. Without making due enquiries, the ruler ordered his half-brother to be disarmed and arrested, together with Zillah Singh. Pucca Senna, who in Frank Grimwood's view seemed to have tried in every way possible to annoy his brother, secretly collected troops to assert his own position; preparations to arm their supporters were also made by Angao Senna and Zillah Singh, who were 'greatly irritated' and 'resolved to die fighting before the throne of their ancestors rather than to suffer the disgrace of either banishment or death'.[7] In the early hours of 22 September 1890, when the Maharaja had retired, Zillah Singh collected a handful of followers and with his brother, Angao Senna, climbed the wall leading to the ruler's apartments, firing rifles through the windows. Sur Chandra recalled, 'I was tying on my turban when it was pierced by a bullet, and as heavy firing began, I concluded that the Palace had been treacherously seized'.[8] Showing little attempt at mounting a defence, instead of rousing his guard to repel the intruders the Maharaja fled through the rear of the palace to the residency with the three brothers remaining loyal to him. A number of sepoys accompanied them, with a great many followers armed with swords and any other weapons they had been able to grab in the confusion. The Manipur Court Chronicle, in its report of events, included the Senapati in the attack upon the palace, stating,

> at six pung hours after the midnight yuthak[9] the royal younger brother Koireng the Senapati, the royal younger brother Aangou the Dulairoi Hanchapa, and the royal younger brother Jilla Ngampa, these three entered in the palace and seized it. The royal elder brother, also called Maharaj Surchandra Singh, Chinglen Lanthapa took refuge at the Bungalow of the Shahep (the residency) ... no king reigned on the throne and there was no market.[10]

Figure 4.1 South Wall of the citadel showing the maharaja's palace through the domed gateway (The Alkazi Collection of Photography).

At the request of Grimwood, a detachment of the 44th Gurkha regiment arrived from the nearest cantonment at Langthobal. The Political Agent elected to defend the Maharaja for as long as possible if attacked, but only had a small force of 65 rifles available in addition to the Gurkha detachment. Sur Chandra later asserted that Grimwood had attempted to persuade him that the Senapati could not be responsible for the attack on the palace, declaring that the root of discontent lay elsewhere and the Senapati was not a 'mad man'. The Maharaja also claimed that the rebel princes, 'being unable to calculate upon the services of the army, had opened the jail at midnight, and released the convicts to the number of about 400, and armed them to join the attack, which they readily did'.[11] However the scale of the insurgency appears to have been less in reality than suggested by his account, and when Grimwood telegraphed the chief commissioner of Assam, James Wallace Quinton,[12] asking for instructions, he stated that he did not anticipate an attack on the residency and that there had been no loss of life. He added, however, that the ruler had been preparing, in conjunction with his brothers, to attack the Senapati if a sufficient force could be raised. This move had been rapidly quashed by Grimwood, who refused to allow him to collect men in the residency grounds.[13] In fact, according to Ethel's account of events, there had been remarkably little attempt at resistance on the part of the Maharaja:

> My husband brought every argument to bear upon the Rajah to induce him to brave the matter out, and allow some efforts to be made to regain his throne; but he would not listen to any reason, and after some hours spent in fear and terror as to what the next move might be, he signified his intention to my husband of making a formal abdication of his throne.[14]

In response to the Political Agent's request for orders, the Chief Commissioner replied that Frank was to protect the residency, to mediate if possible between the parties and, if necessary, to telegraph for troops to Kohima, where the commanding officer had been authorised to send 200 rifles if required. However the Political Agent was strictly directed not to assume the offensive without first informing the Chief Commissioner.[15] Meanwhile Grimwood had already temporarily disarmed the Maharaja's Manipuri sepoys. The firing had ceased entirely in the palace and it was considered unwise to leave the sepoys in charge of their rifles. In Ethel's opinion 'they were under no sort of control, and were ready to fire without any provocation at all, a proceeding which would probably have been attended with disastrous results, as the Senaputti [sic] would not have hesitated to return the fire from his strong position in the palace'. The Maharaja was consulted and agreed to the disarmament, although he was subsequently to deny that he had given his consent. As Ethel wrote bitterly afterwards, 'he has accused my husband of disarming his troops without his consent, thus disabling them from making any attempt to regain the position he had forfeited himself through abject cowardice'.[16]

Meanwhile, during the attack on the palace and the victory of the rebel princes, the Jubraj, Kula Chandra, had taken up temporary residence at Bishenpur, 17 miles from Manipur. In the capital the Senapati occupied the palace (containing four mountain guns and the magazine) with Angao Senna and Zillah Singh from the early morning of 22 September, when he 'took possession of everything, and proceeded to strengthen the palace defences against any attempt to retake it'. Sir John

Gorst, the Under Secretary of State for India, wrote after the event that this action was possibly open to 'sinister construction; but it may, on the other hand, have been commendable, and it had this practical result, that there was no bloodshed, no plundering, no disturbance after the Maharaja's flight'.[17] Tikendrajit recalled that 'The subjects immediately commenced rushing into the palace, and a vast number (over ten thousand men) all cursed Pecca Sing for his evil intrigues and designs, and applauded Angao Sing for his valour and success in becoming a khatri or warrior'.[18] At the time the Political Agent recorded that, of the ministers who had seats in the Durbar, only one remained with the Senapati. The others, including Thangal General and his sons, went to the residency.

On the morning of 23 September the Senapati received a visit from Grimwood who gave him the Maharaja's letter, announcing the ruler's determination to leave the state. At this stage it would have been easy for Grimwood to ascertain the reasons for the disturbance and communicate with Quinton before assenting to Sur Chandra's departure and thereby tacitly accepting the success of the revolt. However the Political Agent, who as an inexperienced officer appears to have forged an unwisely close relationship with the Senapati, failed to confront him and it was agreed that the Prince would arrange for the Maharaja's journey and send for Kula Chandra, who was now in line to become the regent of Manipur.

On 24 September a telegram was received by the Chief Commissioner from Grimwood, confirming that Sur Chandra had voluntarily and formally abdicated in favour of the Regent in order to devote the remaining years of his life to a pilgrimage to the sacred city of Brindaban on the Ganges. The Political Agent had informed the ruler that once he had abdicated he could not return to Manipur or Cachar, however this advice failed to act as a deterrent. After nearly 36 hours in the residency, during which the Maharaja would eat nothing, Frank began to make the necessary arrangements for Sur Chandra's departure for Cachar with Pucca Senna, Dooloroi Hengeba and Samoo Hengeba, under an escort of 35 rifles. As soon as the Maharaja's intention of leaving the state was known, a great many Manipuris flocked to the residency, most of them bringing various sums of money to present to him. Frank commented that 'To judge from the way people wept . . . everyone seemed sorry at his departure.' There was genuine sorrow on the part of several of his ministers, but little regret at the exit of the ill-tempered and jealous Pucca Senna, as he accompanied the Maharaja into his voluntary exile. Grimwood wrote at the time that

> the idea of the Maharaja retiring to Brindaban to lead a religious life is not a new idea; for some time back there have been rumours that he intended to do so, and he was, I believe actually in treaty for the purchase of some land there, where he would live, and his determination to go now was probably the best solution of the situation; at any rate it probably saved bloodshed and I hardly think any satisfactory settlement could have been reached by mediation alone.[19]

The Chief Commissioner telegraphed back to Frank that, subject to the sanction of the Government of India, Kula Chandra might be appointed regent, and early on the morning of the second day after the attack on the Maharaja the Prince entered the palace and formed his new administration. The Manipur Court Chronicle made it clear that at this time there was no doubt concerning the recognition of Kula Chandra as the new ruler of Manipur:

> Shri Kulachandra Singh became king at the age of thirty-seven years. At four pung hours he entered the royal palace ... at three pung hours after the noon yuthak he was enthroned. At the night yuthak the eldest wife of the king was brought from her parental residence. On that day the one who was also called Chinglen Lanthaba (Surachandra) left for pilgrimage to the sacred places.[20]

At this stage Grimwood proved to be highly supportive of the new regime, writing to the government on 25 September that the Senapati 'is popular amongst all classes; he is the only Prince who is said to be poor owing to his generosity'.[21] Suggesting that, far from lacking ambition, he was quite happy to consolidate his position of power, Tikendrajit wrote later that 'credit of victory' during the abdication had been allotted to him by the local populace, and that he, being 'already distinguished for his valour, charity and affability, became more popular and renowned'.[22] The country certainly seemed perfectly quiet, and the people appeared to have acquiesced willingly to the change of rulers. However, on 6 October Sur Chandra telegraphed to the Chief Commissioner to the effect that his abdication statement had been misconstrued following a misunderstanding with Grimwood.[23] In a letter of 14 November the ruler added,

> had I intended to [abdicate], it would have been by a more formal act, and with some stipulation that provision should be made for me and my family by the State. As it is I came away without a single *pice* in my pocket, or even a second suit of clothes or bedding, being dependent for everything upon the assistance of the Government.[24]

To this the Chief Commissioner replied that he would give his full attention to any representation the Maharaja might submit, but that he and the brothers who accompanied him would not be allowed to return either to Cachar or Manipur until further notice.[25]

CHAPTER 5

THE GOVERNMENT OF INDIA

On 31 December 1890 Chief Commissioner Quinton sent a narrative of the current state of play to the Government of India in Calcutta. He informed senior officials that since 17 October 1890, the date when previous correspondence on the subject had ended, Kula Chandra had carried on the government of Manipur, having been recognised as regent by the Political Agent under the orders of the Chief Commissioner. He also pointed out that, 'although the attack on the Maharaja was apparently unjustifiable, the Maharaja had declined to take any active steps to recover the ground he had lost, or to punish the assailants'. Moreover the ruler's assertion that he had been prevented from taking retaliatory action as the result of the disarmament and disbandment of his troops by the Political Agent was completely false. It was true that Grimwood had at the time taken no active steps to reinstate the Maharaja by force, but, as explained by the Political Agent himself, 'it was not possible to do this with the scanty force at his disposal'. The Political Agent had acted on the instructions to mediate between the two parties, but the Maharaja declined to accept his advice, announcing his intention to become a *fakir* and to resign as ruler of the state. He had, moreover, left with Grimwood the official keys and gold ornaments of office, with instructions that they were to be given to Kula Chandra, and he also handed the State sword and jewels to the Ayapurel, the officer in charge of the Maharaja's escort, as was customary on abdication. No encouragement had been given to the Maharaja by the Political Agent to give up the *gadi*. On the contrary, 'he endeavoured to persuade him not to decide too hastily, guaranteed his personal safety, and was authorised and prepared to summon troops to his assistance'.[1]

Having abdicated and left the state, the Maharaja had changed his mind and now wished to countermand his abdication and return to Manipur. The Chief Commissioner did not favour this course unless the Government of India was prepared to support the ruler with British troops. The sons of the late Chandra Kirtee Singh were divided into at least two parties, 'animated by most hostile feelings towards each other'. There was no hope of permanent reconciliation and the weakness shown by the Maharaja made it clear that, if restored, he would only be 'a tool in the hands of others'.[2] Unless fresh arrangements were made regarding the relocation of troops to Manipur, the probability would be that royal hostilities would recur and there would be a constant need for British intervention for as long as Sur Chandra Singh retained the *gadi*.[3]

Somewhat surprisingly for an officer of such seniority, Quinton appeared happy to agree with Grimwood in condoning without question the sudden change of regime, declaring that he was firmly of the opinion that the current state of affairs in Manipur was 'not the result of a revolution in which the people of the State have any interest, of foreign aggression, or of any ascendancy gained by rival chiefs, but ... merely the outcome of a family quarrel between the brothers of a nominal ruler'. Obviously unversed in the history of princely Indian treaties concluded with the British, the Chief Commissioner failed to see that the original recognition by the Government of India of Sur Chandra as successor to his father had any bearing upon the current situation, or justified a claim on the part of the Maharaja for support in attempting to regain a position which he had voluntarily given up. In the view of the Chief Commissioner the succession of the Regent, who had been recognised as heir by the Government of India, 'merely anticipates the ordinary course of events and is generally acquiesced in by the people of the State'. Moreover since Kula Chandra had assumed office 'the administration has been successfully and tranquilly conducted, and the Political Agent expects no opposition to it'.[4] Ethel Grimwood herself reported that the improvements within the state were undeniable, declaring:

> Roads that had been almost impassable in the ex-Maharaja's reign were repaired and made good enough to drive on. Bridges that had been sadly needed were erected; some of them on first-class plans,

> which were calculated to last three times as long as the flimsy structures which existed previously. The people seemed happier and more contented, and my husband found it much easier to work with the Manipur durbar than he had done when there were eight opinions instead of four. There were no more petty jealousies and quarrels among the princes.[5]

However it soon became apparent that the Government of India was far from convinced of the wisdom of maintaining the status quo, despite the failure of senior personnel to take decisive action over Manipur following the September abdication. A confidential letter dated 24 January 1891 from the Viceroy's Council made it clear that the usurpation of an Indian ruler recognised by the Government of India would not be tolerated. The letter declared that Maharaja Sur Chandra had abdicated in 'a state of terror', adding that 'the Senapati has more than once incurred the displeasure of the Government of India on account of his violent conduct, and if the Maharaja, in 1888, had not been afraid of his turbulent brother, he would have been banished from the State'. The ruler had been ousted by a cabal in his family led by the Senapati, and were the Government of India to recognise the Jubraj, Kula Chandra, as ruler of Manipur, the Senapati would 'wield the real power within the State' – as indeed had been shown to be the case. Due to the tribal disorder in the region Manipur was of increasing importance to the British, and the acceptance of an unlawful regime in the state might have 'a mischievous effect upon the lawless tribes adjoining the State – tribes which we are now engaged in reducing to order'.[6] Moreover the Viceroy of India, Henry Charles Keith Petty-Fitzmaurice, 5th Marquess of Lansdowne, was much in favour of safeguarding the territory of British India by maintaining a firm hold on frontier states such as Sikkim, Kashmir and Manipur, which were to be employed as buffer zones against foreign aggressors.

On 9 February 1891 Quinton replied to Calcutta that he did not feel that the restoration of the Maharaja would be beneficial either to Manipur or to its people. Yet again he laid great stress on the weakness of the Maharaja's character, focusing particularly on his failure to act against the Senapati in 1888 following the vicious attack upon two slaves. He pointed out that his return would simply mean that the authority of the state would be wielded by the highly unpopular Pucca

Senna and the two other brothers, Samoo Hengeba and Dooloroi Hengeba, who had fled with the ruler, both of whom were under the age of Kula Chandra and the Senapati, 'who would not easily forego their claims in favour of their younger brothers'.[7] The present government under the Regent had existed for six months and, the Chief Commissioner repeated, was 'conducted with tranquillity' and 'has shown itself in various matters amenable to the advice of the Political Agent'.[8] However Quinton felt that an enquiry into the conduct of the Senapati should be made and that his position in the line of succession should rest upon proof of his good conduct and obedience to the Government of India, unless it was intended to exclude him permanently from the succession.[9]

The Government of India replied that there should be 'a sufficient show' of British strength to eliminate any doubts as to who was in control of the situation; the differences between the Maharaja's brothers should be settled according to 'principles of justice, and for the benefit of good government in Manipur'. To this end Quinton should visit the state for the purpose of making and, if necessary, enforcing a decision based on the merits of the case and should have with him 'a sufficient force to overawe the conspirators'. If it were found that the Maharaja had a reasonable amount of support from the people, he could be reinstated. In that case the Senapati should be removed from Manipur and placed under watch elsewhere. Even if the Maharaja were to prove 'hopelessly incompetent' and Kula Chandra were recognised as ruler, it would be necessary 'to remove his disreputable adherents from the State, and to punish the Senapati for his violent and lawless conduct'.[10]

From this it appears that the real objection of the Government of India to the Senapati's position in Manipur was not that his presence in the country was an obstacle to good government. The local authorities had assured them that the contrary was true. But government policy seems to have been dictated by the fixed idea that it was necessary to 'make it understood' that the British intended to be 'masters of the situation',[11] a view perhaps tinged with pique that Grimwood should have taken matters into his own hands at the time of the abdication. Lansdowne wrote to Viscount Cross, Secretary of State for India, on 25 February 1891 that 'we shall make it a sine qua non that the recognition of the present Regent shall take place under circumstances which will show the Manipur people that he has been accepted with our full concurrence and we shall deport a ruffianly brother of the Maharaja, known as the Sena Pati, who was, I believe, at the bottom of the late cabal'.[12] The words 'I believe' betray a certain lack of determination on the part of the viceroy to mine the facts of the Manipur case. The heart of the elegant, fastidious Lansdowne, who had arrived in India in 1888 at the age of 43, was neither in his viceroyalty nor in his previous post of Governor-General of Canada; he regarded his salary as a means to relieving the debt on his vast estates in England and Ireland, which were his principal interest.[13] Lacking as he did a sense of mission, his relations with the Home Government were poor, and he was disinclined to interfere in the work of Government of India officials[14] – particularly in the running of the Indian states, a task which singularly failed to capture his imagination.[15]

The wider political ramifications of the Manipur abdication reveal the tension which existed between the Government of India and the India Office in London, which was directly accountable to parliament for Indian affairs. It became evident early in official exchanges that the belated response from the Viceroy's Council to the dynastic quarrel between the dethroned Maharaja and his brothers was seen as a highly controversial issue, from which the India Office was determined to disassociate itself as quickly as possible to avoid being implicated. In the immediate aftermath of the Manipur uprising, Cross weighed in to rebuke Lansdowne for his failure to make a full investigation of the situation:[16]

> In your letter to Mr. Quinton of the 21st February you state that the demonstration against the Maharaja was led by the Senapati [who] ought not to go unpunished for his treachery against his brother, however Mr. Quinton's report says distinctly that the Zillah Singh took the initiative; that, after some firing, the Maharaja fled away, and that it was not until then that the Senapati appeared on the scene and took possession of the Palace ... Mr. Quinton, in his telegram of September 24th, says that this arrangement was provisionally sanctioned, and states that the Pucca Sena, not the Senapati, was the primary cause of all the trouble; but your Despatch of the 4th March states that you had fully enquired into all the circumstances of the case, after having had the advantage of discussion with Mr. Quinton.[17]

Cross continued that if the Government of India had determined at the outset not to recognise the bloodless revolution of 22 September, they should have themselves assumed the administration of Manipur pending a decision as to which of the brothers was to be ruler. However as the administration had been conducted with success following the abdication, 'Why then should action have been taken at that particular time? If at all, why not before? If there had been any difficulty, the matter might have been referred home; and, when action was taken, why was the formal enquiry into the conduct of the Senapati, which was suggested by Mr. Quinton, not made?'[18]

For reasons that remain unclear, Quinton's proposals for an enquiry were totally ignored by the Government of India. In a letter to the Chief Commissioner of 21 February it was made clear that the Prince was already found guilty and his punishment awarded without giving him an opportunity to answer British charges and to explain his conduct:

> It is evident that the Jubraj [Kula Chandra] owes his present position rather to the successful issue of his brother's insurrection than to the authority of the British Government, and that, while the Senapatti remains in Manipur unpunished for his treachery against his eldest brother, the Maharaja, the real power in the State will be in the Senapatti's hands. This is not a state of affairs which the Government of India can view with indifference, nor would it be to the credit of the British power, any more than to the interests of the people of Manipur itself, that the Governor General in Council should acquiesce in such a settlement of the case ... the Governor General in Council considers that it will be desirable that the Senapatti should be removed from Manipur and punished for his lawless conduct. I am to inquire where you would recommend that he should be interned, and what steps you consider necessary for carrying out his removal without affording him the chance, which his position as head of the Manipur forces might possibly give him, of making any forcible opposition.[19]

In addition it was stated that Pucca Senna should not be allowed to return to the state and that it was to the advantage of Manipur and the promotion of British interests to recognise the regent, Kula Chandra, rather than restoring the Maharaja – but that a government which could be seen to owe its existence to the Senapati's revolt would not be countenanced. As already laid out, Quinton should visit Manipur to make these requirements known, taking an adequate force 'even though opposition was not expected'.[20] This was not an unreasonable supposition due to the current harmony which appeared to exist between the British and the new regime. It was apparent that at the moment the Government of India determined to inflict their penalty, Grimwood was treating the Senapati with the respect due to his standing under the regency of Kula Chandra (sanctioned provisionally by the representative of the Government of India) and the Prince would have been unaware of the threat to his position. Bizarrely, Grimwood was not warned when it was decided to proceed with the Senapati's punishment that the Prince 'was no longer to be treated with honour, but as a man in disgrace, on whom the wrath of the Government of India was about to fall'.[21] Quinton was placed in a difficult position. He was a fairly long-serving member of the Indian Civil Service, having arrived in India in 1856. However, apart from a short period of service in Burma, he had been posted mainly in north-west India, and had only taken over as chief commissioner of Assam in 1889. His knowledge of the situation in the north-east, and experience in dealing with Indian princely states in general, was therefore limited. He knew that Grimwood strongly supported a policy of acceptance of the status quo in Manipur, and appears to have somewhat blindly trusted his judgement. Moreover he himself had serious reservations about the course of action proposed by his superiors. As a loyal servant of the Crown, however, he had no alternative but to carry out his orders.

On 21 March, Sur Chandra was informed that the Regent was to be recognised as his successor in Manipur.

CHAPTER 6

THE CHIEF COMMISSIONER'S ESCORT

As communications passed between the Government of India and the Chief Commissioner, Manipur was showing disturbing signs of not being as ordered and tranquil as Quinton had imagined. Whether or not the Senapati was implicated in Sur Chandra's departure, during the subsequent five months he appeared to have considerably strengthened his grip on the state. Speculation in the capital had been rife and Tikendrajit and Thangal General challenged Grimwood frequently as to whether or not the British would restore the exiled monarch, who, having, taken up residence in Calcutta, lost no opportunity of pestering the Government of India, 'begging for a reconsideration of his case, and help to regain the kingdom of which he had been unjustly deprived'.[1]

Grimwood himself was not unhappy with the current state of affairs, admitting after the abdication that the Maharaja had been 'a weak ruler, paid little attention to public business, and spent hours every day in worshipping in the temple. He was not at all the person to keep order amongst his brothers, and he is a man who will be much happier, I imagine, as an ascetic than as a ruler.'[2] However in a letter to the Foreign Department dated 9 February Sur Chandra repudiated 'the statements publicly made, that, while ruling my territory, I was a priest-ridden imbecile, neglected my duties and devoted myself to the performance of religious ceremonies and observances', declaring somewhat optimistically that the army remained faithful to him and that 'there was universal regret and lamentation amongst all classes from the time when

I left Manipur until I crossed the border'. The ousted ruler added, in words which no doubt helped to remove any doubts that British officials may have harboured in wielding the imperial stick to arrest Tikendrajit:

> It is a matter of life and death to me, my case is being watched with interest by Native Chiefs as well as by my people to see whether the paramount power will allow a successful conspiracy to deprive a people of its Prince, instead of calling upon the rebels to lay down their arms and not dare to disturb by force the possession of a Prince who ruled, recognised and protected by the British Government.[3]

Despite Sur Chandra's confident assertion that the people of Manipur would 'rejoice to receive me back with open arms and restore me to my throne',[4] it was recognised that his reinstatement would be a difficult operation, as a great deal of bitter feeling existed against the ex-ruler and more especially against Pucca Senna. Adding to the uncertainty, it was rumoured that arms, ammunition and food were being collected inside the palace by order of the Senapati as part of the preparations to resist the Maharaja, should he return to Manipur, suggesting that perhaps the Prince was not as disassociated from the events surrounding the abdication as Quinton had maintained. Confirmation of the stockpiling of arms emerged when Ethel asked her *shikari* to procure some wild duck, 'He said he was not able to shoot, as the Jubraj[5] had ordered him, as well as all the other men in his village, to bring their guns into the palace arsenal, and that all the villages in the neighbourhood had received similar commands.'[6]

On 21 February the Grimwoods were 'electrified' by a telegram informing them of the impending visit from the Chief Commissioner, requesting road and rest houses to be 'put in order' for such a significant event. At the time the couple had two visitors: William Babington Melville, the Superintendent of the Telegraph Department in Assam, whose visit was fleeting; and Lieutenant Walter Henry Simpson of the 43rd Gurkha Light Infantry. Melville was a Scot from Dumfries, who had worked for the department for 21 years and was partially crippled. Simpson, aged 30 and educated at Cheltenham, Rugby and Sandhurst had served with the 43rd Gurkha Light Infantry in the 1886–7 Burmese War, and since 1886 had been an adjutant of the regiment. His task in Manipur was to inspect some military stores which had been left behind at the Langthobal cantonment four miles from the residency when the 43rd Gurkha Rifles went to fight in the Chin Hills, and he was an old friend of the Grimwoods from the hill station of Shillong. A most welcome addition to the residency, Ethel reported that 'He was very clever, and a wonderful musician, and nothing pleased him better than to be allowed to play the piano for hours . . . and he got on very well with the princes . . . who liked looking at his guns and talking military "shop" with him.'[7] When Simpson's work was finished, he wired to the colonel of his regiment for permission to remain in Manipur, his appetite whetted by the chance of a disturbance in the state which might involve military action. The necessary leave was granted.

For more than three years the Grimwoods had been planning a period of furlough in England, and the date of sailing was fixed. Frank felt it would be wise if Ethel arranged to take an earlier steamer in case of trouble; however the suggested alteration of her plans had a drastic effect upon the Durbar – giving the impression, connected with the mystery surrounding the Chief Commissioner's visit, that she was 'flying from danger'. The princes used every possible wile to induce Ethel to remain, and Thangal General came more than once with messages from the Senapati himself. The Grimwoods explained that the steamer fare would be forfeited if Ethel failed to sail on a certain date, but this argument had little effect on the remaining members of the royal family. Their forceful persuasion, added to Frank's 'extreme reluctance' to lose his wife, eventually resulted in the postponement of her journey, a decision which was to have extraordinary repercussions for the sole Englishwoman in Manipur.[8]

The Grimwoods were deliberately kept in the dark as far as Quinton's movements and intentions were concerned. While en route to Manipur on 8 March 1891 the Chief Commissioner wrote from camp to Brigadier-General H. Collett, General Officer Commanding the Assam District,[9] making it clear that he 'thought it very necessary that Grimwood should remain at Manipur and keep a watch on what is going on there', adding, 'I felt that if I communicated with him by telegraph, or even by letter, things might leak out, so I have sent Gurdon [Assistant Commissioner of Assam][10] on ahead to communicate fully with him, and return and meet me between Kohima and Manipur.'[11] There had, in the weeks leading up to Quinton's departure, been a significant amount of discussion over the size of the force deemed necessary to accompany him on his mission. It was common knowledge that the Manipuris possessed two 7-pounder guns and 200 Enfields, plus four mountain guns. In consideration of such a substantial array at the Senapati's disposal, Quinton's somewhat casual approach in suggesting an escort of 200 military police met with little enthusiasm from Collett, who wired back: 'My advice is that you go via Kohima you should take 200 of 42nd [Gurkha Rifles] from Dibrugarh, with Colonel Skene in command ... We cannot afford to have mistakes, and a scratch force of police under a subaltern not suitable escort for Chief Commissioner.'[12] In Calcutta on 20 February Quinton was informed in the Viceroy's Council by the military member, General George Chesney,[13] that 'it would be madness to go with so small an escort' and that to avoid the possibility of successful resistance on the part of the Senapati no less than 400 men should accompany the Chief Commissioner, comprising 200 of the 42nd and 200 of the 44th Gurkha Rifles under Lieutenant Colonel Charles Skene.[14] To this escort Collett subsequently ordered 200 rifles of the 43rd under Captain J. W. Cowley to march from Cachar to form an addition to the garrison at Manipur (100 rifles of the 43rd) and to act as support to the Chief Commissioner's escort.[15] Lieutenant J. B. Chatterton of the 42nd Gurkha Rifles, staff officer of the escort, suggested to Skene the advisability of taking the two mountain guns which were with the 43rd Gurkhas at Kohima. Quinton was, however, of the opinion that they were unnecessary. While these communications were in progress, it was apparently thought unnecessary to refer to the commander in chief in India, Sir Frederick Roberts, regarding the strength or composition of the escort, and the viceroy did not see the papers until 4 March. Roberts was later to write to his predecessor that 'The whole business was kept a secret, and Skene apparently did not know what Quinton meant to do.'[16]

The scale of military support was to prove woefully inadequate. Collett maintained in his own defence after the hostilities,

> I regret excessively that I should not have taken a more correct view of the state of affairs at Manipur ... The universal opinion in this province was that the Chief Commissioner had an escort of overpowering strength, and no one dreamed of the terrible disaster which has occurred. It seemed that an escort of 400 Gurkhas added to the permanent garrison of 100 Gurkhas, and supported

> by 200 Gurkhas en route from Silchar [Cachar], would be ample to overawe malcontents ... I would also draw attention to the fact that an escort of 400 men appeared to be considered sufficient by the Governor-General's Council sitting in Calcutta. That we were all mistaken is now too terribly evident.[17]

Babu Rassik Lal Kundu, head clerk of the political agency in Manipur, stressed the extraordinarily complacent approach of the Government of India:

> Those who have been engaged in the excursion had never guessed the misfortune which awaited them here, and hence it was most unwise on their part to think so little of their antagonists, however inferior in position, and thus to attempt the enterprise, unchallenged, with inadequate strength and armament in a country ever indulged with independence and therefore naturally hostile to foreign interference.[18]

Collett originally gave the order that the escort was to be supplied with 40 rounds in pouch and 50 in box per man; but on learning that there were 13,000 rounds of Snider and 6,000 rounds of Martini ammunition at the Manipur residency, he counter-ordered the amount in the boxes with the result that the escort marched with only 40 rounds in pouch. After some deliberation he gave orders for the police at Kohima to deliver to the escort, should they require it, as much Snider ammunition as was necessary. However, the party departed for Manipur without taking the reserve. Transport was very scarce and Colonel Skene who, having served on the Burmese Expedition from 1886 to 1889 was no stranger to the area, was doubtless guided by the fact that troops marching in Assam did not usually carry more than 40 rounds per man and by the knowledge that they would find ammunition waiting for them at Manipur. The 42nd and 44th Gurkhas were armed with Sniders, the 43rd with Martinis. Unfortunately, out of the Resident's escort one native officer and 33 men with 3,800 rounds of Martini ammunition were at Langthobal, four miles away, and 11 men with 440 rounds were escorting a prisoner to Cachar. This shortfall was, however, not seen to be a problem. A military account of events concluded that 'Colonel Skene did not anticipate much opposition, or that, if he did, that he considered that he was amply provided for.'[19] Had he been able to communicate with Grimwood before departing, he would not have been deluded into thinking that the Senapati would be a soft touch.

By 18 March 1891 Quinton was approaching Manipur with an escort of 414 Gurkhas consisting of nine native officers, seven buglers and 398 sepoys under the command of Colonel Skene. The civil officers who accompanied the Chief Commissioner were William Henry Cossins, assistant secretary, and Lieutenants P. R. Gurdon and Albert Woods, assistant commissioners. The military officers involved in the operation were Captain G. H. Butcher, Lieutenants J. B. Chatterton and E. J. Lugard, DSO, and Surgeon J. T. Calvert of the 42nd Gurkhas, and Captain T. S. Boileau and Lieutenant Lionel Wilhelm Brackenbury of the 44th, together with the Grimwoods' friend, Lieutenant Simpson, of the 43rd Gurkha Light Infantry. From Camp Karong, Quinton telegraphed his plan of action to the Foreign Department of the Government of India in Calcutta. He expected to reach Manipur on Sunday, 22 March with the escort. It was intended that the Regent and the members of the Durbar should meet him on arrival, when he would reveal the decision of the Government of India to arrest the Senapati and inform the Prince that the length of his exile and return were to depend on his conduct and the tranquillity of the country. Quinton further intended to order the Regent to place a gun with the escort during his stay at Manipur and, in order to prevent any disturbances, the Senapati was to accompany him on 25 March on his return. He was of the opinion that the Senapati should not be detained in the neighbouring area of Assam, but elsewhere in India. The conditions to be imposed on the new maharaja were as follows: 'Three hundred troops were to be located in Manipur and a site given for their accommodation; the Maharaja must accept the advice of the Political Agent in all matters; the Pucca Senna was not to be allowed to return to Manipur, and the younger brothers were to be permitted to remain.'[20]

Various other suggestions as to the residence of the previous maharaja and matters pertaining to the allowances to be made to the exiled members of the royal family were also included in the telegraph. On 19 March Quinton's intentions were approved by the Government of India.

As agreed, Lieutenant Gurdon had gone ahead of the escort and reached Manipur on 15 March. The object of his journey was to discuss certain matters with the Political Agent and return to the Chief

Commissioner as soon as possible. In the aftermath of the Manipur revolt this exchange assumed much importance, and Gurdon's confidential report of the meeting formed the subject of a Parliamentary Paper published on 14 December 1891, which, according to *The Times* of the following day, 'fills a conspicuous gap in the history of the Manipur disaster as hitherto placed before the public'.[21] Gurdon stated that upon arriving at Manipur he informed Grimwood that the Government of India had ordered that the Senapati was to be deported from Manipur. Frank expressed the 'greatest astonishment', declaring that he had never imagined this to be the object of Quinton's visit.

The Political Agent stressed that he felt the government's decision was highly unwise for the following reasons: firstly, the Senapati was 'the most powerful as well as the most popular man in Manipur' and 'might give us some trouble to remove from the State'; secondly, if the Senapati were removed there would be no one to administer the affairs of State with the exception of Thangal General, who at 80 could hardly hold a major ministerial role for any length of time; thirdly, the Senapati had been 'goaded' into causing the revolution by Pucca Senna, 'an inveterate enemy of his', whom he wished to remove more than the ex-maharaja, and Grimwood felt that 'the Senapati should be leniently treated for his share in the rebellion'; and, finally, the Senapati would 'never be caught alive, he would sell his life dearly, and all that Government would get possession of would be "his dead body"'.[22]

Gurdon reiterated that the orders of the Government of India were final. In its view the Senapati had been instrumental in bringing about the September revolution, besides having 'misbehaved' on various other occasions. He asked Grimwood if the Prince could be arrested without 'bringing matters to a crisis' in Manipur, and whether he thought that it would be possible to bring pressure to bear on the Regent to deliver up the Senapati. The Political Agent replied that the Senapati had a following in the palace, but he did not know how strong that following was, or whether the Prince's adherents would be sufficiently forceful to resist British attempts to arrest him. At this stage of the conversation, Grimwood showed great annoyance at the fact that the decision of the government had not been communicated to him at an earlier date. Gurdon reported, 'He more than once said to me that as he had not been consulted, he would wash his hands of the whole business.'[23]

Gurdon admitted later that due to the Political Agent's 'pique' he found it very difficult to deal with him, suspecting that Frank had 'a very strong bias in favour of the Senapati, who was a very good friend of his. I came to the conclusion that the Senapati possessed, for some unknown reason, strong influence over Grimwood.'[24] This opinion appears to be been borne out by the fact that, even following his discussion with Gurdon, Frank was happy to make the highly questionable move of going out to shoot with the Senapati on 17 March. However, it appears that at the time of the meeting Gurdon also began to have misgivings about the proposed course of action:

> One thing seemed to me clear, and that was the Political Agent had been at first strongly against the step the Chief Commissioner was about to take. Mr. Grimwood had only slightly modified his first opinion after much argument on my part. I could not help feeling that there was something wrong, and that perhaps after all, Mr. Grimwood was right.[25]

Gurdon suggested that Grimwood should visit the Chief Commissioner himself to give him his views, and on 21 March the Political Agent joined Quinton's party at Sengmai, the final halting place on the journey from Kohima to Manipur. He had a long, private interview with Quinton, followed by a meeting with Quinton, Skene and Cossins. Gurdon stated that, although he was not present, he concluded later that it had been agreed at this meeting to arrest the Senapati in Durbar the following day. This was the first Gurdon had heard of this scheme. He commented, 'After it had gone on for about half an hour, I saw Mr. Grimwood leave and walk some distance away. Judging from his manner he appeared annoyed ... from what passed between Mr. Grimwood and myself before, I am certain that the idea of the arrest in Durbar was repugnant to him.'[26] In her account of events, Ethel recorded the shame that the couple felt in the betrayal of their friend:

> it has been hinted of late that the friendship which we had both entertained for the Jubraj [Senapati] was *infra dig.*, and contrary to the usual mode of procedure adopted by Anglo-Indian officials

in their intercourse with the rulers of native states. But when we first went to Manipur, my husband was told that he must endeavour to establish friendly feelings between the princes and himself ... in order to acquire an influence for good over each member of the Maharaja's family and over the state itself ... if such a friendship were distasteful and unusual, why was it never commented on by those in whose power it was to approve or disapprove, and who knew that it existed? Small wonder was it that we were both very sorry to hear of the fate which was in store for the Jubraj.[27]

CHAPTER 7

THE ARRIVAL OF THE CHIEF COMMISSIONER

Following the meeting with Frank Grimwood, the Chief Commissioner and escort marched stage by stage to Manipur, apparently meeting with great civility from the Manipur officials despite an undercurrent of mutual mistrust. It had been rumoured that Sur Chandra was accompanying Quinton in order to be reinstated, which caused some excitement. Lieutenant C. S. Williams of the 43rd Gurkha Rifles reported that:

> The Manipuris are in no end of a funk; but they say they mean to resist sooner than let the Rajah return. Today we hear that one of the princes with 1,000 men is going out to Sengmai on the Kohima to meet the Chief Commissioner and force. What this means we cannot tell; but it looks like resistance, and, if so, there will be a small battle on the road.[1]

In addition, the correspondent of the Allahabad newspaper, *The Pioneer*, noted that some disruption had been caused in the Durbar by the receipt of a mysterious telegram from Calcutta written in Roman characters, which stated that 'a big tiger would shortly be caught in Manipur'.[2] It appeared more than likely that the Senapati, fearing that he was indeed the 'tiger' in question, intended to resist Quinton's entry into the capital.

Whatever the motives of the Durbar, Thangal General was instructed to meet Quinton at Mao, just inside the Manipur border, with a large force of 700 Manipuri sepoys. While courtesy demanded that the Chief Commissioner should have been given a substantial reception, his officers were no doubt somewhat troubled by the number of sepoys under arms. On 21 Saturday March, the party halted at Sengmai where it was received by Prince Angao Senna with a personal escort of some 50 soldiers. The Prince was given a letter from the Chief Commissioner to the effect that a *durbar* would be held at the residency the next day at noon. Tikendrajit later recorded that:

> Mr. Grimwood was asked the reason of such unusual haste and steps taken by the Chief Commissioner, and it was communicated to the Regent that the Chief Commissioner was anxious to hold the durbar immediately after his arrival in order to expedite his departure for Tammu (on the border between Burma and Manipur) on special duty the next day, for which certain coolies were ordered to be in readiness.[3]

Lieutenant J. B. Chatterton of the 42nd Gurkha Rifles, staff officer to the Chief Commissioner's escort, left a party of 20 men under the command of a *havildar* of the 44th at Sengmai in charge of their own baggage and that of a party of 80 rifles, who had orders to return from Manipur to Sengmai on completion of certain duties which would be explained to them upon arrival. About four miles out of Manipur, the Chief Commissioner and escort were met by Tikendrajit, who had two regiments drawn up in a line on the Manipur side of the river. The Prince was obviously unwell and was carried in a litter, possibly due to the effects of the gallstones from which he had suffered for some time. Captain Butcher noted that the river was 'formerly spanned by a fine bridge, but which the Manipuris had burnt on our arrival at Sengmai, and which was put down to a jungle fire at the time.'[4] Here Quinton had a short interview with the Senapati, who did not join the British party but returned to Manipur to await the Chief Commissioner's arrival in the city.

Ethel recalled that:

> The morning of the 22nd broke clear and beautiful over the valley. Clusters of yellow roses blossomed on the walls of the house and the scent of the heliotrope greeted me as I went into the veranda to

> watch my husband start to meet Mr. Quinton. There was a delightful sense of activity about the place, and one felt that something of more than ordinary importance was about to take place; white tents peeped out from amongst the trees surrounding the house, and the camp prepared for the Sepoys stretched along under our wall at the end of the lake.[5]

About one mile from the palace and enclosure, the Maharaja's troops lined the road on either side. According to the Manipur Court Chronicle,

> Plantains, sugar cane and torches which were to be lit were planted in front of all the houses along the road where the Sahep was to pass, to show that he was the Commissioner Sahep ... Shrijut Kulachandra Maharaj along with all the noble and brave men of the land welcomed him at the Sna Keithen the Royal Market. A thirteen cannon salute was fired.[6]

After Quinton had conversed for a short time with the Regent, it was announced that a *durbar* would be held at 12pm that day in the residency. Chatterton issued orders that all British officers were to be present, together with three native officers from each corps. No man was to leave the camp, which consisted of grass hutting built by Manipuris on some open ground between the bazaar and the residency, and the entire force was to remain under arms.

To his great distress Grimwood was ordered by the Chief Commissioner to arrest the Senapati personally at the end of the *durbar*. Ethel described her husband's reaction: 'To be obliged to arrest a man himself with who he had been on friendly terms for nearly three years, and to see him treated like a common felon, without being able to defend himself, was naturally a hard task, and [he] felt it bitterly.'[7] However Quinton was unyielding and, replying to Ethel's question as to the reason for the arrest, declared that the government alone was sufficiently powerful to make or unmake maharajas.

In the residency precautions were taken to prevent the Senapati escaping. The doors of the *durbar* room were all locked with the exception of the one by which the princes would enter, and guards were stationed in the adjoining rooms, as well as round the house and on the verandas. The correspondent of *The Pioneer* reported that 'With the

Figure 7.1 The Manipur residency with escort and two sons of James Johnstone (The Alkazi Collection of Photography).

80 men warned to be in readiness to march back to Sengmai and with the customary guards mounted in the residency compound and the camping ground adjoining it, practically all the sepoys were under arms.'[8] It was necessary for the written orders of the Government of India to be translated into Manipuri, and Rassick Lal Kundu, the Bengali head clerk of the political agency, with another clerk and the Burmese interpreter were brought to the residency. The orders were lengthy and, having sworn an oath of secrecy, each of the clerks had a sentry placed over him.[9]

Some time before the translation was completed, the Regent arrived at the *durbar* with his brothers and a number of Manipuri officials, escorted by about 100 men. Had there been no reason for keeping the princes waiting at the gate the situation might have had a different outcome; however the delay enabled some of the Manipuri sepoys to enter the residency grounds where they 'made good use of their opportunities, marked the distribution of our forces, saw the Ghoorkhas lining the entrance steps, and the officers in attendance outside'.[10] When the Senapati was informed of the significant military presence in the compound he returned to his enclosure with his brother, Angao Senna, giving as an excuse that he felt too ill to remain in the hot sun. Ethel reported that he had not been well before Quinton's arrival, 'but whether he really felt as indisposed on this occasion as he affirmed is open to doubt'.[11] Tikendrajit later gave his own version of events, in which he declared that

> he was detained over half an hour outside the gate ... This was against etiquette, and the defendant [Tikendrajit], being on horseback exposed to the burning sun, became annoyed and disheartened. He could see the movements and preparations going on inside, and being under suspense, sent [his servant] Dasu Sardar to enquire about the object of such unusual proceedings. Dasu brought news of the armed sepoys being placed in from the rear of the Residency Bungalow, and that the officers were fully equipped and on horseback. The suspicion which the defendant so long entertained, was thus confirmed, that the Durbar was only a trap to make his arrest ... he felt exhausted and unable to wait any longer and consequently returned to the Palace.[12]

The Chief Commissioner informed the Regent through Grimwood that the *durbar* would not be held unless the Senapati appeared; Kula Chandra agreed to send for his brother, waiting for him at the residency with Thangal General who was also apparently ill and was found asleep on the floor before being persuaded by Ethel to rest on a sofa. After two hours the Senapati's messenger arrived with the reply that he was not sufficiently well to leave the palace compound. The Chief Commissioner had refused to see the Regent or his ministers during this time, and at about 3pm the Regent departed 'with great mortification and disappointment'.[13] In hindsight, the insult to Kula Chandra inevitably exacerbated matters. Two days later he was to write to the viceroy, Lord Lansdowne,

> According to previous custom, Chief Commissioners would come down to the Residency bungalow, and having shaken hands with the Maharaja, would welcome him to the darbar. But in the present occasion I could not see the Chief Commissioner even after entering the darbar house. Instead I saw numerous troops ready with arms in the front, back and below in the darbar bungalow; in its stairs and even within the darbar-house. Such an unusual

> arrangement gave rise to suspicion in my mind. Notwithstanding as I was eager to hear the intimation that was sent by the Governor-General, I waited in the darbar-house, having born all the indignities and dishonour.[14]

Later that afternoon Grimwood, accompanied by Lieutenant Simpson and Rassick Lal Kundu, was sent to the palace to confer with Manipuri state officials; another *durbar* was arranged for 8am on 23 March, and it was impressed upon the Regent that his brothers must attend. Ethel noted that there was little doubt that, 'from this moment, some inkling of what was intended penetrated the minds of the princes and their ministers'.[15] To some extent life appeared to return to normal in the capital, although there was an uneasy atmosphere. Captain Boileau of the 44th Gurkhas observed the change of mood at the daily open-air bazaar carried out in the late afternoon, when

> a procession came out of the west gate of the palace enclosure with banners and conch shells. Some women called out: 'The Jubraj is coming'. Just then a bugle sounded in our lines – an ordinary bugle call. I think it was the guard bugle, and some of the sepoys who were in the bazaar at once ran towards the lines, on seeing which, a sort of panic ensued among the women, most of whom rose up, and began to run away. But a Manipuri who was with me, shouted out: 'It is nothing, only the Holi procession', on which they all quieted down.[16]

Quinton later visited the bazaar with Grimwood, and 'officers and men moved freely amongst it purchasing cloths etc.'[17] In the evening the maharaja's band played at the residency during dinner, and Ethel made it clear that 'No thought of evil troubled any of us, for little did we know that it was the last evening we were to spend in peace there all together.'[18]

The following morning no representative from the royal family appeared at the allotted time, the red cloth for the reception was removed, and Grimwood and Simpson made yet another visit to the palace which was to prove fruitless. At this time it was observed that 'a continuous stream of able-bodied Manipuris were pouring into the city by all the roads from the surrounding country and only a few men carrying boxes and some women and children came out. The city gate was also closed and men were seen manning the walls.'[19] On their visits to the palace Grimwood and Simpson had seen Manipuri sepoys handing large quantities of ammunition in boxes out of the magazine near the maharaja's residence. At 3pm Lugard, with 80 rifles, was warned to hold himself in readiness to proceed to the Senapati's residence to arrest and carry the Prince away to Sengmai, while Butcher, with 100 rifles, was told to support him and prevent the Manipuris from following. The order to move was never issued.

It was evident that the Senapati would not make an appearance without some form of ultimatum on the part of the British. Quinton correspondingly wrote a letter to the Regent, informing him of his succession to the *gadi* and advising him that if the Senapati were not delivered up he would be forced to make an arrest. The proposed banishment was not to last indefinitely but would depend upon his brother's good behaviour. At about 2pm Grimwood and Simpson took the letter to the palace, described by Ethel as 'a veritable hornets' nest',[20] and remained there for three hours or so. The Regent made excuses for failing to give up Tikendrajit, writing later that,

> Having informed him [Grimwood] that I will send a reply in consultation with the ministers, I summoned the ministers and all the chief subjects to the darbar. When I put the proposal, none gave his consent in respect of the deportation of the innocent Jubaraj [Senapati]. Especially the Jubaraj having been unwell, I wrote to the Chief Commissioner stating that I will send a reply hereafter regarding the matter when the Jubaraj will recover his health.[21]

When this letter was delivered to the Political Agent, Grimwood repeated that he wanted either the Senapati or a written order for his delivery.

Shortly afterwards Grimwood, Simpson and Rassik Lal Kundu, the head clerk of the political agency, had a brief interview with Tikendrajit, who was carried down in a litter. At this meeting the Senapati informed Grimwood that 'he was willing to obey the durbar's orders'. He was unable through illness to give himself up immediately as requested, but would do so subsequently. Rassik Lal Kundu stated that 'He certainly seemed to me to be ill. He hadn't bathed and was not dressed, and his face was half covered up.'[22] According to Ethel, 'The exertion caused him to faint and my husband said there was no doubt as to his illness, and that he found him in high fever.' Grimwood did his utmost to persuade the Senapati to obey orders and give himself up quietly, 'telling him that the proposed banishment was not to last for ever, but that it would depend chiefly on his good behaviour, and eventually, at the death of his brother, the regent, he . . . would be allowed to return to Manipur, and ascend the throne as Maharaja'.[23] All attempts at persuasion, however, proved useless, and the Political Agent returned from the palace announcing that his mission had failed. He described the Regent as being in a 'very nervous state', having been informed that 'the Government of India would not recognise him as Maharaja, if he did not give up the Senapati, and agree to certain other proposals, but the Regent's fear of his younger brother carried all before it, and the Regent could not be induced to listen to reason'.[24] Grimwood also informed Skene that he estimated the force of Manipuri soldiers in the palace to be between 5,000 and 6,000, and Simpson added that the walls of the second enclosure were thickly lined by soldiers – as was the palace polo ground.[25]

Since political negotiations had again faltered, it was decided after consultations between Quinton, Skene and Grimwood that there was no other course but to enforce the orders of the Government of India. At sundown extra pickets were posted and hourly patrols were arranged. The city had

> a deserted look about it and on the principal road, as a rule crowded with people at that hour, not a soul was visible. The clouds had been gathering up all the after noon [sic], and about seven o'clock a terrific thunderstorm occurred, and darkness set in, which was only lit up now and then by brilliant flashes of lightning.[26]

Ethel reported that a number of the residency servants, including her old ayah, vanished, 'scenting danger', and, according to Captain Boileau,

> no bazar [sic] was held that evening . . . I received reports from two people, not Manipuris, that there would probably be a rush made on the lines that night, and, perhaps, all buildings set on fire, and

> that the Manipuris and Kukis had been collected in thousands. I went and told Colonel Skene what I had heard, and kept one reporter as a messenger to take word out to Langthobal, telling them to come in and join. This messenger was sent out.[27]

Despite these disturbing reports, a remarkable lack of concern existed at the residency on the evening of 23 March. Ethel reported that, anxious to participate in some action, 'the officers and Sepoys were hoping that the resistance would be strong ... but serious alarms for our safety never entered our heads'.[28] As part of the celebrations for the Chief Commissioner's visit, a Manipuri *nautch* had been arranged with dancers from the palace (later alleged by Tikendrajit to be a further venue for his arrest), but Grimwood suspected that the performance was a ruse to find out the strength of the British forces in the residency compound. When by 9pm the performers had not arrived, the Political Agent sent a servant to the palace where he was surprised to find the west gate closed and to be informed that no residency personnel were to be admitted. In place of the *nautch* Lieutenant Brackenbury provided a less exotic form of entertainment by accompanying himself on the banjo, and Quinton participated in a hand of whist.

After dinner Colonel Skene went over a plan of the palace with the military officers. A description of the defences of Manipur had been drawn up by Captain E. Jones, 23rd Pioneers, giving some idea of the scale of the operations. The residency and lines of the resident's escort were situated outside the Manipur fort at its south-western corner. The mud wall surrounding the residency was about three feet high on the north, south and west, but on the east side (facing the west wall of the palace) it was six feet high. While reasonably bullet-proof, it was not loopholed and was never intended to withstand attack. The lower storey of the residency – as described by the former Political Agent, Colonel Johnstone – was raised six feet above ground and built of brick with a two-foot thick wall. The quarter-guard at the main entrance was also built of brick, and two buildings close to it, the hospital and schoolhouse, were raised on a solid brick foundation. The area of the residency enclosure or compound was about 25 acres, and outside the compound walls, on the side nearest the city, there was a shallow ditch, six feet deep and 12 yards wide, with water in some places one foot deep, but mostly quite dry in March.[29]

The defences of the fort consisted of three lines forming an irregular parallelogram, 1,400 yards long on the western face of the outer line and about half that length on the northern and southern faces. The eastern line followed the Manipur River. The outer line of defence consisted of a substantial earth rampart, eight feet high, faced on the outside with a brick wall which rose four feet above the rampart, forming a parapet. The residency enclosure wall was completely commanded by the rampart of the outer line, about 100 yards away. The second line of defence of the fort consisted of another earth rampart of eight feet, also faced with a brick-wall parapet, and small circular bastions provided flanking defence to the inner wall. On the eastern face of the fort the deep bed of the Manipur River, with its steep banks, added greatly to its defensive strength. To the north and north-west the wall was in a bad state of repair and the moat was dry. This was the side on which the Senapati's palace was situated, and the most vulnerable to attack.[30]

The Senapati's palace was a large thatched house with walls of mud and wattle situated between the inner and outer walls of the royal compound. It was within the princes' enclosure, which contained a brick temple and several bungalows built on the model of the residency, surrounded by numerous houses of reeds and thatch, which concealed any persons occupying the enclosure from the view of the defenders in the inner line. The reduit of the fort, commonly known as 'the citadel', consisted of a square enclosure on higher ground than the rest of the buildings; its sides were 150 yards in length, with small bastions at each corner. In the interior was the maharaja's palace with the arsenal and magazine, and two huge statues of lions some 30 feet in height at the entrance, on the outer side of which was the so-called Lion Gate.[31] Between the Lion Gate and the citadel were the *durbar* room and the polo ground. The citadel wall was formed of an earth rampart of 15 feet, faced on the outside by a brick wall which rose three feet above the rampart as a parapet. The fire from the citadel completely commanded the inner or second line of the Manipur defences on the north-east, eastern and southern faces, but the northern and north-western faces were hidden from view by trees and houses. However fire could be directed on the princes' enclosure from the northern face of the citadel at a distance of 500 yards. All the walls in the inner line and in the citadel were well provided with loopholes.[32]

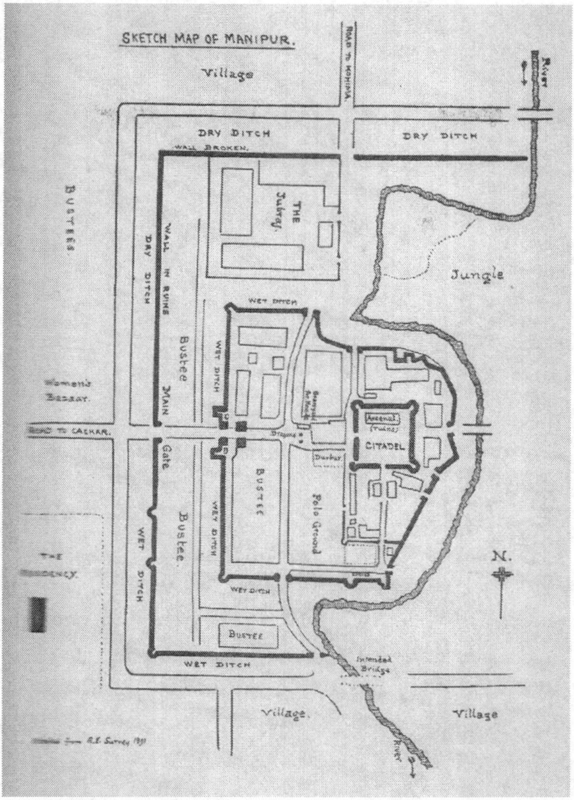

Map 2 Diagram of Manipur fort adapted from R. E. Survey, 1891.

Skene informed his officers that the object was to take the Senapati without force if possible, and not to open fire unless fired upon. It was considered probable that the Prince would be in his own palace rather than the citadel, as the Regent 'feared him greatly, and would be unwilling to shelter him'.[33] The night passed peacefully, and on the bitterly cold morning of 24 March, a little before daybreak, the British party set off to arrest the Senapati in his house within the fort enclosure.

CHAPTER 8

HOSTILITIES

In the early morning of 24 March 1891, orders were given to Captain Butcher, with Lieutenant Simpson as guide, to take 70 men of the 42nd and 44th Gurkha Rifles to cross the moat on the west face of the fort at the point where there was no water, and to 'rush' the Senapati's house from the south side. Lieutenant Brackenbury and Subadar Hima Chand of the 44th were to proceed with 30 rifles to the north entrance of the fort at the rear of the Senapati's house to intercept the Prince if he attempted to escape along the Kohima road. There was no gate to be forced on this face, as the outer wall was in ruins and the moat was dry. Brackenbury had to go almost a mile before entering the northern section of the *pat*, whereas Butcher had only a quarter of a mile to cover before passing over the ruined wall on the north-western face. Shortly after the two advance parties set forth, Lieutenant Lugard, with 40 rifles, was to follow to take up a position in support. A total of 100 men (50 of the 42nd and 50 of the 44th Gurkha Rifles), together with the 43rd Gurkha Rifles comprising the Political Agent's guard,[1] were to remain in the residency compound under Captain Boileau. Colonel Skene, with 100 rifles kept in reserve, was stationed near the polo ground.

At 4.45am, the escort fell in and Lieutenant Brackenbury moved off, followed almost immediately by Captain Butcher. After some delay a shot was heard, announcing the arrival of Captain Butcher's party at the Senapati's house, where they came under fire from 400 or 500 enemy soldiers lining the walls at every yard. The enemy made a stand at the gateway but were 'all despatched by the bayonet', enabling the British to occupy the property.[2] Butcher then posted a number of rifles along the wall facing the inner lines of the fort to keep down the attack. The Manipuris were alert, and the musketry fire very rapid but not straight. Ethel, Quinton and Cossins were in the telegraph office at the end of the residency drive, attempting to send a message to Calcutta, and were driven into the basement below by 'the sudden advent of a bullet through the office window at our elbows'.[3]

Lieutenant Simpson returned to Colonel Skene at about 8am and informed him that Lieutenant Brackenbury, Subadar Hima Chand and one *havildar*, all of the 44th, were wounded. He reported that Brackenbury's party was completely surrounded and in dire need of assistance. Simpson subsequently returned to the Senapati's house with a reinforcement of 50 men and Surgeon Calvert, the medical officer in charge of the Chief Commissioner's escort. At about 10.30am, Calvert, with hospital assistant Haribans Tiwari and two *doolies* reached the Senapati's temple, which had been commandeered by Butcher and in which the wounded were gathered. In the aftermath of the conflict, the seizure of the temple by British forces was seen as a significant event in that it was both insensitive and inflammatory. Babu Rassik Lal Kundu reported afterwards that British troops 'destroyed idols, mounted on top of the temple and polluted it, killed several women and children, and consequently regular fighting commenced on both sides'.[4] However from the British point of view, the temple, despite being shelled by the enemy was, according to Calvert, 'a *pukka* building, and hence deemed an excellent collecting and dressing station. Here all the wounded were dressed, and stimulants and opium give to those requiring them.'[5] It was not deemed advisable to take the wounded back to camp immediately; they would have been exposed to fire, and an attack on the palace was thought to be imminent. The hospital assistant was left in charge of the seven wounded. Lieutenant Brackenbury could not be found and Calvert took one of the *doolies* to search for him.

Meanwhile Lieutenant Lugard had discovered Subadar Hima Chand and a sepoy of the 44th lying wounded in the river and 'at great personal risk' led the doctor to them. Calvert stressed the bravery of the soldiers concerned: 'To reach the wounded men it was necessary to cross a road under heavy fire, and this the *kahars* most gallantly did. Arrived at the other side, they were exposed to an enfilading fire, towards which it was necessary to advance, and from which for some distance there was no shelter.' Field dressings were applied, and the men were placed in the most sheltered place available. Calvert reported that:

> Being now well behind the palace with the party sent to flank the enemy, it was decided to wait here until the assault on the palace took place, since by doing this the wounded would be between the medical officer and the camp, and those nearest the enemy, and consequently most exposed to danger, would be seen first and could be rapidly sent to the collecting station.[6]

At 4.15pm, hearing no news from Captain Butcher, who failed to maintain contact with the surgeon, it was decided to return to camp with the wounded. Simpson, who had been ordered by Skene to take 50 men and clear the left bank of the river, also found himself and his men isolated and joined Calvert on the way back. Calvert reported that,

> as we were passing some houses to the west of the Polo ground, we saw considerable numbers of villagers standing about. Suddenly a shot was fired from their direction, it was very close, very sudden, and apparently startled everybody. The men of Lt. Simpson's party turned round in a rage, abused the people and fired a couple of vollies {sic} into the houses before Lt. Simpson could stop them. Lt. Simpson was very angry with the men who belonged to both the 42nd and 44th for firing without orders and wasting ammunition. I noticed that the telegraph wire was cut, and torn down near the Polo ground and within a few hundred yards of the Residency ... I was very much surprised to find, on arrival, that all other parties had come in and I and Simpson were the last.[7]

British action during the day had not been confined to one area of the fort. Soon after the firing began in the direction of the Senapati's palace, Chatterton was ordered by Skene to take 30 rifles to open the main gate situated in the centre of the west wall, diagonally opposite the residency. The officer crossed the dry ditch at about the same point as Butcher, passed over the wall and, turning to the right, rushed the rear of the entrance, totally surprising its defenders who dropped 'panic stricken' from the upper storey onto the roadway. Boileau describes that 'with splendid dash he {Chatterton} attacked and took the main gate of the enclosure, killing two Manipuris and taking prisoner two Manipuri native officers and 17 prisoners; these prisoners were brought into camp and treated very well'.[8]

Colonel Skene, accompanied by Frank Grimwood, took 80 rifles of the 42nd and 44th through the main gate with a number of tall ladders and a further five boxes of ammunition, and joined the assault party at about 10am. The Senapati was not found, having escaped, it was presumed, to the Regent's palace. This was a considerable distance, and the ground between the two buildings was a network of narrow streets and groups of wattle huts with thatched roofs which 'hid the movements of thousands of Manipuris acting under the Senapati's orders'.[9] On the left front of the compound, which Butcher and Lugard were holding, armed Manipuris in large numbers were seen dropping down from the wall of the inner enclosure and into the bed of the river – at that point, a small, winding stream with steep grass banks. It was at first supposed that they were beating a retreat, but they soon appeared in the jungle to the east and from behind a long, low wall opened heavy fire. In the neighbourhood of the Regent's palace the Senapati now brought his battery of four 7-pounders into action, firing somewhat ineffectually at his own temple, a good target of white masonry topped by a corrugated roof with gilded eaves. It was difficult to see the exact position of the guns owing to the mud huts and trees surrounding the area, and the shelling, although intermittent, continued all the morning.[10]

The British were in no way nearer their objective of capturing the Prince. Skene examined the possibilities of scaling the wall between the Senapati's compound and the inner enclosure. The storming party would be under cover except when crossing a road and a shallow, dry ditch, however in the inner enclosure the arsenal and palace were enclosed by further walls from 15 to 20 feet high which would also have to be scaled unless one of the gateways could be forced. This was hardly an easy matter since the Gurkhas were without artillery or explosives. Butcher was asked to examine the men's pouches to assess the remaining ammunition, and it was found that each man had from five to ten rounds. As *The Pioneer* declared later, 'To have sent a storming party of 100 men under such conditions, against at least fifty times their number, would have been madness.'[11] The party in the Senapati's house did not attempt to advance further, but waited for reinforcements. At this stage Grimwood estimated the strength of the enemy to be 6,000 men, armed with Snider and Enfield rifles. There was also evidence of bullets for Martini-Henry rifles which were used against the British. Apart from the four 7-pounder guns the Manipuris also possessed artillery of a higher calibre, but this appears not to have been brought into action. Colonel Skene returned to the residency at about noon and, after consulting with the Chief Commissioner, sent word by Lugard to the attacking party to withdraw. Chatterton reported that when he asked Skene what had occurred at the Senapati's house

> he replied that 'we had got into a nice fix'. He said he wished we had brought the guns as they would have been invaluable, and, pointing to the residency, he said 'I don't know what we are to do, that place is perfectly untenable ... We have got no men, we have got no ammunition'.[12]

In a letter to Lord Lansdowne, written on 25 March, the Regent insisted that the Manipuris had been forced into an aggressive position as a result of the attack on the royal buildings, graphically detailing British atrocities:

> a large number of armed troops suddenly entered the palace ... having killed eleven keepers of the gate, entered the house [of the Senapati], cut the heads off two boys, killed three boys by shooting. Having entered the temple, smashed the idol and all the articles with it; set fire to a village in the neighbourhood of the palace, and having set fire to a Brahmin's house, burnt the idol, the cows, and everything else. Having tied up the hairs of two girls together, threw them into the fire and got them burnt. One woman was flying away through panic, who was seized and her hands and ears mutilated; she is still alive. The hands and legs of a man were first cut off, and then he was killed with cruelty. Although there was so much cruel treatment, we did not act in opposition, but at last they attacked my palace and set fire to it. And then when it could not be borne any longer, and my subjects turned mad and lost my control, they began to fight to protect their wives and children and religion ... That in the present occurrence the dispute was not initiated on my side is known to all the officers, sepoys, and the subjects of the Empress of India. This was due entirely to the imprudence and obstinacy of the chief officer of the Empress.[13]

However Captain Boileau was to testify later that, as far as he was aware, no cruelty of any sort was carried out by British troops, but he was unable to comment upon what occurred at the princes' enclosure, which was occupied for the greater part of the day by the parties led by Captain Butcher and Lieutenant Brackenbury. Rassik Lal Kundu stated that he had been sent around the Senapati's enclosure by order of the Durbar to see the women and children who had been killed by the British, but could observe none. It was afterwards discovered that three women, who were lying concealed in high grass, had been unintentionally shot by Lieutenant Simpson's party, and a *subadar* in the Military Police testified he had heard that during the attack on the Senapati's enclosure 'a Muhammedan woman was shot in a hamlet; she was shot in a volley fired at some Kukis who were firing into the troops; two or three children were also hit in the same volley'.[14]

During the British incursion into the princely enclosure all had not been quiet at the residency. From about 10am there had been steady infantry fire from the front, and suddenly at about midday a number of Manipuris crept up under cover of the Naga village at the back of the building and fired on the rear face where only a small party of men was posted. Captain Boileau was ordered to burn the village at about 1pm, which had the desired effect of stopping the enemy attack until the fire died down. Ethel and Quinton made another attempt to send a telegram to the Government of India, only to discover that the wires had been cut in all directions. Frank suggested that Ethel should take refuge in the cellars, however she was determined 'to remain above-board, so to speak, until the worst came to the worst'.[15] Windows were shattered and bullets destroyed the Grimwoods' prized possessions throughout the building, but at that stage an evacuation of the residency was not seen as an inevitability. Lugard reported that 'Things were not looking so serious at this time, as later in the day, and the idea of abandoning the Residency was naturally not acceptable to Mr. Quinton, as involving so terrible a political disaster.'[16]

At about 4pm, Captain Butcher's party at the Senapati's house and Colonel Skene's detachment were withdrawn, apparently without ascertaining either the whereabouts or the safety of Lieutenant Simpson and Surgeon Calvert, a severe lapse in duty which was to have its consequences in the aftermath of the revolt. Chatterton and his party at the main gate were also ordered to retire, and Chatterton later detailed the somewhat incompetent British plans which had contributed to the retreat:

> It had been Colonel Skene's intention to hold the main gate permanently, and to occupy the palace wall behind the wet moat in front of the Residency; and orders were given to Captain Boileau to make bamboo rafts to enable men to cross the moat. These rafts were made from green male bamboo, no other materials being available; but they were useless, as green male bamboo does not float.[17]

Unsurprisingly, as soon as the British guard at the main gate guard retired, the outer palace wall was immediately occupied by the enemy and two guns placed in position: one on the wall opposite the residency treasury, and a second on the wall on the north side of the main gate. The Adjutant-General in India, Major-General W. Galbraith, was to comment later that at this stage of the afternoon 'valuable hours were lost in indecision; and even when it was resolved to concentrate for defence, there was inexplicable delay and want of concerted action in recalling the detachments from the Palace and the further bank of the river'.[18]

When the British attacking force had all come in, the enemy moved up and took up a position behind the wall, which was loopholed for men lying down and kneeling. The heavy rifle fire on the residency and entire compound continued relentlessly from about 4.30 until 8pm; according to Boileau,

> it was a perfect hail-storm of bullets, ploughing up the ground; it seemed as if several hundred rifles were being fired off by men firing alternately, there being no cessation of the fire. While the fire from the wall was going on, a cross fire was brought to bear on us alternately from every other side.[19]

After the event, Gurdon detailed the defects of the residency and compound as a military position. He noted that it was commanded by the fort, that the outer walls would take double or treble the amount of men the British had at their disposal to defend them, and that there was cover in villages on the right and rear faces of the building which could be used by the enemy.[20]

In the meantime hospital assistant Haribans Tiwari had brought out all the casualties from the temple through the town gate into the residency compound. Due to the attack on the residency the wounded were placed in the civil hospital in the grounds, which was a thatch-roofed house built on a brick platform with numerous doors and windows on the side nearest to the city moat – dangerously within 100 yards of the wall which was lined by the enemy. On the arrival of the medical officer it was decided to move to the residency cellar, but, as Calvert reported,

> the fire on the hospital became so hot that exit from either door was impossible . . . Bullets now coming through the windows, the medical officer barricaded them with tables put up end ways . . . The wounded were then quickly lifted out through a window in [the] rear of the house, and laid down under cover of the raised brick platform, and a barricade of tables was raised to protect them from the cross fire. Their final removal was determined under cover of darkness.[21]

Lieutenant Brackenbury with a *havildar* and sepoy of the 44th had been discovered lying on the riverbank on the north side of the palace, after losing direction and arriving on the wrong side of the wall near the Senapati's house, where they were exposed to heavy enemy fire. It was a difficult and dangerous task to remove the lieutenant, and a native officer had been mortally wounded in the attempt. However, late in the afternoon Brackenbury was brought into the hospital. Calvert reported that 'I found on him six distinct bullet wounds. He told me then that he had been surrounded and shot in the ankle, and that he had received all the other wounds while on the ground . . . He told nothing about the men of his party, being too weak to talk much.'[22] The commander in chief, Sir Frederick Roberts, stressed later his 'especial regret that from 6am until the afternoon no effectual effort was made to reinforce Lieutenant Brackenbury's party or to rescue this gallant young officer and his wounded comrades from their isolated and perilous position'.[23]

Late in the afternoon, the Manipuris began to use their artillery to greater effect. The shells no longer passed over the residency but lodged in the fabric of the building and grounds of the compound. Moreover the infantry fire from the front showed no signs of slackening: 'the enemy poured in upon us an incessant fire through loopholes without exposing themselves'[24] and 'the tanks and ornamental waters were churned into foam'.[25] It soon became evident that a withdrawal from the residency was vital, and the alternative of taking up a position in the open was discussed by the Chief Commissioner and Skene. It was decided, however, to try first to obtain a truce and reopen negotiations with the royal party. At about 7.30pm, the Political Agent arranged for a ceasefire to be sounded several times by one of the buglers, meeting with the shouted response from the palace, 'You came to fight us, now you want to stop, are you men or women?'[26] After a quarter of an hour a large gong was beaten in the direction of the palace, and a truce appeared to take effect. At this stage the wounded were moved to the residency cellar, where a rough hospital had been assembled.

In a letter to her sister-in-law, Ethel described the horror of the scene in the cellar:

> I pray that I may never see such a sight again. There were crowds of them: some dying. Poor Mr. Brackenbury was the first, shot all over, both legs broken, both arms, bullets in him all over the place; and yet, poor lad, he was alive and perfectly conscious the whole time, and in awful agony. I did what I could to help, but it seemed almost impossible to do anything. In one corner was a poor fellow with his brain shot out on the top of his head, and yet alive. Another with his forehead gone, and many others worse. Luckily, I am rather strong-minded and so I was able to help in bathing some of the wounds and bandaging them up.[27]

Calvert, who had been forced to work with one dim lantern to avoid drawing attention to the cellar, had nothing but praise for Ethel's remarkable performance in assisting with the casualties:

> This brave woman had been under fire all day, her own room had been wrecked by shell fire . . . and yet, with a difficult withdrawal, or a still more hopeless prospect of attempting to hold out, before her, she came down amongst the wounded, after herself preparing soup, beef-tea, etc. and administered it to them, having been without food all day. This enabled the medical officer and the hospital assistant to dress the wounded and begin operating.[28]

Following the sounding of the ceasefire, the Chief Commissioner wrote a letter to the Regent, which was delivered by Manipuri prisoners. Gurdon reported that in an hour's time 'a reply was received ... in Bengali which, after reciting the services rendered to the British Government by the Manipur State, concluded by a promise that the Regent would cease fire if our troops would throw down their arms. These conditions it was of course impossible to accept.'[29]

The Regent also demanded to know why the British had launched an unprovoked attack. There was some doubt about the translation of the Regent's letter, and Quinton suggested that a meeting with Tikendrajit should if possible be arranged to clarify the meaning. At this stage, in a move which appeared to defy all rational thought following the intensity of the hostilities, Grimwood assured the Chief Commissioner that there would be no danger in leaving the residency.

Shortly afterwards a Manipuri messenger arrived with the news that the Senapati wished to meet Quinton halfway between the residency and the palace. When asked if such a confrontation would be safe, the messenger responded, 'Why should we harm you who are our God?'[30] Gurdon recalled the relative ease with which the British officers agreed to the Senapati's proposal:

> After a little hesitation, the Chief Commissioner, on the advice of the Political Agent, proceeded to the main gate of the fort. The Chief Commissioner took the following officers with him: Colonel Skene, Mr. Grimwood, Mr. Cossins and Lieutenant Simpson ... This party went entirely without escort. The military officers even divested themselves of their swords and revolvers. The Chief Commissioner's party proceeded to the fort main gate where they were met by a number of Manipuris. Then a long parley commenced on the bridge.[31]

Lieutenant Henry Senior of the 44th Gurkha Rifles recalled that 'The stillness after the terrific noise of the Manipur fusillade was deathlike. It was full moon, but the sky was covered with thick black clouds which every now and then obscured the moon, and which later on covered the whole sky.'[32]

After two hours there was a shout, and Quinton and the other officers were seen to walk inside the gate accompanied by some Manipuris in white clothes – and, in Gurdon's words, 'we saw them no more. Time went on and we began to feel anxious and we watched the fort gate for any signs of our party returning. Still all remained quiet, and we could not tell what was going on.' At about midnight, a Manipuri shouted from the outer wall, 'the Chief Commissioner will not return'. Almost immediately, firing recommenced along the whole of the outer wall of the fort. The enemy had apparently taken advantage of the truce to get two guns into positions where they could shell the residency more effectively, one of which was almost opposite the building at a distance of about 200 yards.[33] The Adjutant-General in India, Major-General W. Galbraith, later expressed grave concern that at this stage, when the attack was renewed and the men were still at their former posts, 'no attempt had been made to muster them or divide the line of defence into sections commanded by British officers'.[34]

As soon as the firing began again, Gurdon and the remaining party in the residency realised that the Chief Commissioner and the officers accompanying him had been 'treacherously captured'. He commented, 'We wished at all risks to attempt a rescue, but the Manipuris assumed the offensive so strongly that it was all we could do to hold our position.' Shortly afterwards some of the sepoys reported that their ammunition was finished, and it was ascertained that there were only a few rounds left per man. There were 17 wounded and a large number of unarmed followers, together with Ethel, and 'it was essential to place these people in safety'.[35] The alternative of taking up a position in the open was discussed but considered to be impracticable. Captain Boileau took the majority of votes from the officers gathered in the residency, asking their opinion as to whether by staying it might be possible to save the prisoners, the treasury and the residency itself. With the exception of Lugard all were in favour of an evacuation, which had apparently already been decided upon by Quinton and Skene earlier in the evening.

CHAPTER 9

THE RETREAT

Having taken the decision to evacuate, Boileau and Chatterton arranged to go in separate directions from the treasury around the compound wall to collect all the men in the rear of the residency. Bugle calls could not be sounded, as they were well understood by the Manipuris. Boileau wrote that:

> Whilst the collection of men and followers were standing in front of the Residency, a shell, fired from the breach in the Manipuris' wall about 150 yards from the Residency, burst over the heads of all, which scattered them in every direction and shortly afterwards, the Manipuris who must have crept into the compound during the truce began firing from houses in the compound.[1]

Captain Butcher stressed that

> The men were utterly demoralised after being subjected to such a heavy artillery and infantry fire at a close range for such a long time without the hope of being able to return it with any effect. Men fallen in would not remain in the ranks, but tried to seek shelter. Some were actually found out side [sic] the compound wall before the retreat and had to be ordered back . . . The men were so unnerved that they would not go up into the Residency verandah where the ammunition was stored, to bring it down. I had to ascend myself and drag the boxes down, open them and issue which I did with the help of Lieutenant Woods, Assistant Commissioner.[2]

Woods himself wrote later that 'my first baptism of fire has been a severe one, and I hope never to see another with such fearful results to our arms. Had we remained in the residency I do not think there would be a man alive now.'[3]

The soldiers manning the walls were warned to retire by Lieutenant Chatterton and Subadar Mahesh Thapa, and it was presumed that they would make their way along the walls and assemble outside the compound on the Cachar road. However according to Butcher, 'Those on the south wall did not apparently wait for the warning and must have partially withdrawn or closed to their flanks as the Manipuris obtained an entry into the compound on that side before the evacuation took place and had to be driven out.'[4] Captain Boileau led the advance party though a gap in the compound wall, over some rough ground and across the river, where they were fired upon from a village on the opposite bank. Beyond the village, the officer halted the men, fell them in and counted a total of 165. Boileau reported that 'As the men were in a very disorganised state, and as I hoped the remainder of the men were coming along, I went on slowly.'[5]

Captain Butcher was among the last to leave the residency with the *doolies* and a few sepoys, and did not pick up the main party under Boileau until it was over a quarter of a mile from the building. Lieutenant Brackenbury died in the *dooly* as he was being carried out of the residency, and Calvert placed his body in the cellar and covered it with some lumber. The rest of the wounded were carried through the moat at the back of the residency. The group of survivors, including a very large number of servants and followers, set out at about 2am in the direction of Bishenpur to the south-west of the city in order to join up with Captain Cowley's contingent of 200 men which was advancing along the Cachar road. Ethel described how she

> dodged two shells by running behind a tree. We went out at the back of the house, and had to cross first a hedge of thorns, then a high mud wall, then a river before we could reach the road. I hadn't even a hat, and only very thin house shoes on. One of these dropped off in the river, where I also got wet up to my shoulders. We were fired at all the way.[6]

Shortly afterwards Gurdon recalled, 'we saw the whole neighbourhood lit up by a great conflagration in our rear which we soon perceived was the Residency in flames. Whether the building was fired by a shell or by hand is uncertain.'[7]

In the aftermath of the uprising, Butcher was charged at the Court of Enquiry (convened in May 1891) for dereliction of duty in failing 'to collect the men of his battalion who were under his immediate command, in order that the retreat might be conducted in a proper and soldierlike manner' and leaving the residency compound 'before its evacuation by the men of his own battalion was complete'. He stated in his defence that:

> It has never been ascertained that a large number of men were left in the Residency, but that a large number were missing. Even presuming that men had been left in the Residency, I am convinced it would have been impossible to get the men to go back, and I do not think they would have even halted for any length of time where we were ... To maintain order and discipline amongst men utterly disorganised was most difficult. A few shots from villages on the road would cause them to leave it and loose [sic] all formation. A very large party deserted after we had entered the hills taking what they thought was an easier road, and Subadar Mahesh Thapa, 42nd Gurkha Rifles, who was sent after them, had the greatest difficulty in stopping them and making them proceed in the direction in which it was known the Cachar road lay.[8]

Brigadier-General Collett,[9] commanding the British field force which was sent subsequently to relieve Manipur, supported Butcher in his analysis of the situation, writing to the Adjutant-General in India, Major-General W. Galbraith, on 3 May 1891 that 'In my judgment the non-commissioned officers and men did all that men could do in the circumstances in which they were placed; and the officers, both British and Native, led their men with great courage and determination.'[10]

It was estimated that without the wounded there should have been about 430 men in the compound that night. However a number of witnesses called to the Court of Enquiry were able to prove beyond question that at least 140 men were left at the residency, many of whom belonged to the 42nd Gurkhas and were therefore under Captain Butcher's command. Moreover Chatterton stated in his evidence that 150 to 200 men were on the north and west walls and that during the retreat, on joining Captain Boileau on the bank of the river about 200 yards from the compound, he reported that these men had not come up and repeatedly asked Boileau to wait for them, but that he refused to do so until more open country was reached. Captain Butcher was present at the time. There would have been no necessity to take a large number of men back to find those who were left, and the men who had been placed to cover the crossing of the river had already halted there for ten minutes. Not under fire, they could almost certainly have been kept in position during the time required to bring the remainder of soldiers back between the compound wall and the river.

However, leaving the fate of the missing men to chance, Boileau and Butcher determined to press on with the retreat and, at about dawn, having been warned by friendly Manipuris that the Bishenpur *thana* was very strongly manned, struck for the hills over three miles of rice fields. The ascent was extremely steep, but only a foretaste of what was to come. It was covered with short, straggling green grass, interspersed with the rough stubble of the previous year which had been burned. As a result the party was covered with smuts and, according to Ethel, 'after a very short time we all looked more or less like sweeps'.[11] Moreover the party was constantly followed by Kuki tribesmen.[12] At the top of the first ridge was a *thana* held by several Manipuris who did not take the offensive but informed the British party that 'the Regent had ordered that the "Mem Sahib" (Mrs. Grimwood) could go free, but that the Sahibs should all be brought back to Manipur. We however were not inclined to listen to any overtures of this sort after what had happened at Manipur.'[13] Eventually at some 2,000 feet (according to Boileau 'we were able to ascertain the heights, as part of the *loot* brought from the Jubaraj's palace was an aneroid barometer')[14] they halted for a short time, and a young Naga, who had been a groom at the residency for several months, found his way into the British camp and presented Ethel with three eggs, expressing his sadness that he was unable to do more for her, then 'crept back under the cover of darkness to his village'.[15]

In the distance, about 1,500 feet higher, was a Naga settlement through which it was agreed they should pass to find provisions if possible, and perhaps a guide. There was an undefended fort at the extreme top of the hill, and the village appeared to be practically empty. It was necessary to halt until the sick and rearguard arrived, and during this time large numbers of Manipuris collected on the surrounding hills through which the party had to travel in a westerly direction to meet the Cachar road. The trials of the weaker members of the party were at this stage painfully apparent. Lugard wrote that progress was

> heavily impeded by the wounded, whose sufferings must have been terrible, carried in blankets or on the backs of exhausted *kahars* and sepoys. Mrs. Grimwood ... bore up throughout the desperately trying march, marching almost bare-footed (as she only wore thin house-slippers with fancy netted stockings, which were soon torn to shreds) and setting us all an example.[16]

Ethel later admitted the extent of her woes at that stage of the journey: 'We had to eat grass and leaves; but I was too done up to care much. My feet were cut to bits, and my arm wouldn't stop bleeding, and I was perished with cold and having got so wet in crossing the river.'[17] The situation was considerably worsened when, in crossing the valley, they were attacked on two sides. To drive off the enemy from harassing the rear a British group split off down the valley, where it became separated from the others while making too long a detour in the dark.

Boileau describes the difficulties faced by those who remained:

> We pushed on till we got to a position commanding most of the surrounding country, and here about 6pm we halted for three hours; but as we saw fires all round us, and as the cold on this exposed position was so intense, we determined, about 9pm, to push on again, and at 10pm found a secluded bamboo clump, in which we took shelter and halted for the first time since leaving Manipur, – having marched continuously for nineteen hours, no one having had food for twenty hours, and the men having been under arms for forty hours. A party of fifteen men, in their endeavour to find the party who had got detached from us, also lost their way, and in the morning we found ourselves with only 29 rifles. All night we saw fires and expected to be attacked, as at 1am we heard heavy firing, which told us that our detached party had evidently been attacked.[18]

Ethel was well aware that a 'terrible fate would have overtaken any straggler who might have fallen behind without the means to defend himself'. She added, 'His head would have been captured as a glorious trophy, carved off while he was alive, for these tribes never trouble about killing their victim first before taking his scalp unless he offers great resistance.'[19]

The following morning, 26 March, the party departed at dawn and the main Cachar road was struck at about 8am. No trace of elephants signifying Captain Cowley's transport was found. Lugard reported,

> We pushed on some distance with great difficulty, until we found it simply impossible to get the worst of the wounded forward . . . It was decided that the best thing for all was to conceal in the jungle the three worst cases and push on as rapidly as possible to join Captain Cowley, get help from him, and return for the wounded.[20]

After some time a Manipuri advance party was surprised on the road, cooking food, from which they fled. The half-cooked rice was 'greedily seized from the boiling pot by British officer and sepoy alike; caste prejudice didn't stand against starvation'.[21] One man was taken prisoner, from whom it was learnt that the gorge ahead was strongly defended. A stockade was constructed across the road, overlooked by a hill so steep that it was impossible to scale. A British charge led by Lugard with a few men was made against the stockade, and fire opened on the enemy. Shortly after gaining the stockade the 43rd Gurkha Rifles led by Captain Cowley were seen advancing from below. Boileau reported that, 'Bringing up their men at the double, they drove off the Nagas and took up a position on the most commanding hill, and then advancing drove back the Manipuris, and eventually brought up the sick and wounded', with the exception of 'one sick man in the rear [who] was killed by Kukis stealing down the hill, he having left the place to go to the stream for water'.[22]

The combined parties returned to the camp from which Captain Cowley had marched that morning – which was considered a very unsafe position, surrounded as it was by hills. After four hours' rest they marched a further five miles and camped for the night, at which point Cowley produced all of his remaining food, enabling each man to have half a ration and a supply of beer, whisky and cocoa. Ethel was particularly glad to get other luxuries from one of the soldiers, such as 'a brush, a sponge, a grand pair of woollen stockings, and some Sepoys' boots, which each measured about a foot and a half in length and were broad in proportion'.[23] Gurdon asked Cowley whether he was in a position to return to Manipur and attempt a rescue of the captives. After some consultation it was agreed that such a course was impossible, as ammunition and food were woefully short. Some of the men of the 42nd and 44th were without a single round, and the great majority had only a small amount of ammunition left. The 43rd soldiers under Cowley had sufficient rounds for the Martini-Henry rifles, but not for the Sniders of the men of the 42nd and 44th. As far as food was concerned, the retreating party had no rations of its own, and Cowley's supplies were almost depleted after the general distribution.[24]

Cowley himself had hardly experienced an easy journey before he encountered the others, departing from Cachar on 19 March with a well-laden force consisting of '3 British officers, 4 native officers, 4 buglers, 200 rifles, 14 public followers, 14 private followers, 67 ponies, 16 elephants, 61 transport followers, and ten days rations for all except transport animals, for whom rations had been sent on'. Conditions were appalling; on the first night the camp was totally swamped in six inches of water and the crossing of the Jhiri River in flood took over three and a half hours, with only the elephants able to cross loaded. This painfully slow progress continued through the first six miles of the Jhiri Forest as the

> road was intersected by numerous nalas, all of which were almost impassable for laden animals owing to heavy rain, as all bridges were rotten. Over two of the largest nalas the mules had to be unladen and the baggage carried over by the men, and the remainder were only rendered passable by men working hard at them.[25]

For the next three days the detachment was confronted by the constant disruption of heavy rain and continuing operational problems, men crossing rivers by means of floating bridges and animals crossing laden over fords, the mules arriving at camp some six hours before the elephants and rearguard. On 25 March Cowley's force was beset by a number of skirmishes with hostile Manipuris before meeting up with the retreating force of 100 men which had become detached from Boileau's party. The following day contact was made with Boileau himself, apparently only just in time.[26] In submitting Cowley's report of his march from Cachar, Brigadier-General Collett observed, 'It appears absolutely certain that if Captain Boileau's party had not met with Captain Cowley, none of the officers or men, or Mrs. Grimwood, with him could possibly have ever reached Silchar.'[27]

On the evening of 26 March a decision had to be made as to the best course of action to pursue. The British were in enemy territory, many miles from the Assam frontier, without supplies and short of ammunition. The men of the 42nd and 44th were in a totally exhausted condition, and certainly not fit to take the field against long odds with an average of 15 to 20 rounds each. Cowley decided that the only possible course was to march in the direction of Cachar where supplies could be obtained, a decision which was subsequently to come under condemnation from the Military Department of the Government of India. That night the combined forces, including a party of about 100 sepoys under Jemadar Durga Dutt and a number of other stragglers (in all about 367 fighting men and 142 followers, with 66 ponies and 17 elephants) made a forced march from the river near Leimatak, 30 miles from the capital. Taking into account the casualties, of whom there were fewer than 40, over 200 Gurkhas were missing at that stage.

Moving down into the Kampun Valley the following morning it was discovered that the hills were held by Manipuris and it was necessary to send parties up to drive them back, which was carried out successfully in about an hour. Boileau reported that:

> Holding the hills we marched on and took the thana, which had every appearance of having been only just vacated by the Manipuris, who left baskets filled with rice ready to be carried off. Cooking pots, accoutrements, etc. were found and two granaries full of dhan. We divided the rice equally amongst the men and followers, and the dhan amongst the transport animals, burnt the thana, and marched on five miles . . . where there was good water and a good position, and halted there for the night.[28]

For three more days the British party marched on towards its destination of Lakhipur, 14 miles from Cachar. Little opposition was encountered due to the size of the force, and the British burnt the majority of enemy *thanas* on the road. In the deserted Naga villages it was possible to procure rice, pigs and goats, which were either cooked or transported on by elephants.

On 31 March Lieutenant Gurdon went ahead to Lakhipur with 50 rifles to communicate with the government by telegraph. Gurdon was able to provide the first accurate reports of the events of the past week and the names of those safe, missing and captured. A total of 257 officers and men were now known to have met up with Cowley, and a further 73 had reached Kohima; 16 were known to have been killed, including Lieutenant Brackenbury and a native officer, and at least another 21 were wounded. However the main cause for alarm was the inability to account for no fewer than 106 native officers and men, over a fifth of the original force. There was at this stage no real concern for Quinton and his companions. Both civil and military officers believed that they would be used as hostages with whom the Manipuri princes could bargain, and their lives were not seen to be in danger.[29]

In the early morning of 3 April the refugees from the residency limped (literally in the case of Ethel, who had sprained her ankle while running down the hill to meet Captain Cowley) into Cachar. The arrival of the British party and, hard on their heels, a force of 50 of the Regent's soldiers was by no means a trouble-free event for the inhabitants of Cachar. When information of the disturbances had first filtered through, every available soldier in the town had been ordered to march immediately to Manipur. Many of the planters and their assistants volunteered for service with the troops, and those who were unable to go themselves lent horses, bullocks and buffaloes. Some of the volunteers, observing the Manipuri sepoys taking up quarters in one of the Regent's storehouses, grew suspicious and broke into the building, after which a fight ensued and the Manipuris were ordered to surrender their arms. One man was killed, several wounded and 16 locked up in prison. The remainder were punished by being made to act as provision carriers for the march to the capital. In the absence of those participating in the march, the enemy appeared to be flooding down jungle paths with the intention of killing every European in Cachar. Messages were sent to Calcutta asking for 2,000 troops; however until their arrival there was no protection for the European residents, one of whom – M. J. Wright, a tea planter – reported, '30,000 Manipuris about us and hundreds more flocking in from Manipur'.[30]

Wright wrote that for 'three long weeks we were kept in a state of fearful suspense ... We went to bed at night, wondering if before morning the merciless hordes would be upon us and set fire to our bungalow.' One night a large company of the enemy made a raid on a small village, and when the Nagas saw the Manipuris thieving with impunity, according to Wright

> they joined themselves to them, and, indeed, for a time it looked as if there was going to be a general rising of the hill tribes . . . We had to put an extra watch on duty at night and ring the gongs every hour, to let the enemy know that we were on the alert. The windows were all securely fastened, and firearms lay in readiness every night. The punkahs could not be used, because the men working them required a light. With the windows and doors closed, and no punkah, the heat was almost unbearable . . . Our intention, in case of attack, was to make for the jungle which lay right below our bedroom window. Ten times rather would I have faced the tigers and other wild beasts, than the Manipuris in their excited state. One night we did actually get up, and were preparing to make our escape by the window, certain that at last the long-dreaded moment had come, but it proved to be only a tiger growling as he moved past the window.[31]

When British reinforcements did finally arrive from Calcutta there was more than sufficient manpower to quell both the hill tribes and the Manipuris. One company alone, when on the march, was over four miles in length. Wright wrote that 'We often stood and watched them flashing down signals from the hills as they marched forward. Progress was very slow, as they had not only the softening of the roads by heavy rains to contend with, but trees cut down and thrown along the line of march. This was done by the enemy to hinder the advance.'[32]

The European residents of Cachar noted with some satisfaction that when the Nagas saw that the Manipuris were going to be punished for their misdeeds, they came forward and offered to help with the transport for the British relief column.

Despite the undoubted bravery and determined stamina of the retiring party, which was lauded by the residents of Cachar, the retreat from Manipur in itself was hardly a cause for rejoicing. Much criticism was levelled after the event at the gross mismanagement which resulted in a large number of British soldiers and followers being forced to flee from the city rather than celebrating a swift and efficient military defeat of the rebels. It was suggested that Ethel herself was to some extent to blame for the speedy exodus from the Residency, an accusation which she strongly resisted:

> It has been said lately by some that the retreat to Cachar was in great measure due to my presence in Manipur at the time, and that my helplessness has been the means of dragging the good name of the army, and the Ghoorka corps in particular, through the mire, by strongly influencing the officers in their decision to effect 'the stampede to Cachar'. But I scarcely think they would have allowed the presence of, and danger to one women to deter them from what ever they considered their duty; and had they decided to remain at the Residency that night, I should never have questioned their right to do so, even as I raised no argument for or against the retreat to Cachar. I think the honour of England is as dear to us women as it is to the men.[33]

At the time, in another part of Manipur, a certain Lieutenant Charles Grant was undoubtedly upholding the honour of England.

CHAPTER 10

THE SOLDIER'S ACCOUNT: LIEUTENANT CHARLES GRANT

On 27 March news was first circulated of the Manipur disaster. Lieutenant Charles William James Grant, of the 12th Regiment (2nd Burma Battalion) of the Madras Infantry stationed at Tammu, 68 miles from Manipur, volunteered to attempt to rescue the prisoners. Grant, born in Aberdeenshire in 1861, had joined the Suffolk Regiment in 1882 and received his first commission in May of that year. Soon afterwards he transferred to the Madras Staff Corps, and in the Burmese War was on active service in Rangoon. He subsequently distinguished himself in Upper Burma, gaining a reputation for flair and bravery in guerrilla warfare. After a brief illness and a period of convalescence Grant was posted to Tammu, on the border between Burma and Manipur, and, described by Ethel as 'cheery and full of spirits', had met the Grimwoods earlier in 1891 when they paid a visit to the station.[1]

On the same day that he volunteered Grant received orders to march towards Manipur as speedily as possible, and at 5.30am on 28 March he departed with a force of one *jemadar* and 30 rifles (with 60 rounds per man) of the 43rd Gurkha Rifles and one *subadar* and 50 rifles (with 160 rounds per man) of the 12th (Burma) Madras Infantry. There were also one hospital assistant, 28 followers, six transport followers, three elephants, and some country labourers. The sepoys of the 12th were Punjabi Muslims, with a few Pathans. Of their number, 20 were old soldiers but the rest were recruits who had been drilled for merely eight months and had only fired a few rounds of ammunition at musketry practice.[2] The 43rd Gurkhas were armed with Martinis and the 12th Burma Infantry with Sniders, for which ammunition was plentiful.

The 33 men of the 43rd comprised the detachment stationed at Langthobal under Jamadar Birbal Nagarkoti. Prior to the events of March, Nagarkoti had been somewhat derided by his regiment as 'not a success'. He was not a pure Gurkha, being 'a line boy', born on the lines of the regiment, with a Manipuri mother. However he had received a good education and could speak, read and write very good English, despite having a reputation for being 'thick-headed'. The evening before the foray into the palace compound Nagarkoti received orders to bring his detachment into Manipur the following morning. When at dawn he heard firing and learned of the British attack upon the palace enclosure, he reasoned that his valuable stores lying at Langthobal might be looted if he were to march with all his men into the city. He determined to remain and guard the stores and, in so doing, incurred 'a grave responsibility' in disobeying direct orders. It was later considered that his 'willingness to take the responsibility and to act independently in the way he thought right proves far more than his subsequent gallantry and skill that he was no fool and that he was in every way fitted for his position as a Gurkha officer'.[3]

Langthobal had only been roughly cleared for a cantonment, and the roads around it were little better than paths. The officers lived in huts made of bamboo and mud covering, with gardens around them. On the morning of 24 March, building a barricade of bags of rations, mule saddles, sepoys' kit and boxes of horseshoes, Nagarkoti and his men took up a defensive position. Before long a force of Manipuris about 800 strong attacked, retiring after four hours of fighting. The day passed, and at about 2am the following morning the *jemadar* saw the 'light of a conflagration' at Manipur and the sounds of firing beyond the river to the west of the residency. Later in the morning two wounded sepoys of the 43rd brought news of the retreat from the city, the looting of the treasury and the destruction of the residency. A native woman also reported that two Manipuri majors were moving towards Langthobal with three guns and a considerable force. Nagarkoti opted to retire to Tammu, taking the most valuable stores that he was able to transport. He stated later that he had

> half my sepoys in front and half behind. The sick were in the middle, with the transport and the coolies, and also a guard of three men with some Government money which I had. I told them all to be of good heart and that I would take them all right, and I made the coolies slope their bamboo spears on their shoulders to make them look as much like soldiers as possible.[4]

A Punjabi trader, Hafiz Futteh Shah, who travelled with the party and was 'of the greatest use' as a guide, informed Nagarkoti that the Tammu route was preferable to the Cachar road as the villages along it were populated by Muslims, who would be as a rule unarmed. After the Thobal village Nagarkoti was forced to cross a river where the bridge had been partially destroyed by the enemy. His retreat was constantly harassed when the 'pursuers became more than usually venturesome and one or two steady volleys checked their ardour'. To carry his wounded men, *doolies* were improvised out of bamboo, and when soldiers died the force halted under fire to bury them by the road.[5] However enemy fortifications were demolished with little difficulty and a number of hostile villages burnt before the *jemadar* reached British Burmese territory and Lieutenant Grant on 25 March, with minor loss of life.

The progress of Grant's force was slow, as the elephants, each carrying 600 pounds, were only able to travel at a mile an hour over the hills, 6,000 feet high, between Tammu in Burma and the village of Palel south of the Manipur capital. The garrison of Palel was held by 200 Manipuris, who evacuated it on the arrival of the British party. Prisoners taken in the aftermath, including a man who stated he was cook to the Ayapurel, informed Grant: 'all the Sahibs killed or escaped; Mrs. Grimwood escaped to Assam. Poor Melville who had stayed a week before with me at Tummu (telegraph superintendent) killed on march.'[6] Marching on overnight, Grant reached Thobal at 7am on 31 March, meeting only slight resistance until within 300 yards of the river, where he was greeted by 'a hot fire' from mud-walled compounds to the left of a burning bridge and from open trenches on the right across the river. The British force was in fighting formation, with the baggage guard and elephants 300 yards in the rear, and volleys were opened by sections of ten men advancing to within 100 yards of the enemy. Grant reported:

> I had seen one man clean killed at my side, and had felt a sharp flick under arm and began to think we were in for about as much as we could manage; but the men were behaving splendidly, firing carefully and well directed. I signalled with supports to come up wide on each flank; they came with a splendid rush and never stopped on joining the firing line, but went clean to the bank of the river, within sixty yards of the enemy, lying down and firing at their heads.[7]

Grant and his men crossed the river, some 'in over our heads in the water and weeds', and to his 'utter astonishment' the enemy gave way.[8] At the second line of walls the Manipuris attempted to rally then fled behind the hills, followed by the British. At the summit, Grant recalled,

> I halted in sheer amazement; the enemy's line was over a mile long. I estimated them at 800 . . . dressed mostly in white jackets[9] with white turbans and *dhoties*, armed with Tower-muskets, Enfield and Snider rifles, and about two hundred in red jackets and white turbans, armed with Martinis, a rifle that will shoot over twice as far as our Sniders.[10]

Since the rear party and half of Grant's men were still on the other side of the river, a retreat was made to the three lines of enemy compounds to prepare a defensive position. The baggage was carried across the river on the men's heads. No less than 80 of the 160 rounds per man and three out of six days' rations had been used, and with no hope of reaching Manipur it was necessary to sit tight until reinforced from Burma or joined by troops from Cachar. A message from Grant received by the civil authorities in Tammu on 3 April stated, with some desperation:

> We seem to have the whole Manipuri army against us, and only ten miles from the capital. Send with relieving force ammunition, both Snider for us and Martini for Ghoorkhas. I give no details, as this may fall into the enemy's hands, but give your imagination full play ... By all accounts I am the sole representative of the paramount power in this country.[11]

On 1 April at 6am, patrols reported the enemy advancing from their new position. Grant took a single shot into a group of about ten men at

700 yards, when 'The group bolted behind the walls . . . and the little Ghoorkas screamed with delight at a white heap left on the road, which got up and fell down again once or twice, none of the others venturing out to help the poor wretch.' The enemy then retired under cover, but at 3pm they surged forward in full force. Grant lined the wall with 50 men, holding the rest in reserve in a mud fort which had been captured by the British force. The enemy advanced to 66 yards, when volleys were opened:

> after firing at us wildly for half an hour, they again retired to 800 yards and suddenly from the hill a great 'boom', a scream through the air; then, fifty feet over our heads, a large white cloud of smoke, a loud report, and fragments of a 9lb or 10lb elongated common shell from a rifle cannon fell between us and our fort; a second followed from another gun, and burst on our right; then another struck the ground and burst on impact to our front, firing a patch of grass.[12]

Grant confessed his initial horror at this attack, dreading the moral effect on his recruits 'who must have had an enormously exaggerated idea of the powers of guns; but they behaved splendidly'.[13] Soon the British force had calculated the exact range of the shells, and after half an hour – during which the firing became steadily wilder – both guns disappeared and only one appeared on an adjacent hill. When it was dark, men were posted round the compound walls 'which seemed so strong in the morning, but were like paper against well-laid field guns'. Grant, despite feeling 'very, very bitter' at this stage, nevertheless spoke of the great pride he had in his men, particularly 'ten or fifteen old soldiers, who set a splendid example, and talked of what skunks the Manipuris were, compared to the men they had fought in Afghanistan and the North-West Frontier; but they all said they had never seen such odds against them before'.[14]

Throughout the following night the enemy maintained a long-range fire without result. At 3am, Grant started to strengthen the walls against shellfire and to dig places for cover. Fortunately much of the compound was freshly ploughed, and it was possible to fill every available container (such as huge rice baskets, ration sacks, pails, Grant's pillowcase and a postbag) with earth to construct five parapets on the front and the flanks of the compound, each giving cover for eight or ten men. The enemy had at this stage retired behind the hill. At 3pm, a patrol reported a man signalling. Grant wrote that he

> went out with white flag, and met a Ghoorka of 44th, a prisoner in Manipuris' hands, who brought a letter signed by six or eight Babu prisoners, clerks, writers, post and telegraph men, saying there were fifty Ghoorka prisoners and fifty-eight civil prisoners, and imploring me to retire. If I advanced they would kill the prisoners; if I retired the durbar would release them, and send them to Cachar.[15]

Grant replied that if all the prisoners who wished to go with him were surrendered he would retire to Tammu.

For the next three days messages were relayed between Grant and the Regent and his brothers in negotiations for the prisoners. Grant made a point of receiving the emissaries at some distance from his position in order to conceal the small size of his force, and represented himself as his commanding officer, Colonel Howlett, confessing later, 'I had signed all my letters as Col. A. Howlett, Com. 2nd B. Regt., to impress them with my strength and importance, and put on the subadar's badges of rank in addition to my own.' One of the messengers was Signaller C. Williams, in charge of the Chief Commissioner's telegraph camp, who was the only European prisoner of the royal family. Grant's disguise deceived Williams as well as the Manipuri forces, and ultimately prevented an attempt to rush the camp by overwhelming force. Williams informed Grant that the Senapati had declared that he was in no way responsible for the revolt and had 3,000 men in front of the British who had been instructed to 'cut us all up'.[16] Grant, still signing himself as Colonel Howlett, sent a reply with Williams that he would consider withdrawing only if all the prisoners who wished to join him were allowed to do so.

Word came back quickly from Prince Angao Senna, acting as commander in chief, that all the prisoners had been sent to Assam. However Grant refused to retire without holding a hostage of some considerable rank, and sent a letter to the Regent informing him that 'Directly a wire comes to me from Assam that the prisoners have arrived safely I will send him [the hostage] back to Manipur territory', adding that if one of the prisoners were harmed the officers would not be able to restrain the Sikhs and Punjabis from killing every man and burning every house in the country. When offered a Manipuri *subadar* as hostage, Grant demanded in his place the Ayapurel, who was in charge of the territory from Manipur to Tammu. In a final attempt at bribery, Manipuri rations were offered to the British troops, which were sent back with a message from Grant repeating that he refused to move without a member of the Durbar as hostage.[17] However Grant's efforts to intimidate the Manipuri commanders failed to break the stalemate. The Manipur Court Chronicle reported that 'all the people of the land took the decision that since they (the British) had refused (to negotiate) then all of them would go to battle regardless of whether they (the British) would win the battle or the people (of Manipur) would win the battle. Thus the whole country took the decision to go to battle.'[18] On the morning of 6 April the enemy attacked once more.

Grant retreated into the part of the compound which had come to be known as the '12th Burma Fort', and by now was greatly strengthened. By 8am, enemy shellfire had ceased and the Manipuris had gained the hedges and walls from about 200 yards to the front and left. Grant recounts that he:

> Crept out with ten Ghoorkhas and attacking the enemy on the left drove them off with loss, killing six or seven and bolted back to the fort without loss. At 11am crept out to front under my right wall and up to enemy with one havildar and six Ghoorkhas and after driving enemy from one hedge found a party of about 60 in a corner behind a wall 20 yards off. After a very hot two minutes we got to wall and drove them out of their corner, leaving ten or eleven dead. A double-barrelled gun with buck-shot most effective on their heads as they showed up to fire.[19]

By now there were only 50 rounds per man, and Grant 'had to submit to a purely passive defence'. The men were given orders not to fire a shot until the enemy was halfway across the open adjoining compounds, but the Manipuris preferred to remain behind hedges where they kept up their fire until dark. The atmosphere appeared to be remarkably relaxed, 'the men smoking and chatting' and taking little notice of 'bullets cutting the trees a foot or six inches over their heads'. Grant recalled that:

> Thus the day passed, the enemy retiring at dark, and we counted our loss – two men and one follower wounded, one by shell; one pony killed, two wounded; two elephants wounded, one severely; and my breakfast spoilt by a shell, which did not frighten my boy, who brought me the head of the shrapnel which did the mischief – I will send it home to be made into an inkpot, with inscription.[20]

The following day, 7 April, was quiet until noon when two men appeared carrying a flag of truce. One of them was a Burmese messenger who brought a communication from Tammu to Manipur and also a letter from the Regent to the Viceroy, in which Grant was amused to find Kula Chandra complaining about the actions of a certain Colonel Howlett. The messenger also brought a delayed letter from the Government of India to the 'poor killed chief commissioner', Quinton, informing him that a large force was on its way from Burma. In his diary Grant commented sourly that 'A small party three or four days before would have been more use. Maharaja's letter a tissue of miserable lies and stupid excuses.'[21] Grant took the opportunity to write an account of events at Thobal to send via the messenger to his commanding officer in Tammu, Captain Edward Presgrave, asking for reinforcements and medical supplies. To avoid detection Grant wrote in French in Greek characters (Presgrave was later to comment that Grant's French was a great deal less impressive than his military prowess). At noon on 9 April a letter was delivered from Presgrave with orders for Grant to retire at the first opportunity and stating that he had been ordered not to reinforce Grant's party but help it to retire. Grant confessed, 'I *was* sick; but the orders were most peremptorily worded. So at 7.30pm on a pitch-dark rainy night we started back – a splendid night for a retreat, but such a ghastly, awful job!' With two wounded elephants it was possible to travel little more than one mile an hour:

> We were drenched to the skin, and were halting, taking ten paces forward when the lightning flashed, and then halting the column half an hour at times; but the feeble Manipuri, of course, would

> not be out on such a night, and we passed through three or four villages full of troops without a man showing.[22]

At 2am on 10 April contact was finally made with Presgrave who had heard reports that Grant had been captured and all his men killed or taken. With 180 men, 40 of them mounted infantry, and 11 boxes of ammunition, Presgrave had marched for 36 hours without kit or rations, only halting for eight hours. By the time the British parties met up, Grant and his men had been isolated in enemy territory for 12 days. The combined British parties returned to Palel, where they surprised three or four hundred Manipuri soldiers who bolted after firing a few shots. Grant advanced with the mounted infantry and, after trotting to within 300 yards of the enemy, a line was formed in the open and the British advanced in pursuit of the retreating army. Grant had his charger shot from beneath him in the rout and, 'covered with blood from a bullet-wound in the poor beast's foreleg', pursued the Manipuri forces for three miles before the decision was taken after collecting 'the spoil' to return to camp where there were now eight British officers. Congratulatory telegrams appeared from, among others, the commander in chief, Sir Frederick Roberts. Somewhat anxious to press on to Manipur, Grant reported that it was 'all very nice and jolly; but to our disgust we have to halt here for rest of ours, rest of Ghoorkas, two more guns, and General Graham'.[23]

Brigadier-General T. Graham, commanding officer of Myingyan District of Burma and leading a column assembled in Tammu, was advancing with orders from the Government of India to bring about the release of the Chief Commissioner, Grimwood and the other prisoners before 'precipitating a collision which might endanger their safety'. If harm were to come to the British officers 'none of those concerned must expect any mercy at our hands', and if the Durbar attempted to make conditions Graham was authorised to 'promise immunity from punishment of death or transportation beyond seas' to those who had not been guilty of actual murder.[24] Moreover in response to a plea from the exiled maharaja, Sur Chandra, that 'proverbial British justice, generosity, moderation'[25] might be applied when dealing with the maharani and his son, sisters and other relatives still in Manipur, the erstwhile ruler was assured by the Government of India that no harm would be done to any of his family who did not resist and were not implicated in the murder of British subjects. Graham was ordered to treat the maharani and other ladies of the royal family 'with all respect'.[26]

Meanwhile the Manipur Court Chronicle reported that Kula Chandra had held a *durbar* in which he announced:

> While it was being considered whether attack on us by the Saheps might probably cease, we have received reliable information from the western, the eastern and the northern regions, from all these three regions, that the enemy with a large army are on the march to wage war on us. What do we people of the land say we should do? We cannot flee. Probably this is our last stand. All of you come forward shouting, 'Nake, Nake' and I will appoint each one of you to a post befitting each of you. Do come forward.[27]

The *Chronicle* continued that a day or two later a divine apparition appeared to the south-west of the shrine of Lainingthou Pakhangpa:

> a palanquin, together with chong banner and a flag, was seen coming down from the heavens and then disappearing about seven lams distance above ground, but without landing on the ground. Many people of the land witnessed it . . . At this report many pundits were summoned and they were asked to give the meaning of it all. A reply was given to the royal order by Wangkei Pundit saying, 'The palanquin was your Ancestor Pakhangpa's Meeyampa Palanquin and the nine weapons which belong to your Ancestor Pakhangpa will be merged to the great power. Now this shows that the Palanquin Meengampa has already gone ahead. Thus the portent has given the message that there will be peace in the land, long life for the king, and happiness and contentment for the people in the land.'[28]

On 24 April information was received that the enemy, fuelled by this highly optimistic portent, had entrenched themselves in a position about six miles to the north of Palel, south of the Manipur capital, and orders were issued for a reconnaissance to be made to ascertain the strength of the opposition. The following day, at the headquarters of the column, news came from Captain F. M. Drury of the 4th Gurkha Rifles, who was commanding the reconnaissance party, that he had hemmed in a large number of the enemy and needed permission to turn them out. As Drury had only 100 rifles of the 4th, and 50 rifles and 44 mounted infantry of the 12th (Burma) Madras Infantry under Grant to accompany him, Brigadier-General H. Collett – commanding the three columns advancing from Kohima, Tammu and Cachar to relieve the capital – ordered two guns of No. 2 Mountain Battery and 100 rifles of the 4th Gurkhas as reinforcements.

On 25 April Drury and Grant went out from Palel with orders not to attack the enemy. The road ran due north towards the capital, with an open plain on the left and hills on the right where the enemy was stationed. There were additional Manipuri forces in a mud fort 60 feet in diameter situated in the open, 1,000 yards from the hills. Grant worked his way along the hills, driving the enemy out into a trap, and word was sent back to Palel stressing the need for guns and more men to complete the job. The mounted infantry were despatched to the left, to the north-west of the enemy, and the remaining British forces worked behind the hills to the north-east, cutting off the Manipuris from the city. At 11.30am, the column from Palel appeared with the two mountain guns and 100 Gurkhas. The guns were despatched to a hill 1,000 yards to the east of the enemy's fort, and common shell and shrapnel were directed into the fort until the enemy fire was masked. The Gurkhas advanced from the south and Grant's party charged the fort but was unable to progress further due to a deep ditch under the walls, which at that time of year was full of water and concealed by long grass. The enemy put up a white flag and Grant immediately stopped the attack, whereupon the Manipuris 'sprang up' and fired again on the British. Grant recalls he 'felt a tremendous blow on the neck and staggered and fell, luckily on the edge of the ditch, rather under cover; but feeling the wound with my finger, and being able to speak, and feeling no violent flow of blood, I discovered I wasn't dead just yet'.[29]

The 'brave little Gurkhas' led by Captain Drury swarmed over the mud parapets of the fort, and the fighting developed into a hand-to-hand encounter in which the Manipuris, without bayonets, were at a disadvantage. They appear however 'to have asked for no quarter, and none was given'. *The Pioneer* reported:

> The battlefield was a bloody enough sight to suit even the taste of a Rider Haggard. In one or two places bunches of mingled bodies

> were seen, where the shells had done their deadly work. Two large standards – one white and the other red – that had floated gaily in the fort in the morning were now found torn to shreds, also the result of the shell fire . . . The slain were all placed in the trenches, and the mud wall knocked down and thrown over them.[30]

Jemadar Birbal Nagarkoti, showing 'most gallant behaviour', was wounded in the jaw. The bullet appears to have entered his mouth while it was open and, having smashed a few teeth, passed out through the cheek.[31] Grant, sheltering in one of the huts in the fort, discovered that a bullet had gone through the base of his neck, just above the shoulder, and 'carried some of the cloth of my collar and shirt right through the wound, leaving it quite clean'.[32] Only two of his men were wounded – and of the 4th, two killed and eight wounded, including Drury. In contrast British forces gathered 75 Manipuri bodies in the fort and 56 near it, and the shrapnel and mounted infantry killed over 100. Some 20 or 30 of the enemy were discovered in a deep hole in a corner of the fort. Among the dead were two men, one of whom was a prince, who, as reported by the Manipuris of the adjacent villages, participated in the actual murder of Quinton and his party. According to Grant, 'The Manipuris here say we killed over four hundred. So we paid off part of our score against their treachery.'[33]

As a fitting tribute to such fortitude the commander in chief, Sir Frederick Roberts, referring to Grant's report of the operations of his detachment, declared that it 'may be published as an example of what is possible for one British officer with a handful of devoted native soldiers to accomplish by prompt initiative, resolute courage and soldierlike skill'.[34] Grant attributed his success to the magnificent courage and coolness of the men, both Punjabi and Gurkha, and *The Times* reported that 'The men on their part are no less willing to do justice to the gallantry and readiness of resource of their young commander, and they are reported to have said when asked about their doings, "How could we be beaten under Grant Sahib. He is a tiger in fight".'[35]

CHAPTER 11

THE CIVILIAN'S ACCOUNT: SIGNALLER C. WILLIAMS

While Grant was weaving his heroic path through enemy territory, Signaller C. Williams, in charge of the Chief Commissioner's telegraph camp, was brutally exposed to the perils of life behind the lines following the events of 24 March. Leaving Golaghat with the Chief Commissioner on 6 March, Williams reported that all went well until the party arrived at Mao on 17 March. At Mao he was asked by Thangal General, leading the Manipuri advance party, to send two messages to the regent, Kula Chandra, which he declined to do having been ordered not to accept messages from any outsider without Quinton's sanction. Quinton subsequently gave orders to his tour clerk to write out the messages, but Thangal General was not satisfied with the contents and asked Williams to add several words, offering him 'presents of milk, rice, fowls, ducks, vegetables and Manipuri shawls' if he would comply. After a discussion with the assistant secretary the words were duly added.[1]

At Sengmai, following Quinton's meeting with the Senapati, Williams was informed by the Chief Commissioner that he was to remain behind with 20 sepoys for reasons that could not be divulged at that stage. On the evening of 23 March, in heavy rain, William Melville, the superintendent of the Assam Telegraph Department and his Eurasian assistant, Signaller James O'Brien, came into the camp, sharing Williams' tent with wet instruments and furniture, and, no doubt due to the acute discomfort, leaving him early the following morning. At that stage it was discovered that the line to Manipur was cut. On 25 March Williams was informed by the *havildar* of the local *thana* that the officers and the Chief Commissioner had been killed, all the sepoys had retreated via Tammu and the Regent wished no British subjects to remain in Manipuri territory. At this news Williams prepared to make a hasty exit from Sengmai, and upon emerging from his tent encountered a large number of enemy sepoys approaching the camp. The Gurkhas loaded their rifles and filled their pouches with cartridges, at which the Manipuris took cover in the jungle and fired at the signaller and the soldiers: 'bullets came like rain drops upon us and 100 Manipuris with rifles, spears, bows and arrows, made a rush at us'.[2]

Braving the heat of the grass jungle, which was set on fire by the enemy, Williams hid alone in the bush until 11pm. He emerged into 'a bright moonlit night' and set off for Kohima, walking eight miles until 1am when he fell into an ambush of six Manipuri sepoys, who simultaneously fired a volley at him. Williams took some delight in the incompetence of his foes, noting later that 'all six missed me, though I was only 10 or 12 yards away from them', and, escaping up a hill, he remained in hiding until 11am when he continued his journey in a desperate attempt to find food and water. At 2pm on 26 March he was stopped by more Manipuri sepoys who, upon discovering that he failed to possess a pass from the Senapati, prepared to shoot him. Williams described how

> all my clothes were taken out except a flannel banian and flannel drawers. I was then made to sit down on the ground; the sentry taking aim at me. Just then a Manipuri Major arrived who had seen me at Mao Thana, and was one of the men who offered me presents if I added his words to the messages from the Thangal General. This Major on seeing me told the thanadar not to shoot me.[3]

Half an hour later a number of servants came into the *thana*, bringing some of Melville and O'Brien's possessions, which Williams instantly recognised from the night they had spent in his tent, and he was informed that 'the Telegraph Sahibs were killed'.[4] It transpired that Melville and O'Brien had been attacked in their bungalow at Myangkhang by a group of Nagas armed with spears and rifles. O'Brien was hit by a bullet in the lung and died immediately, whereupon he was decapitated. Melville, severely wounded in the thigh, managed to escape at night through the high grass jungle to a stream about 100 yards from the rest house. He lay there until noon of 26 March, when he was discovered by a party of Nagas and, according to the correspondent of *The Pioneer*, as 'he lay in a pool of blood unable to move from weakness, he was brutally murdered, one man sweeping off his head with a dao, while another cut and carried off his hands'.[5] A *havildar* in the Manipuri army later reported that he had received a letter with the Senapati's seal upon it, confirming that the Chief Commissioner and other officers had been killed, and giving orders to the outposts to kill all British subjects on the road to and from Kohima. Naga tribesmen had been called upon to further this gruesome task.[6]

The following morning, 27 March, barefoot and still in his underwear, Williams was taken to Manipur jail, where an iron chain and rods were placed around his feet. The jail was divided into three buildings: one for Nagas, one for Hindus and one for Muslims 'and other castes,' in which the signaller was placed. The conditions were primitive in the extreme: 'this latter house was the smallest, being about 70 feet by 14 feet. In this house there were 38 sepoys, eight pony drivers, 14 Muhammedan servants of the Chief Commissioner and officers, 19 Cachari construction coolies with Sub-Inspector Moosai, and four syces of the officers, and five wounded sepoys, making a total of 88 men.' Williams rebelled against the standard prison fare, informing the jail *subadar* that he was unable to eat 'that kind of red rice and the rotten dried fish', with the miraculous outcome that the next day 'I got fine white rice, four large fresh fish, salt and some curry-stuff, which I took and the servants cooked for me separately.' This largesse, it transpired, was due to the desire of the Rajmantri of Manipur to learn about telegraphy and the construction of various telegraph instruments, having removed the instruments and battery from the residency office and the Chief Commissioner's camp. The Rajmantri declared that he was able to procure Williams an appointment in the service of the Maharaja with 'a fine house, good eating, good living, and a laichabi, i.e. a woman', an offer which the signaller politely declined.[7]

Having been cross-questioned as to the number of sepoys and quantity of ammunition in Kohima, Williams was sent for by the Senapati who ordered his release from jail, 'gave me a pant and coat (most shabby looking things), also a pair of boots which were so loose

I had to tie cloth around my feet, as I had no socks and my feet were cut and blistered all over' and sent him to a Muslim bugler's house. The following morning the signaller met the Prince again, and was requested to go to Thobal to ask the British sepoys to retire. Orders had been given for all prisoners to be released and sent to their homes as soon as a British retreat was evident. A 'fine horse, with Manipuri ornamented saddle with fringe tassel and white thread balls' was given to Williams and two sepoys, one a bugler and one a flag signal man, were released from jail to accompany him. Upon their arrival at Thobal the party found 2,000 Manipuri sepoys gathered in some anticipation with four 7-pounder guns, and Williams was taken to Prince Angao Senna who informed him that if he could produce an amicable settlement with the British troops he would receive a large reward. The Manipuri sepoys were constructing huts along the fort walls, 'in the field of some zemindar; the field was well enclosed with mud walls, and large fields of potatoe [sic], ginger and garlic trees, which were being trampled upon indiscriminately by everyone.' Williams and the two sepoys scaled the wall, from where they sounded the bugle several times, giving the call of the 43rd Gurkha Rifles and then that of the officers. No response was given and the flag sepoy advanced on the road with a white flag, where he was met by a British officer who arranged to meet the signaller early the following morning. Dinner that night, organised by Angao Senna, was a lavish affair

> in a large brass plate, which consisted of rice, fine clean rice, on a plantain leaf, and plantain leaf cups were made, which each of us had separately; one cup contained peas and potatoe fried, three cups contained three kinds of dal, one cup of fish, potatoe, and peas curry, one cup of some tamarind chutni, one cup of curd, and one cup some sugar, and one with some ghi. All this was enough to feed ten persons which three of us got.[8]

At this stage of his story, Williams' account agrees with that of Lieutenant Grant. The signaller met Grant – presuming him to be his commanding officer, Colonel Howlett – in the paddy fields the following morning, and informed him that the Chief Commissioner had been beheaded with Skene, Grimwood and Simpson, and that the headless corpses of Melville and O'Brien had been seen lying on the road in the moonlight. As has been described in his account of events, Grant under Howlett's name wrote to Angao Senna, 'saying that he did not come to fight but came to take the prisoners, and that the Manipuris first fired at his men, when they also defended themselves'. After about an hour Williams was forced to return to Manipuri quarters, as he had been advised that if he failed to do so all the other prisoners would be killed. Grant's letter was given to a Manipuri sepoy who was instructed to ride at full pelt to carry it to the Senapati. Tikendrajit's reply indicated that all the prisoners had been released and upon Grant's retirement would be despatched to Cachar. Receiving this reply, Grant responded that if the Regent would let him have the British sepoy prisoners and some rations, the British force would retire. This time the information was relayed back to the Regent, and back in Manipuri quarters a somewhat jaded Williams received his 'usual dinner, but did not eat anything, as I got the dyspepsia by eating all this kind of food'.[9]

The next morning, 5 April, 'the reply came, and with it came 500 lbs ala,[10] 50 lbs ghee, 50 lbs dall, 12 packets candles and a dozen bottles of Manipuri liquor'. However the Regent had not sent the British sepoy prisoners, who had apparently been despatched towards Cachar and Kohima. Grant refused to take the stores without the sepoys and, in the name of Howlett, wrote to the Regent demanding as hostage 'a man of high rank either of the military or civil employ'. Willliams wrote that he reluctantly took the letter, believing it to be 'a most outrageous demand'. Angao Senna retorted by sending the 'Colonel', a mere *subadar* whom, as Grant described in his account, he refused, demanding the Apprai Major, who held a high post in the Manipur Durbar. According to Williams, Angao Senna irately responded,

> 'first Colonel Howlett wanted the prisoners; then he wanted rations. Then he wanted a hostage, and now he wants a Major; next time he will want a Brahmin, and then he will want the Senapati himself; that Sahib is a great fraud. I will teach him to play the fool with us again. I don't know why the British Government is doing all this; ... we look upon them as our father and mother; but if they want to fight with us forcibly, we will then defend ourselves. If Government wants to take me prisoner, they will never get me alive; but can take my corpse a prisoner', – and laid his hand on his sword.[11]

He then ordered Williams to go back to Manipur where he would not be harmed. Williams reported that 'I made a salam {sic} to him and turned round to go, when he ordered all the bugles to sound, and his war bugle, a large brass-horn-shaped instrument, was sounded, which means war is declared.'[12]

Williams and the two sepoys arrived at 8pm in Manipur and were met in the palace compound by the Senapati who promised them an escort, rations as far as Kohima and some clothes. The men were taken to the Muslim bugler's house where they had dinner and the Senapati sent them sweetmeats, with three Manipuri shawls and a turban for Williams. The next morning, 6 April, the party remained in the city, as fighting continued in Thobal and the Senapati was too occupied to attend to them. However the Political Agent's clerk informed Williams that that all the prisoners had already left and that the signaller's pass had been made out so that they could leave the next morning. On 7 April the jail *subadar* arrived with 'three brass cooking pots, rice, fresh fish, some peas, curry-stuff, oil, salt, etc. for our journey and asked me to give him the Kashmir shawl which the Senapati had given me. I gave it away at once, thinking the sepoy escort might rob us at night on the way.' At the point of leaving, Williams was asked to see the Senapati once more in order that the signaller could 'speak the truth' from the Prince's narrative of events when he was, as was bound to be the case, interrogated by British officers.[13]

Tikendajit stressed his 'disgust' at having had to wait for a considerable time at the first *durbar* proposed by the Chief Commissioner when he was very ill, and explained that no one from the palace was prepared to attend the second *durbar* as they had been so badly treated. That evening the Chief Commissioner had written to him, stating that arrangements had been made for them to leave Manipur together the following day, 24 March, and to arrange for servants to be prepared, but at 4am the Chief Commissioner's sepoys came to his palace and began firing. The Prince reported that, following the assault upon the palace compound, he 'to defend himself, ordered his men to fight'. The Chief Commissioner had come to him attempting to apologise for all the disturbance, but the Senapati had told his soldiers to arrest the British officers, and, as Williams reported,

> the men were very angry with this business, and in their rage they beheaded them; but he said he is quite innocent of the murder;

> he did not order them, and all rest [sic] that has been done was done by his sepoys, who were most uncontrollable just then, and the Nagas and Kukis did all the mischief; that if the Government wants to fight, he is quite prepared to do so, but let Government come with five or six thousand troops; why come with three or four hundred and have so many lives lost.[14]

In the words of Tikendrajit, 'Government has given us this country, and now after so many years wishes to take it away; we will fight and die before we give up our country, and as for me, Government will never get me alive. I am very sorry that all this has occurred, but I am not to blame.'[15]

The signaller reported that the two men then discussed

> various matters regarding my family, home, pay, service etc; then I asked to go on my journey, to which he assented, came out in the compound with me, wished me good-bye, and shook hands. The word 'good-bye' was expressed in English; to which I replied by saying the same word.

Accompanied by two servants, two sepoys and two escort sepoys, Williams travelled unmolested, despite the fact that there were fortifications along the road. On 9 April the party arrived at Myangkhang where the signaller went to see the corpses of Melville and O'Brien: 'I found them on the side of the road a little distance from one another. The ravens picked all the flesh, and only the skeleton was seen.' On 11 April the men reached Mao *thana*, where they were caught in a heavy hailstorm, and in Kohima the following day Williams related his adventure to the deputy commissioner of the post and two other officers. He reported that the line from Manipur to Myangkhang was 'completely taken out, post and all, about 35 miles of wire; and from Manipur towards Tamu the line is entirely taken out to Palel, 30 miles . . . I saw on my way every Manipur sepoy going had coils of line wire with them for making rods and fencing.'[16] In Kohima the signaller no doubt also saw evidence of one wing of the massive field force which was setting out to assert British supremacy in Manipur.

The adventure was not without personal cost to Williams. At the end of the typewritten account of his version of events he made the following heartfelt plea:

> Sir, – In concluding this narrative, I most respectfully solicit you will kindly sanction a bonus for me . . . as I am at present without anything, and my loss is over Rs. 400; besides the few things that were left behind at Golaghat were sold off, my family believing I was really dead. It is a most unfortunate event that befell me. Some kind of reward for all my information may be given me. The good grade will be most acceptable. I have already passed the Code test, and can pass the same any time required.[17]

It has not been possible to establish whether or not the signaller was ever compensated for the traumatic role he played in the events of 1891.

CHAPTER 12

THE THREE COLUMNS

The first news of the difficulties experienced in arresting the Senapati reached the Viceroy in the North-Western Provinces very late on the evening of 29 March. Lansdowne immediately interrupted his tour and returned to Simla, where his council was assembled with some speed. From the north, south and west troops were ordered to advance on Manipur – at first with the hope of saving the prisoners, and later in greater strength to take the city.

As soon as rumours of the disaster reached Kohima, the Political Agent at the station, A. W. Davis, collected 150 military police and marched towards the Manipur border. By 30 March they had covered the 40 miles to Mao and, after a brief skirmish with Manipuri defenders, occupied a well-fortified stockade and awaited reinforcements. Davis despatched a messenger to the Regent, demanding details of the anti-British activity. He then returned to his post in Kohima. The response from the Manipur palace purported to be a copy of a telegram sent on 25 March from the Regent to the Viceroy, Lord Lansdowne, setting out details of the abortive *durbar* at the residency at which the Regent was treated with such disrespect. The letter claimed that the British had later attacked the palace without warning, whereupon the Manipuri soldiers in the Senapati's compound were compelled to fire in self-defence. However there was no mention of the truce or the night *durbar* in the palace, and the impression was that the British officers had been killed in the general hostilities. In the final sentences the Regent took pains to convey his personal innocence:

> I regret very much the sad occurrence. All Her Majesty's employes [sic], troops, and subjects surviving are well cared for. I took no aggressive part ... This disaster has happened only on rash ill-advised acts on the part of officers concerned. It is not known to my policy. Such barbarous acts have been committed, and I think my subjects were justified to fight for the cause of their religion, wives and children.[1]

However the Regent's insistence upon his personal lack of support for the violent response of his subjects appeared questionable when it was ascertained that two days after the attack on the residency there had been a 'General Thanksgiving', followed by a great procession through the city as Manipur was proclaimed free and victorious over its enemies.[2]

Babu Rassick Lal Kundu, the head clerk of the Manipur Political Agency, was taken prisoner in the palace. In a letter that he was ordered to write to the Assam authorities the clerk, no doubt to save his own skin, stressed the conciliatory tone which had been adopted by the princes. He reported:

> It was during the night of the 24th that all Bengali Babus and all British subjects with our families having left the town sought shelter in the interior, and during the next day we were gradually brought into the Palace as captives. We found about 200 sepoys, followers and servants kept under chain there in the jail, and from them I have learnt that our soldiers having run short of ammunition could not stand the heavy firing ... The telegraph line has been cut into numberless pieces, and all houses belonging to the British Government ... are burnt down. The treasure and all Government properties, stores, ammunition, and all the merchandise of British subjects and properties of the Babus are looted ... it is the lenient disposition of the Maharaja and Jubaraj to release the captives as per the attached list, who are supplied with provisions, apparels and other necessaries, and permitted to proceed to Cachar and Kohima under proper escort, but I regret very much to state that my own liberty is not granted, and I am detained against my will under the reasons that I, being the Head Clerk to the Political Agent, resident of fourteen years here and conversant with Manipuri language, would prove useful in making

> the Government convinced through any officer, civil or military, who might come to re-establish British concern in Manipur, that the Jubaraj would plead and prove himself innocent from the very beginning of the unhappy dispute, and all his subsequent undertakings especially his self-defence in this present unfortunate action. He states that as a Khatri by birth, he has only done the duty of his fighting race in self-defence, and yet in case the Government deem it expedient to ruin him, he is least afraid of his mortal life, but it would add discredit on the Government of such superior strength to ruin a feudatory state of such inferior position.[3]

On the morning of 5 April the Regent released 46 captive soldiers with a sum of Rs 5. The remaining telegraph officers were also set free, and the following day the six political agency clerks were despatched to Cachar. On 21 April lists of the prisoners that the Regent was sending to Kohima and Cachar were sent to British officials and it was reported that the Kohima party had arrived, but not those men travelling to Cachar. A Naga spy returning from Manipur stated that 62 captives remained in the city. They had set off for Cachar under an escort of Manipuri sepoys, but on hearing that British troops were on the road the escort had returned 'through fear'.[4]

By the first week in April the Manipur field force had been assembled to march on Manipur in three columns from the west, north and east. Overall charge was entrusted to Brigadier-General H. Collett, who was to lead the column advancing from Kohima in the north. The western column, assembled at Cachar, was under Lieutenant-Colonel R. H. F. Rennick, and Brigadier-General T. Graham commanded the eastern column coming in from Tammu. Collett was a veteran of the Indian Mutiny and also well acquainted with the north-eastern border of British India, having served in the Burma War of 1886–90. However even for a seasoned campaigner the movement of troops from as far afield as Poona and Madras created major logistical problems. The transport of the Kohima and Cachar columns consisted of hired carts, government and hired elephants,[5] mules, ponies and pack bullocks. Stores for the Kohima column were sent by rail to Goalundo or Dhubri on the Brahmaputra, and then by river steamers to Nigriting. Many of the boats ran aground or had to be unloaded and their cargo transferred to smaller vessels owing to the uncertain state of the river.

Upon leaving the Brahmaputra, Collett's column consisted of the 13th and 36th (Sikh) regiments of the Bengal Infantry and a mountain battery of four field guns. The troops had to cover the route from Nigriting to Kohima, a distance of 117 miles, before they could start the 87-mile advance on Manipur. To carry the massive amount of supplies required by the field force, Collett commandeered over 13,000 pack animals and 500 bullock carts (often from unwilling planters). A total of 500 mules were ordered from Burma for the transport of supplies to the Manipur garrison, but interpreters were not provided. As interpreters were essential for working the creatures, three sepoys of the 43rd Gurkhas were found who could speak Burmese and it was reported that 'The mules worked splendidly but the drivers required a very firm hand and much tact when dealing with them.'[6]

The route was daunting in the extreme. The road to Kohima rose to over 5,000 feet over unmetalled tracks which became impassable in heavy rain, and the path from Kohima to Manipur, although fairly well travelled, wound its way through several ranges of hills down to the valley. With the onset of the monsoon Collett relied eventually upon human bearers. The Deputy Commissioner of Kohima managed to procure no less than 1,500 Nagas and 'by his personal influence kept them together, as they are very averse to going to Manipur'. Described by the correspondent of *The Pioneer* as 'wild-looking ... many naked, save for an apology for a waist-cloth, and others boasting nothing but a blanket or a stout cotton sheet', they were employed in the fields at the time of the expedition and particularly objected to doing transport work.[7] Demanding high wages, they required no clothing or food from the British Army, only officers who had knowledge of the tribesmen and their language. The Nagas in the immediate vicinity of Kohima, the Angamis, were said to be the finest hill men to be found in Assam, most of them 6 feet tall at least, broad shouldered and powerfully built. Cachari bearers were supplied by the Civil Department but 'were found useless ... and had to be employed in building lines, cutting grass for transport animals and other similar work'.[8]

The journey from Nigriting, officially 11 marches, severely taxed the column and it was not until 20 April that, having picked up soldiers from the 42nd, 43rd and 44th Gurkhas, 1,200 men moved off from

Kohima towards the Manipur border. Little opposition was encountered. The Manipuri *thana* at Myangkhang, where the telegraph officers had been murdered, was only lightly defended and was soon abandoned in the face of the substantial British presence. *The Pioneer*'s correspondent accompanying the march described with some flourish how the column

> winds like a gigantic snake along the road which itself is sinuous in the extreme, as it follows the contour of spurs which stretch down from a precipitous range, on our left, into a valley . . . Spear heads, shining in the sun, indicate where our Nagas are toiling along, and splashes of brown among the bright green of the jungle show that our sturdy Gurkhas, in khaki, have set their faces towards Manipur. 'Our kookaies are thirsty for blood' is the significant phrase uttered by one of them.[9]

Along the route a Gurkha sepoy had been found lying in a narrow gully in the hillside. Roughly 300 men had marched past without seeing him, and he had remained either asleep from exhaustion or too weak to call out. He was 'tenderly lifted out and carried forward . . . The poor wretch was too weak to stand, being terribly emaciated.' Belonging to the 42nd, he was one of three sepoys released by the Regent who had never reached Cachar and had been hiding for days, creeping out at night for water. Nagas had taken his rifle but spared his life, a decision which elevated the tribesmen in British eyes.[10] Indeed Collett's praise for the Naga bearers was unstinting, declaring that it was only due to the assistance of 'these wild people' that the trek to Manipur could be accomplished. Upon his arrival in the capital, Collett reported that

> The spirit and behaviour of the troops have been throughout excellent. Much rain fell during the march, and as we had no tents, the men suffered considerable discontent in bivouac, but it was cheerfully borne as becomes good soldiers. The only complaint I ever heard was that the enemy did not stay to fight.[11]

The Cachar column under Rennick consisted of the 3rd and 18th regiments of the Bengal Infantry, the 1st battalion 2nd Gurkhas, a mountain battery of two guns, a detachment of the Surma Light Horse and about a dozen volunteers from the Calcutta Pioneer Corps who proved their worth as the intelligence arm of Rennick's troops. Also due to travel with the column was R. B. McCabe, deputy commissioner in Assam, as the replacement for Grimwood. McCabe had been originally described in glowing terms as an 'excellent' political officer by the Viceroy and well acquainted with the area, but was relieved of his duties when it was discovered that he was in an advanced state of alcoholism and quite unsuitable for the task.[12]

The stores for the column were sent by rail from Calcutta to Goalundo or Dhubri, and from there via steamers of the India General Steam Navigation Company as far up the river as was possible. The road from Cachar to Manipur was about 126 miles and, although easier than the route from Kohima, it crossed nine ranges of hills with narrow deep valleys and several rivers. At the height of the rainy season it was virtually impassable due to steep gradients and a lack of bridges. During the first stages of its advance the progress of the column was uneventful. A temporary bridge was constructed over the river Irang and positions secured along the route; however at Laimatol, where the road rose to nearly 5,000 feet before cutting through the final range of hills, the advance party came under fierce attack. In a course of action which to some extent exonerated him from his dishonourable performance during the retreat from the residency, Captain Boileau with a small detachment cleared three strongly fortified Manipuri stockades, in the process of which the enemy lost ten men and the commander was taken prisoner. Meanwhile Captain Butcher led a second party of Gurkhas to outflank the Manipuri position on the rocky heights further ahead, at which the enemy withdrew taking their wounded with them.

The British had suffered no casualties although conditions were appalling. The rains had begun in earnest and many of the men were without tents. The Cachar column had the added distress of a number of cases of cholera, and rest hospitals were set up along the route to Manipur. It was recognised that if severe sickness occurred it would be difficult to carry patients back over passes of 4,900 feet. The full force of the misery of the march was described with much feeling by Rennick in a despatch along the route:

> Heavy storm and rain last night, continuation of which makes me most apprehensive as to the possibility of keeping up the lines of communication . . . Half the elephants are wild, unruly brutes, and

> I have already dropped over 120 bullocks as useless up to date; my Naga coolies from Lushai are broken down and unhealthy; and they with local coolies have cholera in their way, which will cause numerous defections; the rivers might rise at any moment and utterly paralyse all attempts to supply the column; there is no grazing for bullocks, and bamboo leaves are distant from all stages; the ponies from Lushai have almost done their work. I have found it hitherto impossible to establish any heliographic or lamp signalling as the weather is so cloudy . . . I am prepared to carry out the orders I may receive after this warning, which I consider my duty to submit.[13]

However despite the severe conditions the troops displayed remarkable resilience. It was reported that the Pioneer Company 'having left half their strength foot-sore at Silchar [Cachar], and having been attacked with cholera, nevertheless did most useful work on the line of communications. The Surma Valley Light Horse did excellent service in carrying despatches, escorting officers, mails etc.' The muleteers from the Punjab and the North-West Province were found to be ideal for the task, although those from Madras were 'very much wanting physically and were constantly falling sick'.[14] Praising the entire column, Rennick noted the 'splendid behaviour' of both officers and men, declaring that 'Exposed throughout the march to the inclemencies of the season, to hardship, sickness and privation, all answered cheerfully to the call of duty, and worked with a zeal and energy rarely surpassed.'[15] Singled out for his contribution to the march was Major H. St John Maxwell,[16] deputy commissioner in Cachar, whose posting as Political Agent in Manipur in place of Frank Grimwood, and subsequently the incapacitated McCabe, was confirmed by the Government of India on 15 April. Maxwell had pursued a successful military career and had served in the Naga Hills, where he later acted as political officer. Described as 'an English gentleman and very kindly and considerate' he was an obvious choice, as few officers existed with any knowledge of the north-eastern area of India.[17]

The Tammu column was to face the strongest opposition from Manipuri forces. Under the command of Brigadier-General T. Graham, commanding officer of the Myingyan District of Burma, were 200 men of the 2nd Battalion Oxfordshire Light Infantry, half a battalion of the 4th King's Royal Rifle Corps, a regiment of the 2nd Burma Battalion of the Madras Infantry, a regiment of the 4th Burma Battalion of the Madras Infantry, the 2nd Battalion of the 4th Gurkhas and four guns of a Royal Artillery mountain battery. The advance column of this substantial force, consisting of 400 men, 40 mounted infantry and two mountain guns, pressed ahead to relieve Presgrave and Grant, as described in Grant's narrative. Civilians also played a part in the action: Hafiz Futteh Shah, the Punjabi trader who had acted as guide to Birbal Nagarkoti, accompanied the column from Tammu and carried water and ammunition to the fighting line, 'showing as much bravery as any soldier'.[18] Following the violent encounter with Manipuri forces in the hills to the south of Manipur, in which Drury, Grant and Birbal Nagarkoti were wounded, the column started for Manipur at 4.30am on 27 April. Severely delayed by the bad state of the roads and bridges, Graham and the Tammu column reached the capital at 11am. The columns from Cachar and Kohima arrived from the west and north just before him.

According to *The Pioneer*, when the three columns arrived in Manipur, having been marching in the heavy rain, scarcely a human being was to be seen and the capital was 'wrapped in silence'. Inquiries were made as to what had occurred during the previous days. It was reported that a *durbar* had been called in the palace at which it had been agreed to evacuate the city. The Manipur Court Chronicle stated:

> money and other gifts were presented to all the Brahmins and Baishnabs. All the royal wives were made to pack up their belongings and leave with their mothers for their parental homes . . . All the tools of trade and weapons of war were presented to the Institutions where they belonged. At six pung hours after the noon yuthak a large number of the people of the country came out. With love and devotion for the Institutions which each of them served and to which (they) belonged, they left them all in tears. Shri Govinda and all the other images (from the temples) were moved into the house of Takhur Tas (Das), the king's personal priest, near Khongman.[19]

A witness confirmed that earlier he had seen 'the Brindaban idol brought into the Raja's place. The idol had been stripped of its jewels. The idol was naked.'[20]

It appeared that the Regent, the Senapati, and Angao Senna had decided to take flight with a bodyguard of 200 men, eight elephants, ten ponies and four Shan guides. The royal party left at 9.30pm on 26 April in the direction of Chassad, six marches eastwards from Manipur. The four mountain guns with six other pieces of artillery had been placed in the magazine, in which were stored shells, cartridges, boxes of percussion caps and small arms. The magazine had then been fired and the adjoining maharaja's palace reduced to ashes. The explosion of shells had been heard during the night in Colonel Rennick's camp, and the fire was still smouldering when the columns arrived in the city. Traces were found of the royal fugitives, with some Martini Henry rifles, Sniders, sporting rifles and ammunition scattered in the jungle. One rifle was inscribed as having been presented to the Maharaja of Manipur by the Viceroy in 1872, and there was a 'double-barrel express' which was identified as the property of Lieutenant Simpson.

The sepoys of the Manipuri army scattered to their villages taking their arms with them while the townspeople fled temporarily to neighbouring settlements, fearing that the city would be looted. Also departed from the capital were the Nagas and Kukis, 'always ready for fighting, drink and plunder', who, in an old established tradition, had been called in at short notice to support the Senapati and had been concealed in the enclosed area of the palace.[21] Collett confirmed that on his arrival the houses in the immediate neighbourhood of the capital, the city itself and the palace enclosure were totally devoid of inhabitants. *The Times* elaborated upon the picture, reporting:

> The Maharaja's palace, from which so tremendous a fire was poured upon the Residency, is a heap of ruins. It has been gutted of everything it contained, and nothing remains but its crumbling walls. It is a singularly dramatic termination to the whole melancholy affair. Retribution came from north and south and west with strides as inevitable as fate, and when its forces closed in upon the doomed town they found it nothing but a desert. An entire population has disappeared leaving no trace ... They have left behind, however, ghastly relics of that terrible struggle in the Residency. Lying in the courtyard of the wrecked palace our soldiers have found the heads of the British officers treacherously massacred by the Senaputty.[22]

However the 62 Indian British subjects who had been held in captivity by the Regent were found safe and well, and ample accommodation for the troops of the three columns was found in the buildings adjacent to the palace.

Queen Victoria, avidly following events in Manipur, expressed the view that,

> While wishing murderers, if possible, to be caught and duly punished, [I] would earnestly deprecate any wholesale punishment of the innocent, or incitement to bloody revenge: this only too easily encouraged, would not redound to our honour, or add to our power for the future.[23]

Sir Frederick Roberts, commander in chief, reassured the monarch that 'Generals Collett and Graham are humane men of great experience, excellent judgment and proper feeling, and I am certain they will keep their troops well in hand and will not allow them to commit excesses in any form.' Roberts did, however, take the precaution of sending the generals a telegram, impressing upon them that:

> As it is possible that the strong indignation which has been aroused in the public mind by the Manipur disaster may cause our troops, particularly the Gurkhas, to wreak their vengeance in a cruel manner, please do all in your power to prevent them from resorting to unnecessary bloodshed, or taking the law into their own hands after the fighting is over. Remember it is absolutely essential there should be no indiscriminate punishment.[24]

In this Roberts was no doubt attempting to combat the tendency of many British members of the relief force to lump 'Asiatics' into a hostile mass, a view expressed by General Sir James Willcocks, who wrote many years later of his participation in the event, 'I was on my way to help in avenging the massacre of our officers in the very country I had left only four years previously, to all outward appearances peaceful and friendly; but there can never be real peace in lands where the palm trees grow.'[25]

A proclamation was issued by Collett disarming the population of the Manipur Valley and the peoples of the neighbouring hill tracts, formerly subject to the Manipur Durbar. An order was also issued for the immediate return of property looted from the residency together with cash, notes and stamps from the treasury, from which it was calculated that Rs 1 *lakh* 90,000 had vanished. Any outstanding amount was to be levied from the villages in the valley.[26] No less than 26 elephants, the property of the Durbar, and 50 ponies were made over to the Transport Department with some struggle. When it had become evident that British troops were reaching Manipur, the elephants had been let loose in the swamps of the valley and sent off with a deep spear wound in the buttocks. Many of the animals were only half tamed and soon became wild, with the result that collecting them was no easy task. With experienced army elephants and the use of chains they were eventually all secured, but not before some of the transport *mahouts* had experienced narrow escapes.[27]

The following guns and ammunition were captured in the palace arsenal: four 7-pounder rifled muzzle-loading guns, eight 3-pounder smooth-bore bronze guns, one 2-pounder muzzle loading bronze gun, one 4½-inch mortar, 1,290 fire-arms of various patterns, 910,000 rounds smooth-bore balled musket ammunition in boxes, 972,000 percussion caps for smooth-bore muskets, 180 barrels of powder and, finally, elephant gear for the 7-pounder mountain guns.[28] Following a subsequent enquiry, it became clear that 'an accumulation of ammunition has been going on stealthily for years, and the gravest deceit has been practised upon the Political Agents by the Durbar'. It was apparently the custom for the political agent to inspect the maharaja's magazine from time to time to check that the stock of ammunition tallied with the quantity shown in the stock book. The inspection invariably showed a correct balance as the Durbar took pains to conceal any surplus supply, and never more than 60,000 rounds of ammunition were declared to be in stock. In fairness to Grimwood, who was no doubt aware of the surreptitious stockpiling of arms, it was accepted that 'even a Political Agent cannot always be discrediting the word of a native prince'. The ingenuity of the local craftsmen was apparent: both gunpowder and caps were manufactured locally, and it was reported that a blacksmith had actually turned out several Martinis from his workshop. Moreover, in several of the guns which were surrendered there was a Snider breech block on a smooth bore.[29]

Under instructions from the Foreign Department of the Government of India proclamations were issued to hill tribes in the Manipur area, offering a reward of Rs 5,000 for the apprehension and surrender of the

Regent or Senapati, and Rs 2,000 for minor members of the royal family or leading officials implicated in the murders of the British party.[30] Swift retribution was the order of the day, and the instructions given to the officers commanding the columns as to the punishment of the culprits were precise and unequivocal:

> If the Regent or any other member of the royal family falls into your hands and is suspected of murder or abetment of murder or of having acted as a leader or instigator of revolt, he should be tried by a court consisting of three officers, including at least one Political Officer. Their sentences to be subject to confirmation by the Government of India. The punishment of convicted offenders should be public and striking, but it should be completed as soon as possible.[31]

A proclamation was to be issued demanding the surrender of all swords and firearms within one week, on pain of death or deportation, and it was suggested that some form of penalty should be imposed upon the Manipur people in general and a fine levied to cover supplies needed by the British force. However, it was advised that:

> Indiscriminate punishment of the rank and file would be neither humane or politic . . . remember that it is not desirable to drive the Manipur people into further resistance, or to make them more difficult to deal with hereafter. Let any penalty imposed be just and deliberate, and take care that, when punishment is being inflicted, the strictest discipline is maintained. If the palace buildings are demolished take care that any sacred objects are as far as possible respected.[32]

News, of varying reliability, was trickling through as to the facts of the murder of Quinton and the British officers. On 15 April the following account, given by a member of the Chief Commissioner's escort, Palkem Kahar, was sent with its gruesome content to the Foreign Secretary of the Government of India in Simla:

> I was taken prisoner soon after Lieutenant Brackenbury was wounded and kept a prisoner inside the principal entrance to the

> palace enclosure. The Sahibs came in at about 8 pm; it was bright moonlight then. The Sahibs had about half an hour's conversation with the Jubraj and Senapati. After this they were seized and killed. The Manipuris first cut off their hands, then their feet, and then their heads. Their hands were tied and then cut off. Their feet were cut off as they stood. The Chief Commissioner was killed first, after that I was unable to see anything as a crowd got around. I was about 20 paces off only from where the prisoners were killed. The Jubraj and Senapati saw all that happened from about six yards off. I do not know what was done after this. I was alone a prisoner when the occurrences took place. I have lost all I had, including rupees 100 I had on me. About 1,000 men must have been present when Mr. Quinton and the others were killed. I did not see the corpses of the Sahibs. I saw the Chief Commissioner killed with my own eyes. I am not merely telling you vague surmises.[33]

According to *The Pioneer*, a report from Dhonosing Sajol Senba, the public executioner, corroborated the soldier's account of the violent course of events. The executioner confirmed that:

> The four Sahibs and a native sepoy came out of the house; the sentries marched them to the gate and made them over to me. The whole place was crowded with Manipuri sepoys. The Sahibs were killed one by one. Chains were on their legs, and their hands were tied behind their backs. Each one was placed in a standing position facing the west, and I was on the north side and gave the dhao[34] stroke. I don't know one Sahib from another. The execution occurred at night, but it was bright moonlight, as bright as day.[35]

The newspaper also confirmed that a Gurkha sepoy had found the skeletons of Melville and O'Brien in a ditch at Myangkhang, 34 miles from Manipur. Howard Hensman, correspondent of *The Pioneer*, and H. T. Pinhey, assistant superintendent of telegraphs, had buried the remains, and the funeral service had been read over the grave by Pinhey.[36]

A special committee set up by Collett inspected the residency and grounds on 28 April and found that 'the building has not only been burnt, but every brick thrown down and every shrub rooted up. The out-houses have also been levelled, as well as the mud walls round the Residency. Large holes had been dug in different places.' British soldiers were asked if they wished to undertake the work of finding the bodies of the victims, and informed that if they were unwilling to do this men would be ordered from a native regiment to deal with the appalling task. After consultation the men agreed that the work should be done by British men, and they preferred to act without native help. They dug throughout the day, one party relieving the other. The graves of Major Trotter and Mr Heath had been disturbed, but apparently not with the object of burying any of the murdered officers. Mr Heath's grave was then investigated and in it, buried deeply, two of the bodies of the murdered officers were discovered. The working parties cleared the ground floor of the residency, and special attention was paid to the examination of the cellar where Surgeon Calvert indicated that Lieutenant Brackenbury's body had been left by the retiring party. No trace of his remains could be found among the debris and it was presumed that his body had been cremated in the residency fire.[37]

From information received in the afternoon the committee moved to an area half a mile from the residency where Nagas and criminals were buried, and discovered further bodies of murdered men. Various officers, personal friends of the deceased, were asked to identify the bodies and it was generally agreed that two of them were Lieutenant Simpson and Quinton. Several medical officers were consulted as to which of the other bodies belonged to Europeans, but on this point there was much difference of opinion. The committee then proceeded to the ground outside the palace, under a large tree, where some of the heads of those 'executed by the order of the Raja' were believed to have been buried, and three heads in small brick graves were found. One head appeared to be that of Grimwood and another that of Colonel Skene; however due to advanced decomposition even Major G. G. Grimwood (the late Political Agent's brother) was unable to be certain in his identification.[38] Lieutenant Colonel St John Michell, Graham's adjutant-general, described later that he 'had never experienced anything more ghastly than poor Grimwood bending over this head and by the light of a lantern, trying to decypher his brother's features'.[39] At last Major Grimwood recalled that there was a scar on his brother's head which an army doctor was able to identify.

Figure 12.1 The Lion Gate leading to the durbar room and polo ground (from a private collection).

The heads were taken to the bodies and placed in a large grave in the residency compound, next to that of Major Trotter. The committee considered that they had found all the parts of the murdered officers. The only mutilations were hands, feet and heads, and the bodies had not been damaged. On 30 April a military funeral was held and 11-minute guns were fired by No. 2 British Mountain Battery from the open ground outside the west gate of the palace while the cortege was proceeding to the graves. Each regiment in the field force detailed one company, made up to 100 rank and file, to accompany the cortege, and the street from the gate of the inner palace enclosure to the site of the residency quarter-guard was lined by troops of the 42nd, 43rd and 44th Gurkha Rifles. In the evening the stone lions overlooking the site of the murder, supposedly smeared with the blood of the murdered officers, were blown up with dynamite.[40]

On 10 May the Viceroy informed the Secretary of State that Thangal General had surrendered himself on the 7 May and was in custody. The younger princes were tracked down by a party of Manipuri police sent out by the new political officer in Manipur, Major Maxwell, and on

9 May the Regent was arrested and kept prisoner under a military guard.[41] According to the correspondent of *The Pioneer*, when apprehended he 'looked very cheery and was not a bit cast down'.[42] Tikendrajit was discovered on 23 May, hiding in the house of his stepmother near the palace. After some resistance he was overpowered by Maxwell's men and brought in semi-conscious.[43] Collett reported that 'The Senapati detected officers, and ran, but was caught by Subadar, and they rolled together on ground ... and after further struggle he gave in and was hastily taken the six miles into fort.'[44] It was also revealed that Manipuris had opened the grave of the infant son of James Johnstone and scattered the remains, despite the fact that the grave was situated in Naga country 12 miles from the capital. Six out of seven of the guilty men were apprehended and publicly flogged.[45]

The villagers were fast returning to their houses, offering submission and voluntarily producing supplies for the British force,[46] and the leading Brahmin priests were instructed to continue their duties, according to the *Court Chronicle*, allowing 'the cart festival for Shri Govinda to take place in order not to disrupt the (religious) practices'.[47] *The Pioneer* reported that:

> Bazaars are now crowded with women selling fish, fruit, cloth, grain, vegetables etc.... The climate is still deliciously cool and as pleasant as a hill station in the Himalayas, but mosquitoes and flies are very bad ... The clearance of all unused huts and buildings in the palace enclosure has made a tremendous improvement in the appearance of the place, which would hardly be recognisable by old inhabitants. We have polo on captured ponies twice a week.[48]

Fresh meat was available from cattle which the local populace was unwilling to sell and 'had to be seized when wanted'. Sheep were supplied by traders from Cachar, although the rate was high. Biscuits and tinned meat were also issued to the soldiers, corned beef being recommended over and above the somewhat 'tasteless and insipid' boiled mutton. Goats for the native troops were not procurable at Manipur and had to be brought in from Cachar; however many were destroyed owing to diseases contracted in transit. The issue of pigs to the soldiers who were prepared to eat them was suggested but not recommended on medical grounds, and a few buffalo were made available to Gurkhas.

Tea, sugar, rice, *atta*, *dal* and *ghee* of reasonable quality were all available. A small bakery was also set up in the city to supply fresh bread to the Europeans.[49]

With the rains in full force, urgent plans were put into operation to accommodate the British troops. There was little Manipuri labour for building work, and few tools for either the troops or the Manipuris. Proposals involving major demolition or earthwork movement were therefore considered impractical, and it was agreed that whilst there was cholera the Gurkhas should not be taxed with heavy duties. In the meantime it was possible to use the remains of some of the buildings within the fort. The Manipur Court Chronicle reported with some feeling on the speed and thoroughness with which the British commandeered the royal compound:

> The Bara Sahep (Maxwell) stayed in the queen mother's palace. The Bara Sahep became the king of the Meeteis.[50] The Meeteis presented a large amount of pressed rice to him. The sepoys also stayed in the palace {compound} ... All the horses, cattle, buffaloes which they had confiscated from the Meeteis were kept in the Konthoucham homestead {the former Residency compound} ... Nine cannons and all the guns which belonged to the Meeteis and those which belonged to the Manipur Levy were broken and piled up at the front of the Garot Court. All the weapons of all the Meetei army were confiscated and broken up. Every door and gate was guarded by a British sepoy.[51]

To reinforce the utter disgrace of the Manipur royal family, the site of the Jubraj's palace was to form the lines of the 43rd Gurkha Light Infantry during the rains and the spare transport animals were to be accommodated on top of the citadel. The *nautch* house, used for female dancing displays, had the potential to make 'an excellent commissariat godown' and with little regard for religious sensitivity the golden temple was proposed as the magazine for reserve ammunition.[52] In addition there was a 'good shed' which might be used as a hospital. Measures for defensive purposes included the erection of a stockade surrounding the fort, and the demolition of the residency and the buildings adjacent to it to obtain a clear field of fire. The terreplein of the citadel was to be cleared to improve the 'ventilation' of the area, and fresh huts constructed for 300 or 400 men. Huts on the citadel were also to be used as alternative quarters for the treasury, political officer's quarters, jail and post office.[53] The telegraph office at Manipur reopened on 11 May after repairs to the line which had been almost entirely destroyed between the capital and Kairong, two marches away, with many of the posts broken down or pulled up.

In October the 1st battalion 2nd Gurkha Rifles returned to British India, and the following month the Mountain Battery marched to Burma. The 44th Gurkha Rifles returned to Shillong and were relieved by a wing of the 42nd from Kohima, who with the 43rd Gurkha Rifles formed the permanent garrison at Manipur. The majority of the field force had not fired a shot in the whole campaign, and more had died of cholera than had been killed in action. As James Johnstone observed bitterly after the event, there had been little need for 'such a formidable muster of troops, at a vast expenditure of money and suffering, to retrieve a disaster brought about by such an extraordinary want of courage, nerve, forethought and common sense'.[54]

CHAPTER 13

THE COURT OF ENQUIRY

In the aftermath of the events of March the Government of India was all too aware of the mounting criticism in India and Britain of both the actions of those masterminding the expedition to arrest the Senapati and the military performance during the uprising. Not only had British forces been soundly defeated by supposedly ill-trained native troops, but they had also been forced to retreat in no little disarray from the capital. In an effort to deflect such criticism as early as possible, orders to hold a Court of Enquiry were issued soon after Collett left Kohima. Among other matters, the court was to investigate the suitability of Quinton's escort and the sufficiency of the available ammunition. The president of the military enquiry was Colonel H. M. Evans, assisted by Major Eaton Travers of the Gurkhas and Captain A. Birch of the Royal Artillery. The Calcutta newspaper *The Statesman* was quick to point out that the court consisted of men who were 'servants of the state, immediately subordinate to the Executive Government and dependent upon it for their promotion' and therefore unable to be impartial.[1] Colonel Evans was hardly a neutral observer, being commanding officer of the 43rd Gurkha Rifles, of whom 100 had been stationed at Langthobal as the Political Agent's escort. It was later suggested that Evans chose to blame the European officers of the 42nd and 44th rather than to believe that his own men of the 43rd had deserted under fire.[2]

Having examined a considerable amount of evidence from key witnesses, the members of the Court of Enquiry found it impossible to clear with any conviction the names of the principal players, now dead, who had been involved in the fiasco surrounding 'the punishment of the rebellious durbar'. In a telegram to the Viceroy of 9 May Viscount Cross made it clear that 'As to Quinton, I am not prepared to defend all he did; impossible to do so. There seems to me to have been a series of blunders both by the Civil and Military authorities.'[3] However, in what transpired to be a vain attempt to avoid public censure of the Government of India, the findings of the court underplayed the severity of the shortcomings of the British senior civil and military officers responsible for the planning of the expedition. It was maintained that the escort of 400 men detailed by Collett to accompany Quinton was 'sufficient for the purpose of ensuring his safety and securing the objects which, as far as was then foreseen, his mission was designed to accomplish'. From his evidence it appeared that Chatterton had suggested to Skene the possibility of taking the two mountain guns at Kohima; however the court deemed it reasonable that Quinton considered these to be surplus to requirements, since 'neither the Chief Commissioner nor the Officer Commanding contemplated the employment of the escort on any duty in which guns or reserve ammunition in excess of 13,000 rounds, known to be at Manipur, could be of use'. As a result senior members of the Government of India were absolved from responsibility since, due to Quinton's lack of concern, 'it was apparently thought unnecessary to refer to the Commander-in-Chief in regard to the strength or composition of the escort, and His Excellency [the Viceroy] did not see the papers until the 4th March'.[4] As far as the sufficiency of ammunition was concerned, the court commented that 'All the officers unite in saying that no man was out of ammunition, but that all were very short of it.' Little mention was made of the negligence on the part of Quinton and Skene in failing to ensure that adequate ammunition was available.

When dealing with the execution of the mission it was less easy to remove culpability from the British officers involved. The findings of the court noted that the determination to arrest Tikendrajit before daylight was 'infelicitous' as 'it was expected that his personal servants and adherents would resist; and it should have been foreseen that to the Regent and his troops, who were not in the secret, the first sounds of conflict at night would appear the commencement of a general attack'. But for some reason, as stated by Captain Boileau, Surgeon Calvert and Lieutenant Chatterton in their evidence, Colonel Skene imagined that there would be no reprisals. When the attempt to seize the Senapati had failed, two courses were open to the British: to storm the citadel or to 'withdraw to some point of vantage' and await the arrival of reinforcements. However, considerable time was wasted in indecision and even when agreement was finally reached to assume a defensive position, there was no evidence of a well-considered plan of action to assemble the various detachments operating in the royal compound and on the far bank of the river. The fact that from 6am until the afternoon 'no effectual effort was made to reinforce Lieutenant Brackenbury's party or to rescue this gallant young officer and his wounded comrades from their isolated and perilous situation' was a source of much concern.[5]

Referring to the final fateful departure of the British officers into the palace, the commander in chief in India, Sir Frederick Roberts, declared that he was unable to

> sufficiently express his regret that at this juncture Colonel Skene did not carry out his original intention and insist upon retiring to some position, where he could have held his own until reinforcements reached him, instead of trusting to the forbearance of a semi-barbarous army, inflated with victory.[6]

The Pioneer agreed bitterly that:

> Of the last scene of all when he [Skene], as senior military officer, accompanied Mr Quinton into the palace, it can only be said that he and his companions made the fatal error of trusting Asiatics, flushed with success and probably bent on completing their triumph by treachery.[7]

The sheer senselessness of both men, supposedly officers of some considerable experience, in accepting Grimwood's naïve belief in the Senapati to the point of entering a stronghold which had been directing hostile fire upon the British residency throughout most of the day was implied, if not spelt out.

Summing up the entire proceedings of the Court of Enquiry, the Commander in Chief arrived at the conclusion that the escort of 400 men, detailed by Major-General Collett to accompany Mr Quinton, proved insufficient only because it was unexpectedly employed in attacking a strong defensive position, a task for which it was unsuited in strength and equipment. He continued that there was little doubt that

> had the General Officer Commanding been aware that such a contingency was possible, he would have insisted upon the Chief Commissioner being accompanied by a much larger force; but it seems equally clear that, had it not been for the chivalrous but fatuous decision to place themselves in the power of the unscrupulous Senapati, Colonel Skene with the Chief Commissioner and his companions could at any time have secured their personal safety, by withdrawing beyond the range of the Manipuri guns and effecting a junction with the Langthobal party and Captain Cowley's detachment.[8]

However despite its condemnation of the senior personnel involved, the summary stressed that the painful story of the occurrences of the 24 and 25 March was

> relieved by many well-attested examples of the excellent behaviour of the men; the three brave sepoys who volunteered to rescue Lieutenant Brackenbury and other wounded; the Native officers and men who on the morning of the 25th remained at their posts awaiting orders when others had retired; the treasure guard, who defended their trust until overpowered by numbers; the sepoys and kahars, who, without food or rest, for many weary hours, carried wounded men under the devoted supervision of Surgeon Calvert.

In the opinion of Sir Frederick Roberts, 'no stigma can attach to troops for a failure ennobled by such instances of soldierly and gallant conduct'.[9]

Missing from the findings of the court was the burning issue of the failure to divide the line of defence into sections commanded by British officers and subsequently to assemble the British troops in the residency in the early morning of 25 March. As a result, at 1am when it was agreed to retreat nearly two-thirds of the force were left behind without orders from their officers. Comment on such a grave dereliction of duty was withheld while the conduct of Captains Boileau and Butcher was under consideration with a view to disciplinary action. Statements were given from Boileau, Butcher, Lugard, Calvert, Chatterton and Woods, as well as evidence from commissioned and non-commissioned

Indian officers, which was pivotal in determining the military future of the two captains.

In his evidence Havildar Gunjabir Rai of the 43rd Gurkhas denied all knowledge of the retirement and stated that he left with a small party for Kohima, eventually arriving alone. Jemadar Dhunbir Karki of the 42nd was told 'to close his men to the left' by Lugard but received no further orders before retiring with 15 soldiers 'when the morning star was high in the heavens'. He later met up with Jemadars Durga Dutt and Gaj Bahudur of the 44th attempting to reach the Cachar road with 102 men, where they joined the 43rd detachment under Cowley at Kowpoom. Naick Kabiraj Thapa and 20 men of the 42nd and 44th heard sounds of the main party moving out at about 2am but since they had received no orders, nor had the bugle been sounded, they remained at their posts until the enemy closed in and they were forced to retreat over the river. Thapa reported in his evidence that he saw 'a large body of sepoys, about one hundred and fifty of them, some going one way and some another. I could see neither British nor native officers. I asked where they were and was told they had gone on.' With eight men, he eventually arrived at Kohima. Some soldiers made their way to Sengmai, where they found the British camp burnt down, and others set off for Tammu, where they met up with Grant's party. Among those men who had stayed at their posts until surrounded by Manipuri soldiers, Sepoy Man Sing Thapa of the 44th attached to Brackenbury's party was taken with other prisoners to the palace and kept in chains for 11 days.[10]

Chatterton admitted that 'there had been no regular "fall in" and no muster, prior to the commencement of the retirement, because I knew there were still men posted at the North walls'.[11] Lugard's evidence also revealed that the junior officers had little confidence in their superior, stating that when he had declared his opposition to the over-hasty departure from the residency on the night of 24 March, Boileau

> seemed to waver at my words, indeed he certainly did waver and said something to the effect that perhaps we had better not go. This startled me as it seemed to throw the responsibility of changing the decision to go on me, the junior officer of the garrison, and I said something to the effect that the decisions must rest with him and not with me. I also felt that it was too late to change as the movement had actually begun.[12]

Following the submission of this body of evidence, Boileau was called upon to submit a defence against the allegations formulated by the adjutant-general in India, Major-General W. Galbraith, that he abandoned the residency

> without observing established rules for conducting a retreat, that he did not parade his men or detail advance and rear guards before retiring, that he personally left before the evacuation was complete, that on ascertaining that a large number of men had remained behind, he took no measures to communicate with them, but left them to their fate, that he failed to maintain discipline and order in retreat, and that he allowed the retreating party to straggle and separate in a perilous and unsoldierlike manner.[13]

It was agreed that 'the excellent behaviour of many of the native commissioned and non commissioned officers shows that they would, as a body, have responded freely to any vigorous call from their own commanding officers'.[14]

In response to the charges against him, Boileau's defence did little to improve his position. A despatch emanating from the Viceroy's Council, dated 15 August 1891, declared that the captain's statement 'practically admits the truth of the charges against him' and that the 'demoralisation' of the men during the retreat, upon which Boileau placed great emphasis, was 'doubtless due to their having seen their own British officers retreating in haste, without any proper military preparations or precautions'. In declaring that he 'hoped the remainder were coming on', the captain unsurprisingly failed to impress senior Government of India officials.[15]

Boileau made an impassioned plea that he had served nearly 21 years in India with one year in the Forest Department before joining the army. During that time he had only been home for 11 months. Under normal circumstances he would have obtained his majority with the requisite increase in pay in a few months, and as a married man with three children the loss of pension would be 'a very heavy blow'.[16] The final verdict of the Viceroy's Council was that there was no alternative but to recommend to the Secretary of State that Boileau be compulsorily retired from the service as a captain, but that, in consideration of his previous service and as an act of compassion to his wife and children, he should be granted a pension of £200 per annum.[17] Despite the adjudication, upon returning to England Boileau was able to find employment as an army tutor preparing public school boys for entrance into Sandhurst and Woolwich, and officers for promotion examinations. In 1914 he was employed as a recruiting officer in Kent for five months, and on the grounds that he received no pay or gratuity for this work Boileau applied for an addition to his compassionate allowance following the war. The case was referred to the War Office, which promptly refused the application.[18] In the 1960s his son, Colonel Digby Boileau, was still attempting to prove that his father's dismissal was engineered to detract from the shortcomings of the Government of India and that Boileau was

> made the scapegoat for those really responsible, and sacrificed to public opinion chagrined at the loss of British prestige, and quite possibly wounded pride at a very high level. That a cloak of secrecy was cast over the whole business, was not, I believe, out of consideration for my father, but to hush it up as quickly as possible.[19]

However Boileau fared better than his subordinate, Captain Butcher, who was called upon to raise a defence on much the same lines. The charges stated that he failed to recall Lieutenant Simpson's party on the afternoon of 24 March or to ascertain Surgeon Calvert's whereabouts before he left the Senapati's temple; that he failed to collect the men of his own battalion, in order that the retirement from the residency might be conducted in a proper manner; that he left the residency compound on the morning of 25 March before its evacuation by men of his own battalion was complete; that as the next senior officer to Boileau at the time of the retirement he failed to offer him 'any support or counsel'; that on ascertaining that a large number of his men had remained in the residency compound 'he took no measures to communicate with them, but left them to their fate'; and, finally, that he failed to maintain discipline and order during the retreat, when his men were allowed to straggle and separate.[20] As with Boileau's defence, Butcher stressed the utter demoralisation of the men, stating that they were 'so unnerved' that they would not go up into the residency veranda, where the ammunition was stored, to bring it down. The captain stated that when the main body of the retiring party was moving off he was unable to say even roughly how many men were with him at the time: 'It was very difficult, or almost impossible, to fall in the men in such a place, owing to the heavy fire which was constantly kept up by the enemy.'[21] However to have 'presumed' that the men on the residency walls would retire and assemble outside was viewed as a highly irresponsible reaction to the critical situation on the morning of 25 March, as was Butcher's comment that in retrospect he failed to see what advice he could have given Boileau in the circumstances.[22]

In a despatch to the Secretary of State, Lansdowne concurred with the Commander in Chief's low opinion of the captain's behaviour during the night of 24 March and the subsequent retreat from Manipur. The Viceroy made it clear that in his opinion 'Captain Butcher's conduct showed such an unsoldierly disregard for the welfare of his men and such neglect of the duties manifestly imposed on him by the situation' that his retention in the army was undesirable, and his compulsory removal from the service was recommended.[23] As he had served for only 12 years he was granted a compassionate allowance of five shillings a day.[24] Butcher appealed against the decision later in the year, submitting a further statement in his defence, and requesting a court-martial, a request which met with little success. A letter from the Adjutant-General in India dated October 1891 confirmed that the Viceroy

> finds nothing in it to lead him to alter the opinion he has already expressed, that having regard to the orderly retirement of the parties who retreated under their Native officers, he is forced, reluctantly to believe that the demoralisation of the men under Captains Boileau and Butcher was due to their seeing their British officers retreating in haste and confusion, abandoning the greater portion of those under their command. He sees no reason to modify his former recommendation that Captain Butcher should be retired from the service.[25]

In January 1892 Butcher took his appeal to the Under-Secretary of State for India with the plea that he had a right for his case to be heard in open court 'to afford me an opportunity of clearing my character, and defending my honour which has been unjustly impugned on unsworn evidence'[26] and was again refused. A request by Butcher in April 1892 for a new Court of Enquiry fell on equally stony ground. In a final blow to the captain, the North-East Frontier clasp sanctioned for participants in the expedition to Manipur was, following a submission to the Queen, withheld from him 'on account of unsoldierlike behaviour'.[27]

Disciplinary action was not called for in the case of Lieutenants Chatterton and Lugard.[28] It was deemed that the former had done 'good service' as adjutant of his regiment and the latter was wounded in the residency while helping to move disabled sepoys to a place of safety. Captain Cowley did not receive as favourable a judgement. In reviewing the retreat to Cachar, Sir Frederick Roberts expressed his 'severe notice' of Cowley's 'want of enterprise and soldierly instinct' in retiring from Leimatak on 26 March without attempting to rescue Grimwood and the other British officers who were at that time believed to be prisoners in the hands of the Senapati. However, somewhat grudgingly the Commander in Chief was forced to admit that, having recently met up with Ethel and the bedraggled party in flight from the residency, without reserve ammunition or adequate provisions, Cowley was hardly in the best position to enter into combat. Moreover it was suggested in his favour that he was 'doubtless influenced by the opinions of his seniors – Captains Boileau and Butcher'.[29] On a more positive front the court commended Jemadar Birbal Nagarkoti, officer in command of the detachment of the 43rd stationed at Langthobal, for his initiative and bravery.

The Bengalee newspaper expressed 'grave dissatisfaction' with the procedure which the court had followed, declaring that its judgements were highly unsatisfactory and failed to command the respect of the Indian people.[30] There were grounds for such criticism. The speed with which the proceedings were conducted, the lack of a court-martial and the fact that the findings of the Court of Enquiry were never published pointed to an undeniable reluctance to reveal the full facts of the British role in the uprising. However, the accusations tabled against the Government of India of using middle-rank officers as scapegoats to draw attention away from the shortcomings of its own senior officials were less credible. Both Butcher and Boileau were undoubtedly guilty of wilful neglect in carrying out their duties at the time of the retreat, and the charges, substantiated by a number of witnesses, were hardly trumped up.

CHAPTER 14

REACTION AT HOME

In Britain, a somewhat less lenient view of events was taken than that held by the Court of Enquiry in Manipur. *The Times* of 6 April 1891, at which time the fate of Quinton and the other captives was still unknown, suggested that there was general agreement at home that the Manipur disaster must have resulted from a 'series of blunders' on the part of the officers on the spot. The characters of the Regent and the Senapati were well known, and it was hard to imagine how the experienced political staff of the residency could have failed to obtain some knowledge of the 'mischief which was brewing in the palace and the town'.[1] In a letter to *The Times* of the same day, James Johnstone stressed that it was 'of questionable wisdom for an officer in a position of the Chief Commissioner of Assam . . . personally unacquainted with the people, to have undertaken a task more within the province of the Political Agent'. It was recognised that in Manipur it was at times exceedingly difficult to ascertain the intentions of the Durbar, but an accurate view of affairs should have been possible and the result foreseen. In Johnstone's damning view, 'As it was, the telegrams seem to indicate that every one went blindly to work.'[2]

The newspaper noted that:

> The neglect to seize the palace guns and magazine immediately on the first outbreak of the disturbance; the retreat to the Residency before native troops; the attempt to treat with their victorious leaders, in defiance of the rules of British diplomacy in India, are all facts which need to be explained. The failure of ammunition at a later period in the fray is equally unintelligible.

However it was suggested that individuals were not entirely at fault:

> The eyes of our Indian Government naturally and necessarily have long been fixed on the North-West. The road to success and to promotion in all grades of the service is felt to lie in that quarter, and by a process of natural selection the ablest men are chosen for the many and arduous duties which confront us there. It seems possible that this circumstance has led to some comparative disregard of our difficulties in the North-East. The Manipur disaster may be a 'blessing in disguise' if it awakens us in good time to the fact that there, too, we have important and even vital interests.[3]

Inevitably the question was raised of how to deal with Manipur when 'the British flag again flies over the ruined Residency'. Writing to *The Times* of 10 April, Johnstone again entered the fray, addressing the subject of annexation, to which in the case of Manipur he was determinedly opposed. He argued that:

> the Manipuris from long habit obey the Rajah de facto. They feel their first allegiance due to him; and the Sepoys who fought against our people, did so knowing that a refusal to obey would mean death. We have never made it clear to them that they have a duty to us except under compulsion. Thus it would seem that we have a military outbreak, headed by two usurpers, to deal with, and not a rising of the legitimate ruler against the paramount Power. This necessitates the condign punishment of all who bore arms against us, but not the absorption of a most interesting little State and race in British territory, and the obliteration of much that is of surpassing interest in the lives of the people, by reducing them to the dead level of a British district, with its cumbersome system utterly unsuited to them.

By administering Manipur through a new young ruler, educating him according to British standards during the course of a long minority, it would be possible for Britain to retain the 'free passage through the State which is indispensable to us'.[4]

In addition, if annexation were to take place Manipur would produce an annual deficit for many years. Every official would demand high wages and every road would have to be paid for 'at a ruinous rate', whereas under the native system, 'every official is paid by a small assignment of land, and handsomely rewarded in his own eyes by some sumptuary privilege, and the roads are made by the people without any cost to the State whatsoever'. Moreover Manipur had for some time maintained a state of peace among the hill tribes. Taxes were not demanded, but 'an amount of invaluable labour is willingly conceded' and throughout the hills there were excellent paths cut out by the hill men in their spare time. Undoubtedly the rule of Manipur had at times been harsh, and bribery and corruption were painfully apparent; however, a long minority with the state administered by a British officer would enable these problems to be addressed 'while we maintained the native system of administration in its integrity'. The independence of Manipur had been invaluable to the British in the past, providing the huge asset of the short route into Upper Burma, and it was likely to be of equal worth in the future.[5]

Johnstone admitted that in some cases, British direct rule was far from ideal:

> We are not a highly imaginative race, and our system is often ill-suited to the people. We all readily acknowledge the blessing, the unspeakable blessing, of the 'Pax Britannica', and may feel proud to think that India is, on the whole, the best governed country in the world; but while our system suits the inhabitant of the plains of Hindoostan and Bengal, it is not quite the same to the inhabitant of the Eastern jungles, and we hardly take in that some of them are better suited by the rough-and-ready rule they are accustomed to than by ours.[6]

The former Political Agent concluded with a plea for tolerance:

> let us not destroy native life, with its many charms; let the people be content with their picturesque surroundings, and . . . leave the native Court to encourage all the various little arts and manufactures which are found here alone and would soon die out, as they have done in Assam, but for the encouragement thus given. Let the people enjoy their stately little processions, their titles, their Royal festivals, their boatraces, their dances, the

> thousand and one pretty ceremonies inseparable from a native Court which give a zest to native life; let them, in a word, retain their individuality as a people, and while exacting what we require and have a right to expect, leave them the right to consider themselves as subjects of their hereditary chief.[7]

Needless to say, Johnstone's view attracted an instant reaction from the pro-annexation brigade. The day after his letter appeared in *The Times*, the newspaper printed a riposte from Sir George Campbell, lieutenant-governor of Bengal from 1871 to 1874 and subsequently Liberal member of parliament for Kirkcaldy, stressing the advantages of a swift move to gather the state of Manipur into the British fold. In Sir George's view, Manipur was 'wholly an enclave in British territory' – occupying a special position between Bengal, Assam and Burma – and it was 'impossible to imagine a better, more central, and more commanding position midway between those British countries; a healthy position for troops, officials and tea planters, and a centre for dealing with the Indo-Burmese tribes'. He continued that in the light of the treacherous murder of British officials, the reigning family of the state

> can have no claim to consideration. And we are no more called on to restore the old Rajah than we were bound to restore Louis XVIII to the Throne of France, unless for reasons of our own we find it expedient to do so. Sir James Johnstone is what is called in India a 'political' as distinguished from a civil officer . . . Such officers are always given to favour the system of a native State under the guidance of a Resident, and his native sympathies are natural and creditable. But, after all, there might be native colour, and regattas, and polo under British rule. We must look to expediency in the matter.[8]

During the course of the weeks following the revolt, when the fate of the British officers was discovered, parliamentary criticism was heaped liberally upon those in charge of the punitive expedition, although to spare the Government of India from the full force of volleys from both Houses, the Viceroy and Secretary of State for India took great pains to edit the material on the uprising which was eventually published in

England.[9] Perhaps unfairly, bearing in mind his repeated requests for an enquiry into the Senapati's behaviour during and after the abdication of Sur Chandra, Quinton was perceived as the villain of the piece. *The Times* declared that it was

> unhappily too plain that the whole expedition was planned in overweening confidence by a man who did not choose to ask or to listen to advice, and who took every precaution to conceal his intentions. Four hundred men with only forty rounds of ammunition were led into a town defended by twelve thousand rifles and ten guns, to back up a cool request to the master of these forces that he would quietly surrender himself to exile. Unfortunately this even is not the worst. For as things stand at present it does not seem that we have much right to complain of the Senaputty's treachery, seeing that he was to be asked to a durbar and seized as he went away. It may be hoped that some better face may yet be put upon a transaction which at present seems to have been bad both in plan and in execution.[10]

The view of the newspaper was no doubt heavily influenced by a letter in *The Times* from Ethel herself, stating that Frank had informed her of the proposed course of action:

> viz., that the Government of India had decided that the ex-Maharaja was not to be allowed to return, but that also the Jubraj [Tikendrajit], the Prince who turned him out in September, was to be banished for a term of years to India. This decision was to be announced in the durbar, and when the Princes got up to go the Jubraj was to be arrested then and there and conveyed out of the place that day by some of the 42d' [sic].[11]

Writing to Lansdowne, Cross admitted that 'Mrs. Grimwood's letter has caused much agitation here, as it is supposed to say that Mr. Quinton inveigled the Senapati to the *durbar* for the purpose of treacherously arresting him there.' He added, 'my information does not lead me to believe that your Government contemplated that such a course should be taken and that I should have been much surprised if they had done so . . . Mr. Quinton must, I think, have lost his head.'[12]

However, a letter to *The Times* from Sir William Hunter[13] dated 5 May 1891 strongly defended Quinton. Hunter maintained that the Chief Commissioner had gone to Manipur under the orders of the Government of India with instructions to carry out a specific policy. Far from ignoring information regarding the situation in Manipur, the Chief Commissioner had sent Gurdon ahead to determine the extent of possible resistance and had come to the conclusion that any such resistance would be of a scale with which his escort and troops could easily cope. As to the supposedly treacherous plot to seize the Senapati, according to Gurdon's official report to the viceroy, Lord Lansdowne, Quinton had 'sent a written ultimatum to the Regent warning him that unless the Senaputty was surrendered he would be arrested'. Hunter declared that he had 'sat side by side' with Quinton in the Viceroy's Legislative Council for four years and found him 'an experienced, cautious, high-minded man, without any special gift of the initiative and apt to lean on the judgment of others rather than to assert his own'. The former viceroy, Lord Ripon, in a statement made in the House of Lords agreed that 'it is incredible from my acquaintance with Mr. Quinton's character that he should have had any hand in such an unworthy proceeding'.[14]

Reviewing the facts, *The Times* took the view that the Government of India could be acquitted of 'anything that can be branded as a deliberate design of treachery'. But Quinton's plan, which the Viceroy defended as 'the most straightforward and the safest' was 'foredoomed to failure, and ... wanting in that frankness and boldness which constitute the moral strength of our position in India, and which alone are worthy of our Imperial responsibilities'. The newspaper declared that if Quinton had at the outset made clear his intention of dealing with the Senapati as a traitor 'whom it was expedient, for the good of the State, to deprive of power and send into exile', he would not have been at a disadvantage and 'would have kept the Indian Government free even from the shadow of a suspicion of bad faith'. In as much as there was 'a failure to master the conditions of the problem before attempting to solve it and an imperfect adaptation of means to ends', Quinton alone was responsible. However, the Government of India had formally approved his proposals for summoning the Senapati to the *durbar* without warning him that he was to be treated as a criminal. The newspaper came to the conclusion that 'This also was an error, and a very grave one, though it may well be that the officials at Calcutta had not fully thought out the meaning of

Mr Quinton's proposals, and still less their effect upon the native mind, when they gave them a hasty and casual approval.'[15] Such a view was given some credence by Sir Frederick Roberts, commander in chief in India, who wrote to his predecessor that 'to my surprise all the members {of the Viceroy's Council} took the view ... that an officer, acting under the orders of Government, was as much justified in seizing a person in Durbar as a bailiff would be in arresting anyone in his own, or his neighbour's house'. Roberts himself had opposed the general opinion of the council, declaring that 'Quinton should I think, have sent for the Jubraj and told him the terms on which he would have been permitted to become maharaja. These terms included the deportation of the Senapatti {sic}. If the Jubraj refused to give his brother up, Quinton could then have taken such action as seemed necessary.'[16]

In the House of Commons Sir Richard Temple,[17] Conservative member of parliament for Evesham, agreed that if there was an intention to arrest the Senapati in the *durbar*, 'a durbar which was peaceful to all others, save to him', this intention 'was not properly justifiable and it will do no good, either for the honour of England, or its influence in British India'. Sir Richard conceded, however, that Manipur was

> essentially a point – strategically and politically – on our Eastern Indian frontier which must be traversed by all expeditions of a political and military character between Bengal and Burma ... If we did not remove the Senapati there would have been another revolution and another exiled Sovereign – I maintain that we are bound to interfere in a very effective manner, and that the Government of India, from among the many possible modes of interference, chose the best.[18]

In this opinion, Temple was echoing the views of the Viceroy expressed in a letter to Cross dated 23 June 1891, in which Lansdowne stressed that

> If we were to admit the principle that when discontented members of a royal family eject by force the Chief recognised by us and ... {we} acquiesce in the change of rulers, a very dangerous precedent would be established ... We should be stepping down from our paramount position, and bringing all sorts of disorder and trouble on the Native States, if we reverted to a policy of non-interference.[19]

As had occurred in other cases involving friction between the British and Indian rulers in the second half of the nineteenth century,[20] there was a certain amount of sympathy in Britain for the Senapati despite his history of violence. *The Times* declared that he 'was not an exemplary character, but the beating of natives, however reprehensible, is not an uncommon exercise of power by an Oriental Prince, and does not seem to be a reason for attempting serious political change'. What should have assumed more importance to the British as rulers of India was Grimwood's report that the government of Manipur was being successfully transacted. The exiled maharaja had failed through 'sheer weakness of character', and his restoration was judged to be out of the question. As the Senapati was de facto ruler of the state and fairly amenable to advice, 'it seems at least doubtful whether there was any pressing necessity for his expulsion'.[21] The Prince was 'quite tractable, and disposed to work harmoniously with the Resident'. The newspaper pointed out:

> The Indian Government will have its hands full if it means to depose every native ruler whose character is less than perfect in European eyes. The beating of a couple of natives was not the reason for deciding upon the expulsion of the Senaputty, and so far as the real genesis of the decision can be made out, Manipur was neglected altogether under stress of other business, and finally taken up and dealt with offhand without due and careful examination.[22]

In the Commons Sir John Gorst, under-secretary of state for India, expressed the cynical opinion that the Senapati was removed for the simple reason that he was 'an able man intriguing against the Paramount Power'. In an extraordinarily critical statement for the second most senior official at the India Office, Sir John maintained that the Government of India was merely acting 'in accordance with their customary policy of cutting down the tall poppies, setting aside the man of ability and strong character in native States in favour of the mediocre or incapable'. Sir George Chesney, who while serving on the Viceroy's Council had insisted that Quinton equip himself with a more substantial escort, expressed his disgust at 'the mischievous effect' of Gorst's statement,[23] declaring that 'the policy of the Government of India, in their dealings with native States, has uniformly been the opposite of such machiavellian courses; it has always been their aim to secure the services of the ablest men that could be found'. In Chesney's opinion the Senapati's conduct in dealing with the Government of India was not in question: 'The matter at issue was not one of danger to the peace of India in leaving him at Manipur, but whether this would be compatible with the maintenance of quiet within that little State'. The quarrels of the Manipur family had been occurring relentlessly for the last 70 years, consisting of 'a dismal succession of palace intrigues and revolutions, usually accompanied by brutal murders, of father by son, or brother by brother' and the most recent coup, in the course of which Sur Chandra had fled, appeared to be the only one without bloodshed. Since Manipur was immediately adjacent to British Indian territory 'it was impossible to tolerate these excesses any longer'.[24] Chesney stressed that the veneration of the Senapati in the Commons debate of 19 June, by which 'it may be thought that even the Nana Sahib[25] would find supporters nowadays', was quite misplaced. The Prince appeared 'to be simply a cruel and truculent ruffian unredeemed by personal courage'.[26]

Despite parliamentary criticism of the Government of India in the Manipur debacle, Sir John's 'extraordinarily flippant and ill-judged performance' was universally condemned in the House of Lords on 22 June. Lord Cross, in 'language very rarely used by a Cabinet Minister in speaking of his Under-Secretary' declared it 'utterly opposed to all common sense', although *The Times* was quick to point out that in defending the Government of India from the charge of repressing men of ability and encouraging mediocrity, many of the speakers in the Lords were 'perhaps opportune if not excessive in their praise'. An editorial of 23 June insisted that at a high level of officialdom in India there had been 'a certain laxity and want of grip in the management of the business'. The revolution in Manipur had been practically accepted and friendly relations had sprung up between the British resident and the men whom the Government of India had placed in power. To accept one of these men while punishing the other who gave him his position could not be regarded as 'a conspicuously sound bit of statesmanship'. If the government had wished a de jure ruler, the old maharaja ought to have been reinstated. If not, it was patently absurd to expel the Senapati while retaining his 'puppet'. However it was now necessary to move on 'with the simple hope that our officials will adhere to the direct and straightforward ways which are the source of our strength'.

As far as the future of Manipur was concerned there was a general desire, expressed by almost every speaker in the House of Lords, that annexation should be avoided. It was agreed that there was no requirement for more Indian states to be absorbed into British India, and that if there were a way of maintaining 'a tolerable native rule in Manipur' it should be found. *The Times* pointed out to its readers that:

> The native Princes dislike annexation because it reminds them unpleasantly of their own tenure of power. Probably the inhabitants of Manipur would rather jog on in their old slipshod way than be squeezed into uniformity by British tax collectors. Indian finance is not so flourishing that any new burden need be assumed except under pressure of overmastering expediency.[27]

Queen Victoria followed the debates of both Houses closely, having communicated with Lansdowne and the India Office throughout the passage of events in Manipur. As early as 8 April the Queen had expressed her opinion that 'there must have been great ignorance and imprudence' and her fear that 'bad advice was given from Calcutta. We never had any quarrel with them before. If former Maharaja had been reinstated, nothing of all this probably would have happened. *This* is opinion of well-informed people who have lived in the country.'[28] Victoria undoubtedly deprecated the attitude of many British officers in their attitude to Indians of all classes, stating:

> Our dealings in India should be dictated by straightforwardness, kindness and firmness, or we cannot succeed. This disaster is most unfortunate, and the effect may be very serious in other parts of India. Our system of sending out people who merely get appointed for passing an examination must be altered, or we shall have some trouble in India. There is no doubt, from what the Queen hears from many sides, that the natives (though they are very loyal to the Queen-Empress and Royal Family) have no affection for the English rule, which is one of fear not of love, and this will *not* answer for a conquered nation. One of the Royal Family ought, if possible, to be constantly there to encourage the good feeling and

> loyalty of the people, which no private individual could in the same way, and certainly not people like many of those who are now in Indian employment.[29]

Not surprisingly Maxwell was in the firing line. Cross reported to Lansdowne that the Queen 'had grave doubts as to the wisdom of appointing as Resident one who had been so actively employed in capturing the Senapati as Major Maxwell had been and she desired me to telegraph her own views at once'.[30] The royal opinion of events in Manipur was undoubtedly heavily influenced by the view of Victoria's 'Indian Secretary', Munshi Abdul Karim, who, to the scorn of the court, had succeeded in ingratiating himself to an alarming degree with the monarch. Cross's own view was that

> her Indian Munshi tells her that there is in India the greatest devotion to herself and all her family, but at the same time distrust and dislike of the Government, and that the Native Chiefs think that the Residents are rude and overbearing.[31] I have done my best to disabuse her of this feeling.[32]

Lansdowne was quick to respond to the Queen that he respected her view that at the end of the nineteenth century commissioners and political agents tended to be of a lesser breed than their predecessors, and agreed that an endeavour should be made to employ 'people of higher calibre socially, and more conciliatory as well as firm'.[33] However he stressed that Quinton in particular had been 'much respected' by all who knew him, and, although it was possible in this case that he may have misjudged the situation, or been misled by others,

> the Viceroy is sure that he was not open to the charge of wanting in the attributes to which your Majesty rightly attaches so much importance. He was for some time a member of the Viceroy's Legislative Council, and was consequently well known both to Lord and Lady Lansdowne, who liked him much . . . a man who was certainly incapable of acting, as some people apparently believe he intended to act, in a treacherous manner towards the Manipur Princes, or towards anyone else.[34]

Lansdowne added that in his view it seemed 'natural that the representative of the paramount Power should command the rebellious subjects of a Native State to appear before him in open court, and should, if they refuse to accept his decision, then and there proceed to enforce it', adding with some acerbity that 'the tendency shown by the House of Commons to interfere with increasing frequency in Indian affairs, with which it has at best a superficial acquaintance, greatly impairs the efficiency of the Government of India, and seriously affects the authority of your Majesty's representative'.[35]

Unwilling to let the Government of India off the hook when it came to apportioning blame for the course of events, Victoria had expressed her unhappiness that action was taken so late against the Senapati if he was 'as bad a man as to necessitate his expulsion from Manipur',[36] to which Lansdowne responded with the less than convincing argument that:

> It was absolutely necessary to consult both the Chief Commissioner and the Resident, and the Viceroy fears that the English public will not realise the fact that a letter takes about a week to travel from Calcutta to Assam, and several days to travel from Assam to Manipur.[37]

Cross, continuing to distance the India Office from the shortcomings of the Government of India, informed the Queen that many members of the Cabinet agreed with her in questioning

> the length of time that had intervened, the quiet way in which the State was being ruled, the absence of any enquiry into the conduct of the Senapati, etc.; but the broad ground was wisely taken that the Viceroy must either be recalled or supported, and that he could not be recalled and must therefore be supported.[38]

On 1 July the Queen gave a private audience to 'a much worn and weather-beaten' Ethel at Windsor Castle, and was very moved by her first-hand account of the revolt and subsequent harrowing march across the state. Possibly due to a tacit agreement among press and politicians to avoid condemnation out of respect for Ethel, thus far Frank had surprisingly escaped public censure. His lack of judgement may have been seen in a sympathetic light on the grounds that he was a young, inexperienced officer sent to what was now identified as a barbaric, remote corner of India, whose unhealthily close attachment to members of the royal family should have been recognised and overridden by his seniors, Skene and Quinton. In the absence of any criticism of her husband, Ethel stressed to the Queen her own high opinion of the Senapati, stating 'she could not, and would not, believe he intended to kill the prisoners', as opposed to Thangal General who was 'a horrible blood-thirsty old man of eighty-six, who had killed no end of men, women and children, when he went out to punish tribes'.[39] In this view she was preaching to the converted. In a telegram to the secretary of state, the Queen had already declared that 'hanging Senapati would never do; it would create bad feeling in Manipur and in all India. But shut him up in some distant part. Think no prince was ever hung.'[40]

The final decision lay in the verdict of the court still in session.

CHAPTER 15

THE TRIAL OF THE PRINCES

During May 1891 Major Maxwell heard the charges against three high-ranking officers in the Manipur administration: the Ayapurel, who had been in charge of the maharaja's escort and the arsenal; the Luang Ningthou, the member of the Top Guard, who had been in control of the south gate on 24 March and had failed to intervene to protect the British officers from the mob; and the army commander, Mia Major. The Ayapurel and the Luang Ningthou were both charged on the counts of waging war against the Queen Empress, abetting the murder of Grimwood, and abetting the murders of the other four British officers. Both men received the death sentence. Mia Major was accused of waging war against the Queen in the palace on 24 and 25 March, and subsequently participating in the attack upon Grant at Thobal, and was also sentenced to death. However, on the grounds that the accused were subordinate to the royal family and were forced to obey orders, none of the sentences were carried out and the three officers were given transportation for life. In the same month Kanjao Singh, the man who had actually speared Grimwood, and Niranjan Subadar,[1] a British subject found guilty of treason, were hanged.

The last case heard in May was that brought against Thangal General. A rumour had been circulated that the general had addressed the Manipuri mob in the palace, informing them that it was written that there would be a great war in Manipur which would not be won by them unless the heads of five of their enemies had been buried under the sacred tree and the blood poured down the throats of the lions.[2] However there was little or no evidence to substantiate such a theatrical call to violence on Thangal's part. It appeared conceivable that he may have given orders from the Top Guard in the palace for the prisoners to be made over to the executioner, but it was by no means a certainty that such orders originated with the general since two of the prosecution witnesses distinctly stated that the order to fetter the British officers came from members of the royal family. Moreover the case for the defence stated that Thangal had been in great pain on the night of 24 March and had been carried some distance to a pool where he was massaged by a doctor, returning to the Top Guard after the executions.

It was also attested by witnesses for the defence that earlier in the evening Thangal had gone to the west gate of the palace to warn Quinton and his party not to enter the palace by night. Thangal himself declared in a statement that he had informed Prince Angao Senna that 'it was not advisable for such important Sahibs to enter the Fort after dark' and 'called out from inside the gate to the chief commissioner and asked him to hold a durbar in the morning', but was informed that 'the Senapati has asked the Sahibs to come in and who are you to go contrary to his orders'.[3] However this evidence appears to have failed to sway the court. Maxwell stated in his judgement:

> The question naturally arises that when the accused warned the British officers not to enter the Fort at that late hour of night why did he not insist on seeing them safely to the gate ... All the witnesses depose to the crowd being great and in an excited state and it was the accused's duty to have given the officers a safe conduct to the Residency compound.[4]

Thangal General was condemned to death for murder and 'waging war against the Queen' despite the fact that Maxwell agreed that he had not even been in the palace compound when hostilities began. The general – who, according to those present was seriously ill during his trial – refused to cross-examine the witnesses and, despite submitting an appeal, his death sentence was not commuted.[5]

In July and August Maxwell tried three more cases in his court: the first against the Wangkheirakpa, the chief judicial officer of the state and second in command to the Senapati; the second involving a group of nine men accused of murdering Quinton and his party; and the third in which seven Manipuris and a Naga were charged with the murders of Melville and O'Brien. The Wangkheirakpa was accused of waging war against the Queen, both in the palace on 24 March and at Thobal; however no evidence was found to implicate him in the murder of Quinton and he was sentenced to transportation for life and the confiscation of his property. The nine men – consisting of the eight guards ordered to protect the British in the *durbar* room at the palace and subsequently to take them to their execution, and the executioner himself – were all sentenced to death for their involvement in the death of the British officers. However, as with the high-ranking Manipuri officers, their sentences were commuted on the grounds that they were simply obeying orders. The seven Manipuris tried for the murder of Melville and O'Brien were sentenced to transportation, but the Naga who had actually beheaded Melville was hanged.

Following the hearings conducted by Maxwell, the trial of the Manipur Princes (called later a 'mockery of justice') was heard in June 1891. Observing the instructions of the Viceroy a special court was convened under the presidency of Lieutenant Colonel St John Michell, Graham's adjutant-general. The other members of the court were Major R. K. Ridgeway of the 44th Gurkhas and the civil officer, A.W. Davis, deputy commissioner of the Naga Hills. From all reports the proceedings, lasting for 32 suffocating days, were beset by problems – among them, the deaths of two men in court from cholera. Michell, described as having 'a keen intellectual face' and 'a rich sympathetic voice',[6] favoured a court-martial on the grounds that the Manipuris were feudatories and therefore guilty of rebellion. He was later to write that the 'Abominable trials were a perpetual anxiety to me.' Reporters from a number of newspapers sat in court all day with no restrictions on their extremely profitable output. Captain du Moulin of *The Pioneer*, writing for *The Times of India* and *The Civil and Military Gazette*, received Rs 3,000 for his accounts of the trials. Observing such financial reward, Ridgeway's 'iratenesss took an apoplectic form, because officers who only strolled into the Court for a couple of hours a day were making thousands a day while he had to sit from morning to night for nothing'. In addition Michell admitted that 'Davis knew less of law than either Ridgeway or myself, as he had been in the Naga Hills all his life, and is a careless young man not given to unnecessary study.'[7]

Based on the evidence given by a number of witnesses in the palace on the night of 24 March, a summary of 'material facts' was gathered on behalf of the prosecution against Kula Chandra and Tikendrajit. It was mainly upon these facts that the charges faced by both men of waging war against the Queen and abetment of murder were based, carrying the death sentence. The summary stated that Quinton – accompanied by Grimwood, Skene, Simpson and Cossins – approached the Durbar Hall in the palace for the purpose of coming to terms with the Manipuris. Tikendrajit, who been 'lying down' in the Top Guard, came to meet them, and some of the ministers of state were also present at the interview which took place in the open a few yards from the hall. The Regent was not present, and was later to claim that he had been quite unaware that any of the British men had come into the palace that night. The Senapati complained to the Chief Commissioner that

> he had been first attacked by the British troops, his people killed, and property looted; that he himself was unwell, and was unable to attend the Durbar previously ordered; that he was now distrustful of the British and could only treat on the understanding that the troops laid down their arms.

The Chief Commissioner replied that he could not comply with this, as 'the arms were the Queen's'.[8] This discussion lasted about half an hour, but no settlement was reached. When Quinton and his party rose to depart there was much shouting from the crowds who had assembled, and Grimwood requested Angao Minto, one of the ministers of the Manipur Durbar, to see the party out in safety. Angao Minto asked the Senapati, who was leaving in the opposite direction, if he should accompany the British and the Senapati replied, 'Certainly'.[9] As the party was leaving, it was attacked by the mob. A young British officer (believed to be Simpson) was wounded in the head, and Grimwood was speared. He died almost immediately.

The keeper of the maharaja's stores, Jatra Singh, burst open the door of the Durbar Hall, which was closed from the inside, in order to save the British officers. On hearing the noise of the attack Tikendrajit returned and drove the Manipuri soldiers away with a stick. He then (according to his own statement and that of his witnesses) helped the wounded officer up the steps and after a short conversation with Quinton, the substance of which was not disclosed in the evidence of the defence, went away, ordering Angao Minto 'to take care of the sahibs and keep them in the bungalow'.[10] Angao Minto placed Quinton and his companions under the care of some sentries in the Durbar Hall, and went away to bathe and eat. Jatra Sing gave some water to the wounded officer, at his request, and some time later Thangal General informed Usurba, one of the guards in charge of Quinton's party, that 'the sahibs should be killed'. Usurba went to the Senapati to ascertain if he had requested the death of the British, and on hearing Thangal General's words Tikendrajit replied, 'Did the old man give such an order? Don't do such a thing; I am coming.' Usurba returned to Thangal General and told him what the Senapati had said, to which Thangal replied, 'The Jubraj is a fool. We can never make it up with the sahibs. What is the use of saying such a thing as this?'[11]

Thangal General and the Senapati subsequently had a discussion, the precise nature of which was not disclosed by any of the witnesses,[12] and some time later the order came from Thangal General that the British were to be made over to the public executioner. The prisoners were put in fetters by a blacksmith, taken a distance of 20 yards through the Lion Gate to the stone lions, and shortly afterwards beheaded together with Gunna Ram, the bugler of the 44th who had accompanied them. Two of the men needed two strokes of the *dao* before the head was severed. Finally the body of Grimwood was brought out and decapitated. These events occurred within three or four hours of the time that Quinton first entered the palace grounds, and shortly after midnight the Manipuris resumed the attack upon the residency. Neither the Regent nor the Senapati punished any of the persons concerned in executing the British, but both were instrumental several days later in sending a false version of events to the Viceroy to the effect that the British party had been killed in action. The Summary of Facts ended at this stage.[13]

Mano Mohun Ghose,[14] who had received his legal training at Lincoln's Inn before becoming a barrister at the High Court in Calcutta, was permitted, to his 'profound dissatisfaction', to support the appeals of Kula Chandra and Tikendrajit against the charges before them through a Memorandum of Arguments alone, rather then a viva voce argument before the Viceroy as a Court of Appeal. The publication of this memorandum caused a sensation throughout India. Ghose, a great patriot and an early participant in organised national politics, argued that the Manipur princes were not legally tried under the Indian Penal Code[15] or any other Indo-British or British law. Nor was the court which tried them constituted under any legal authority derivable from any Act of Parliament, or any legislative enactment of the Governor-General of India in Council. Ghose stated that 'in creating this special tribunal at Manipur the Government of India was simply exercising the rights of a conquering sovereign force, for the purpose of bringing to justice persons accused of committing grave offences, but who, not being British subjects, are not triable by British Courts, and are not governed by the municipal laws of British India'.[16]

Ghose also maintained that of the officers comprising the special court, two military and one political, none had any legal training and it was clear that the court was far from familiar with the procedure followed during criminal trials in British India.[17] Each of the accused persons was subjected to an inquisitorial cross-examination ('a procedure utterly repugnant to the humane tradition of British justice') through the medium of two languages, Hindustani and Manipuri, and subsequently recorded in English. There was no vernacular record to preserve the exact words spoken by the prisoners, and the examination was not signed by them. Moreover some of the questions were of such a complex nature that even witnesses of normal intelligence would find it difficult to answer them with precision. Finally, and of the greatest importance, the princes were given no opportunity of being defended by counsel, or by a professional lawyer of any kind.[18]

The Senapati was charged not only with waging war against the Queen but also with abetment of murder. To the first charge Tikendrajit clearly stated that the princes were compelled to use arms only in self-defence when troops 'forced an entry by crossing walls before daybreak, demolished and polluted the temple of his household god, Brindabun Chandra, plundered the ornaments of the said god, killed a number of his domestics, slaughtered the whole family of one Dasu Sardar, a Mohammedan minister, without the least provocation' and that 'he, the defendant, an uneducated ignorant prince of savage wild tribes, is not aware how actions taken in self-defence under such critical circumstances can be deemed hostility and mutiny against the Empress'.[19] Ghose maintained that under the Indian Penal Code only subjects of the Queen or foreigners residing in British India could be guilty of waging war against the Queen. Manipur was an independent sovereign state and, Ghose stressed, its sovereignty had been recognised by the Chief

Commissioner when he sent his political agent into the palace on 23 March to request the Regent to hand over Tikendrajit. The Senapati did not wish to fight the British, and had they not tried to take him by force 'he would never have sanctioned the firing of a single shot against the British troops'.[20]

As far as the second charge was concerned, the 'actual intention' of the defendant during the events of the night of 24 March was seen to be crucial. The considerable body of evidence marshalled by Ghose indicated that Tikendrajit did not give the instructions which led to the death of Quinton and those who were with him. It did, however, prove clearly that he remonstrated with Thangal General, an old minister of near 50 years' service to the state, and rebuked him for entertaining such an idea as the putting to death of the British officials. Meanwhile he himself gave instructions, after personally assisting the wounded Lieutenant Simpson up the Durbar Hall steps, for eight sentries to mount guard over the officers in the only suitable and safe place for Europeans in the city.

In Ghose's opinion it was the duty of the prosecution, and indeed of the court itself, to establish the meaning of the words spoken by the witness Jatra Sing that Tikendrajit 'made no reply' to Thangal General's demand that the British be killed. Whether Jatra Sing meant to say that the Senapati remained silent, or that he, the witness, did not hear the reply was of the utmost importance. If the Senapati took the trouble of going to Thangal General to remonstrate with him, was the Government of India justified in inferring that he eventually agreed with the general? Or could Thangal General have assumed responsibility for the executions without further reference to the Senapati, taking advantage of the physical and mental state of the prince after the tiring events of the day?[21]

In addition 'a matter of serious importance' had been disclosed in the affidavit of Babu Janoki Nath Bysak, a trader with some knowledge of the Manipuri language and the ability to read and write in English, who had been requested by the Senapati to write a statement of the court proceedings on his behalf. After the Prince had signed the statement it was submitted to the court, who suggested that the Babu's English was faulty and required verbal corrections. Subsequently 'grossly misleading' additions and alterations, of which the Senapati remained ignorant, were made to the document by the President of the Court and by Captain du Moulin, the special correspondent of *The Pioneer* (supposedly hostile to the Manipur princes), subtly changing the meaning of certain sentences relating to the interchange between Tikendrajit and Thangal General on the night of 24 March.[22]

Ghose made it clear that the following factors should be taken into consideration: the considerable power exercised by Thangal, an old general of the state from the time of the Senapati's grandfather; the ill-defined authority of the Senapati in 'a barbarous state like Manipur'; the possibility that Thangal General may have supposed that the Senapati had 'lost his senses' in objecting to the executions, but would eventually be won over; the absence of a *durbar* to discuss what was to be done with the British; the lack of public execution to fulfil a ceremonial or legal function, but instead 'a foul idea treacherously carried out at dead of night, although the public executioner was employed'; the reality that Tikendrajit was 'an uneducated Prince belonging to a hill tribe, and ... ought not to be judged by the same standard of probability by which men belonging to more advanced races and brought up under a differently organised state of society are judged'; the possibility that the Senapati might have supposed that Thangal would do nothing without calling a formal *durbar*; and, finally, the beheading of the bugler without any order – which showed 'how little the sentries and executioners cared for any formal order from a competent authority, and how hastily and irregularly the executions were carried out'.[23]

However the judges chose to concentrate on the three major omissions on the part of the accused, which in their view led to the murders of Quinton and his party: the failure of the Senapati to warn the sentries against carrying out the order of Thangal General; his failure to remove the British to the citadel, or to a more secure place than the Durbar Hall; and the fact that 'he made no efforts to see the officers safe to their camp'. In his support of the Senapati's appeal, Ghose responded that his client had ordered eight sentries to take care of the British, that he did warn the officer in charge of the sentries, Usurba, in unmistakeable language that Thangal General's order was not to be carried out, and that the Durbar Hall was in fact the only place where Europeans could be comfortably lodged. They could not be taken to the citadel or any other part of the palace 'on account of the religious scruples of the Manipuris, who do not admit Europeans into their private apartments'.[24] Moreover Tikendrajit in his defence stated that three of the six officers (Grimwood, Simpson and Brackenbury) were among his 'best friends', declaring that 'A man of charitable disposition is hardly capable of manslaughter, while killing one's own friends is beyond the bounds of probability.'[25]

The judges in the case had also arrived at the conclusion that there was no truth in the allegation that the accused was unwell. Yet the evidence of Rassik Lal Kundu, the head clerk of the political agency, and a telegram received from Mrs Grimwood on 25 July declaring that her husband had declared the Senapati to be ill on the evening of 23 March, appeared in Ghose's opinion to establish beyond doubt that the Prince was in bad health at the time. In his defence Tikendrajit stated that in September 1890, at the time of Sur Chandra's abdication, he had been suffering greatly from a stone in the bladder and undergoing treatment at the residency hospital which prevented him from taking any active part in the hostilities surrounding the ex-maharaja's departure.[26] The judges stressed the 'apparent improbability' of the accused going to sleep; however Lieutenant Chatterton gave evidence that he himself went to sleep after dinner, when the occupants of the residency ought to have been anxiously waiting for the return of Quinton from the palace or devising means for their own safety. Considering the rigours of the day and the anxieties of the two previous days, not to mention ill health, Ghose countered that there was nothing improbable in the Senapati's action.[27]

Much attention was paid to the fact that neither Thangal nor any of the parties directly concerned in the execution were punished by the accused. However, Ghose emphasised that after 24 March the Manipur state was in a 'highly disorganised condition' and that the princes were hardly in 'a proper frame of mind to consider calmly and deliberately what was the best course for them to pursue'. The Senapati would naturally presume that the British Government would never excuse 'so atrocious a crime, and in his ignorance of the strictness and impartiality of British justice he would come to the conclusion that the vengeance that the Government of India would exact would be of the same indiscriminate character, confounding the innocent with the guilty, as was ordinarily wreaked by the semi-barbarous tribes of Manipur and its neighbourhood'. He would therefore take it for granted that he would be subject to the general retribution which would overtake the Manipuri population following the arrival of British forces. Moreover the accused would be unwilling to create a rift in the Durbar, or civil war, by attempting to punish Thangal, the oldest minister of the state whom he addressed as

'Ipoo' (Grandfather), and no useful purpose could be served by punishing underlings who had been falsely informed by Thangal that the death sentence on the British officers had been ordered by the Senapati.[28]

In summing up, Ghose submitted that as regards the charge of abetment of murder, the evidence adduced by the prosecution entirely failed to establish the complicity of Tikendrajit; that, on the contrary, there was sufficient material on record to suggest that he was entirely opposed to the murder of the British officers and that the orders of Thangal General were carried out in spite of his protests and without his knowledge. Ghose expressed his conviction that

> in spite of the very natural desire to 'exact full and signal retribution' for the crime, the Government of India will hold the scales of justice evenly; and its ultimate decision in the case of the unhappy Prince will be such as to proclaim to the Eastern World, that the British Government, although powerful enough to crush all its enemies, will not, even in the face of so atrocious an outrage, follow Asiatic examples, and wreak indiscriminate vengeance; but that, no matter how grave the crisis, and how strongly national passions may have been aroused, British justice will always assert itself, and take care to distinguish the innocent from the guilty.[29]

However, Ghose's expectations of scrupulously fair British justice were over-optimistic. The court ruled that Tikendrajit's action in challenging the attack upon his compound was an act of war, and found him guilty on the first count that he had waged war against the Queen Empress. As far as the second charge was concerned, the court virtually dismissed the evidence presented in the statement of the accused. Witnesses for the prosecution whose evidence supported the case of the Senapati were described as unreliable and, despite his obvious illness at the time, the assertion of the accused that he fell asleep in the Top Guard following his conversation with Thangal was deemed 'beyond the bounds of credence'. The court was in no doubt that he had acquiesced to the order of Thangal which resulted in the execution of the British officers. This certainty was shared by Lansdowne, who wrote to Cross that

> It is to my mind absolutely inconceivable that our officers could have been executed without the Senapati's knowledge and consent.

> The evidence before us justifies the belief that the execution took place with his distinct approval. His abetment of the murder amounted to a great deal more than 'omission to prevent it'.

Suggesting that his opinion was to a large extent dictated by policy, the Viceroy added that if the leading criminals behind the rebellion were allowed to escape with their lives, there would be 'a general feeling that the Government of India has signally failed to inflict a suitable and exemplary punishment'.[30]

As in his half-brother's case, Kula Chandra Singh appealed against the charges of waging war against the Queen Empress and abetting the murder of the British party. As far as the first charge was concerned, Ghose maintained that the available evidence indicated that the British Government had dealt with Manipur previously as a sovereign power in alliance with, and not owing any allegiance to the Queen, as was the case with certain of the other native states of India. If, therefore, Manipur was an independent state, were the soldiers and officers of the maharaja guilty of any offence in repelling an attack made upon the palace by British soldiers[31] in the small hours of the morning without even a declaration of war by the British Government? Or, on the contrary, would a sudden armed invasion of the palace of an independent sovereign by the troops of another power be an act which it would be the duty of the soldiers and officers of the invaded sovereign to resist?[32]

Facing the second charge, Kula Chandra in his defence stated that he

> being naturally of an indolent disposition had ever maintained a neutral position towards his other step brothers ... Being corpulent and consequently inactive it was never his ambition to be a scion of his race ... to acquire this Kingdom and become its King, and he was more content with his former position as Juba than being installed as a puppet on the gaddi by his younger step brothers with neither power nor influence.[33]

During the fighting he had shut himself up in the citadel, and neither he nor his personal troops had been involved in the hostilities. He had strongly condemned both Thangal General and the Senapati when he had heard that the British officers had been killed, but felt insufficiently powerful to punish them. To this defence the court responded that, since

Figure 15.1 Kula Chandra Singh, Regent of Manipur, and Thangal General, after their capture (Pictures from History).

the guns could not be fired from his citadel without his permission and no fire could be opened from his ramparts without his knowledge, as the ruler of Manipur the Regent could not abdicate responsibility for the anti-British revolt.[34]

The sentences of the court were subject to confirmation by the Viceroy, and until such confirmation arrived the two men were detained in Manipur with no special privileges – to the disgust of the Regent, who complained that he was a prisoner in his own palace with irons on his legs like a common criminal.[35] Thangal General, who submitted his appeal several days after that of the Regent, was in no better a state. He was still ill, and had been given the news that his property had been looted and his wives and children were destitute. Not unexpectedly, Ghose's appeal on behalf of the Senapati was wholly unsuccessful and on 10 August 1891 a telegram was sent from the Foreign Secretary of the Government of India to Collett stating that Tikendrajit was 'properly convicted' of waging war against the Queen and abetment of murder, and confirming the death sentence given by the court. However, the impassioned pleas for clemency made by the Manipuri royal family did not entirely fall on stony ground. Although the Regent was also convicted of waging war against the Queen and abetment of murder, his sentence of death was commuted to transportation for life, with forfeiture of all property. The sentence of death was also commuted in the case of Angao Senna who, argued the court, in his command of the main west gate must have known of the attack on the British officers and failed to help them. Moreover it was, the court maintained, inconceivable that he had not been aware of the subsequent murders. Yet, as in the case of Kula Chandra, the Prince in his defence stated that he had no real power to restrain or disobey Tikendrajit.[36] Zillah Singh was never brought to trial, no doubt due to his young age and the fact that there was no real evidence to suggest that he had participated in the fighting.

Ghose's memorandum, with a transcript of the trials of the Senapati and the Regent, was published in Britain in the summer of 1891, highlighting the shortcomings of the British rush to justice in Manipur and the cavalier approach of the court towards much of the evidence. After the findings of the court had been communicated to Queen Victoria, she immediately despatched the following telegram to Lord Cross: 'Trust Senapati will not be executed. He was not found guilty of murder and the effect is sure to be bad in India.'[37] On 8 August Cross informed her that the Viceroy had commuted the sentences in the cases of the Regent and Angao Senna, but the sentence in the case of Tikendrajit had been confirmed. Much distressed, Victoria replied,

> I can only say I regret the decision as to the Senapati and trust my approval is not asked, for I wish to give no opinion. We shall see whether it will be of use in deterring others. I cannot consider that the Senapati was not aware of our *intention to seize him* and thus HAD CAUSE for resistance. The Queen ... thinks we seem not quite clear in this deplorable affair, and ought *not* to hang the Senapati, though certainly Tongal.[38]

Cross himself appeared to agree in the light of the fact that Tikendrajit was convicted only of abetting murder, not of committing it. Whilst expressing satisfaction at the reprieve of Kula Chandra and Angao Senna he 'was sorry to find that the same careful consideration of the evidence and of the petition led the Viceroy and his advisers to a different conclusion in the case of the Senapati'. However he pointed out to the Queen that:

> By long custom all such questions rest with the Viceroy;[39] it was only on account of the gravity of the occasion that in the case of the princes Lord Cross ordered that there should be a reference home. For his guidance he had consulted Lord Salisbury, the Lord Chancellor, and the Cabinet. It was very far from his desire to ask for your Majesty's express approval, or even to seek for an expression of opinion from your Majesty, in such a painful case.[40]

On 11 August the Queen acknowledged the Secretary of State's letter, writing that she had

> a great and strong feeling that the principle of governing India by fear and *crushing* them, instead of by firmness and conciliation, *is one* which will never answer in the end and which the Queen-Express would wish to see more and more altered. To these reasons the Queen would add that hanging a person (and he a Prince) so long after he has been kept a prisoner has something cruel and cold-blooded about it. These are the Queen-Empress's feelings, which, however she will not write to the Viceroy. She intends neither writing nor saying anything to him about it, as he is evidently very sore about it.

No doubt persuaded by Ethel's opinion of the General, the Queen added that 'The Tongal richly deserves [hanging], though he is eighty-six! He is a very cruel, wicked old man. The other commutations of all the other sentences are quite right.'[41]

The following day, 12 August, Ghose himself appealed directly to the Queen for clemency for his client, and she immediately sent a telegram to Lansdowne asking if this were possible. The reply came back from India the same day: 'Your Majesty's telegram of 12th: I entertain no doubt commutation of sentence would be a grave public misfortune, and I regard as now absolutely impossible.'[42] Two days later the Viceroy informed the Queen that the sentence of death on Tikendrajit had been carried out in the presence of a large crowd in Manipur, later defending his decision in a letter which declared that

> the case was not one for the extension of your Majesty's clemency ... the Senapati was the prime mover, both in the conspiracy which led to the downfall of the lawful ruler of the State, and in the rebellion which led to the massacre. Your Majesty will have noticed that, while the fighting was in progress on the 24th, and at a time when it was impossible to contend that the Senapati was merely acting in self-defence, he brought up guns from their position inside the palace, to a position on the outer wall, from which, at a distance of a few yards, fire was opened upon the British Residency, a defenceless building, which at the time contained several wounded men, and an English lady ... it would be impossible to show mercy to one convicted of these crimes without gravely endangering our supremacy in this country.[43]

However, British supremacy in India had already been severely damaged. The *Amrita Bazar Patrika* expressed the views of other newspapers in its unwavering belief in the innocence of the Senapati and the fact that the Prince had been used as a pawn on the imperial chessboard, suggesting that 'once the idea of annexation was given up, the next alternative was the execution of the Senapati'.[44]

Lieutenant Colonel Alban Wilson of the 44th Gurkhas reported that when the day of execution came,[45] a guard of 400 rifles surrounded the scaffold, as it was expected that with over 8,000 spectators there might be an attempt to rescue the prisoners. Wilson stated:

> The Tongal pretended to be too ill to walk up to the gallows, and was carried up in a chair and placed beneath the noose, but the Senapati walked up and stood upright like a man. A sergeant of gunners, who was executioner, adjusted the rope around the Senapati's neck, tapped Thangal General on the shoulder and said, 'Now then, old man, stand up or I can't hang you'. Thangal gazed at him blankly, and then at the interpreter who translated the remark, on which the old fellow shook his head and roared with laughter. The interpreter said, 'Sir, the general states he will not

> rise'. The sergeant said, most persuasively, 'Just tell the old gentleman I'm not going to hurt him'. This, too, was translated, but the Tongal would not budge. Then ensued a most ghastly pause, whilst a man climbed up to the top of the gallows to lengthen the rope, and when it was adjusted both criminals were loosed off. The moment the drop fell, all the women in the crowd set up the most desolate wailing, which showed that the Senapati was a great favourite with the fair sex, but no regret was expressed for the Tongal.

As Wilson added mournfully, 'No one who had seen the mutilated bodies of his countrymen, or the desecrated graves in the little cemetery, felt much sympathy for any of these people, though, as is customary, there was plenty of it expressed in England by those who sat at home in comfort.'[46]

CHAPTER 16

THE AFTERMATH

The Times of 27 May 1891 announced that the Victoria Cross would be given to Lieutenant Grant, together with promotion to the rank of captain in the Indian Staff Corps and to the brevet rank of major. The official statement ran:

> For the conspicuous bravery and devotion to his country displayed by him in having, upon hearing on the 27th of March, 1891, of the disaster at Manipur, at once volunteered to attempt the relief of the British captives with eighty native soldiers, and, having advanced with the greatest intrepidity, captured Thobal near Manipur, and held it against a large force of the enemy. Lieutenant Grant inspired his men with equal heroism by an ever-present example of personal daring and resource.

The newspaper declared that it was difficult 'to over-estimate the value of such an exploit on the morrow of a serious defeat, were it only as a means of restoring the spirit of our native troops' and reflected somewhat bitterly that 'had the Manipur expedition been handled with ability and resource equal to Lieutenant Grant's, the errors of its conception might have been obliterated by the brilliancy of its execution'.[1] The Victoria Cross was awarded to Grant by the Governor of Madras at Government House, Ootacamund, on 6 July 1891 and as he was led to the dais the band played, suitably, 'See the Conquering Hero Comes'.[2] Every one of Grant's men received the Indian Order of Merit with six months' pay. Grant was promoted to Lieutenant Colonel in 1904, and retired in 1913. In World War I he was Deputy Commanding Officer attached to the 3rd battalion of the Royal Scots, and he died at Sidmouth on 23 November 1932.

After much spirited correspondence between the Government of India and the India Office, the India Medal with a new clasp inscribed 'N.E. Frontier 1891' was granted to all troops and followers employed in the Manipur expedition.[3] Such recognition was by no means taken for granted.[4] Following a certain amount of unwillingness on the part of the India Office to deliver such an accolade,[5] a letter was sent from the Viceroy's Council to the secretary of state, Lord Cross, suggesting that the grounds for objection could only be 'associated with the retreat of the troops ... and also with the circumstances attending the unfortunate death of the gentlemen and of the officers who accompanied them into the palace of Manipur on 24th March 1891'. Urging him to reconsider, it was stressed to Cross that 'the disaster which occurred under such peculiar circumstances was completely, and even brilliantly, retrieved by the forces which united at Manipur on the 27th April, under the command of Major-General Collett'[6] and that the march to Manipur had taken a substantial toll. In addition to casualties in action, 42 British and 122 native officers and soldiers had died from cholera and other complaints in eight weeks.[7]

The Times of 8 June announced that Queen Victoria was to confer upon Ethel Grimwood the distinction of the Royal Red Cross, 'in recognition of her devotion to the wounded under most trying circumstances, during the attack upon the Residency at Manipur'. The Secretary of State for India awarded Ethel a pension of £140 a year for life, and 'as a mark of appreciation of the special services rendered by Mrs. Grimwood at the time of the attack on the Manipur Residency and in the events which followed it' a sum of £1,000 was granted to her, irrespective of any compensation which might be given by the Government of India for 'the destruction of her husband's property at Manipur'.[8] Upon hearing of this remuneration Lansdowne, in whose eyes Ethel's halo had slipped considerably, was quick to point out to Cross that:

> Mrs. Grimwood has, I thank, been very generously dealt with. I had rather, however, say no more on the subject, except that I trust that, if any further proposals are made on her behalf, you will

> not listen to them without giving us an opportunity of telling you what we think about them.[9]

It is probable that Lansdowne was swayed by the appearance of a letter sent by Pucca Senna to Sir Mortimer Durand, foreign secretary to the Government of India, in which the behaviour of both Ethel and Frank in India was deemed to have been less than immaculate. Flattered by their closeness to the royal family the couple appear to have lost their judgement, presuming somewhat arrogantly that their actions were beyond reproof. It was alleged that the Senapati procured young girls for *nautches* and visits to the residency, supposedly for Frank to take their photographs. The protests of their parents and guardians, who declared that as a result of this familiarity 'their girls were not likely to be accepted for matrimonial purposes', appeared to fall on deaf ears, and Frank was seen publicly with Tikendrajit and the girls 'rowing and amusing themselves in a pleasure boat in the tank within the Residency compound'. As the matter became a local scandal of some importance, it was the subject of a discussion in open *durbar* in the presence of the Maharaja and his ministers, who insisted that the matter should be 'hushed up'. According to Pucca Senna, at this stage Sur Chandra remonstrated with Tikendrajit and, in doing so, incurred the animosity of Grimwood.[10]

Weight was given to these allegations by details contained in a petition sent to the Viceroy by the relatives of Kula Chandra and the Senapati at the time of the princes' trial, stating that Thangal General was responsible for the murder of the British officers, hoping to destroy Kula Chandra in order that the former maharaja, Sur Chandra, might be restored to the throne. According to the petition the 'lazy and unwise' Frank, who had 'plunged deeply into mirth and merriment'[11] while Ethel enjoyed herself in Shillong from March to December in 1889 and April to December in 1990,[12] had formed an attachment to Thangal's 'beautiful and gay' daughter who was seen visiting the residency in broad daylight. Thangal, deeply shamed by this, remained behind on the night of 24 March when the Senapati had left for the Top Guard, and 'with a view to avenge himself, instigated the people to murder Mr. Grimwood first'.[13]

The Viceroy's private secretary, Colonel John Ardagh, was also vitriolic in his opinion of the couple, believing their behaviour to have been a prime cause of the abdication of Sur Chandra which in turn led to the Manipur revolt. In a secret memorandum condemning the fact that she had received the Royal Red Cross plus a large pension, Ardagh wrote that had Ethel remained with her husband, Frank would not have consoled himself with Manipuri girls, producing the scandal which resulted in a quarrel between him and the royal family:

> If he had not taken Tikendrajit into his friendship, as the companion in his orgies, the latter would never have dared to oust his brothers, nor would he have relied upon Grimwood's support of the revolution.

Ardagh concluded that 'The answer to the question "Cherchez la femme?" is therefore that Mrs. Grimwood's conduct led to the revolution of September.'[14]

In addition, it was said that in India 'strong feeling' existed as to the truth of Ethel's account of events during the uprising. Having spoken to a member of the Court of Enquiry, Lansdowne wrote to Cross in June 1891 that credit was no doubt due to her for her attention to the wounded in the residency,

> but the danger was evidently much exaggerated, and I am assured that she showed herself by no means such a heroine as she would have the public believe. I am told that she was much nearer being the first than was the last to leave the Residency. I learn from the same source, and from others, that the closeness of Mr. Grimwood's relations with the Senapati formed the subject of a good deal of disagreeable criticism ... Upon occasions of this kind the British public likes to have a hero or a heroine, and I cannot help fearing that the mark has been a little overshot in the present instance.[15]

Lansdowne appears to have been influenced also by a letter from Sir Charles Elliott, lieutenant-governor of Bengal, informing the Viceroy that Ethel 'talked very freely, and, among other things, she told the Chief Justice that she used to ride out every morning with Koireng, the Senapati, which shows an extraordinary degree of intimacy with such a scoundrel'.[16]

In his role as General Graham's adjutant-general, Lieutenant Colonel St John Michell added to the rumours, having completed the 'fullest investigation into all the facts' when Ethel and the other fugitives arrived in Cachar after the retreat from the residency. Michell examined all the officers concerned both officially and unofficially, with evidence from both sepoys and Manipuris. It was alleged that Ethel had been on intimate terms with Captain Butcher and 'slept under the same blanket on the way down, to the scandal of the party'.[17] Michell declared:

> Mrs Grimwood acted most injudiciously before the disaster, especially in writing to the Jubraj [Tikendrajit] (she carefully abstains from mentioning this fact);[18] her account of hospital running with blood, etc., is absolutely incorrect. She was never wounded or under fire, for the lower rooms of the Residency are shot-proof; only two or three shots were fired at the retreating party at long distance. She seriously embarrassed our officers by pressing them to retire. She never showed any one the way, for there was no way to show, the road being perfectly straight and well known to all. Her relations with her husband were very strained, and it is quite probable that he never spoke to her. In no way did she act heroically.[19]

Despite the criticisms of her which were voiced on the Indian front, Ethel's aura as the heroine of the Manipur disaster remained undimmed at home during 1891, boosted by the publication in November of her account of events, *My Three Years in Manipur*, which was a great success and highly profitable, running into three editions. Such fortune proved to be short-lived. In May 1895 Ethel married Andrew Cornwall Miller, the proprietor of a paper mill in Surrey, who emigrated to America four years later, leaving Ethel to follow him. After a number of years in Oregon, the couple separated and Ethel became a music teacher. Following increasing bouts of mental illness, she died in Portland on 11 August 1928, aged 55.[20] Memorials to Frank were placed in the Winchester College cloister and the ante-chapel of Merton College, Oxford. The Winchester school magazine expressed the mixture of admiration and exasperation held by many who followed the events in Manipur, declaring that 'We may express our sorrow that the career of so promising a young Wykehamist should have been so soon and so fruitlessly cut short in the service of the country.'[21]

As far as the welfare of the families of the other British victims was concerned, a representative of Mrs Skene enquired as to whether compensation was recoverable from the state of Manipur, since Colonel Skene had been killed 'during a truce by people of an independent State'. It was agreed by the Military Department that the state was extremely poor and it was doubtful whether compensation could be exacted; however under the provisions for widows of military officers killed in action Mrs Skene was granted £200 a year for herself and £25 a year for each child.[22] Quinton's family fared somewhat better and it was agreed that in view of the 'lamentable circumstances' under which the Chief Commissioner met his death, a special pension of £300 a year should be granted to his widow for life. Moreover following an application from his two brothers, informing the India Office that Quinton had regularly contributed over 30 years to the maintenance of his mother and sisters 'whose means were very scanty', a pension was granted to his mother of £100 a year during her life, and after her death £50 a year to his sisters so long as they remained unmarried.[23]

Mrs Melville was forced to plead to the Secretary of State that her husband, William, had been employed for over 21 years in the Telegraph Service of India, during which time his conduct 'had entirely merited and received the approval of his superiors'.[24] The day before Quinton's mission, she pointed out,

> my husband was allowed without any warning of danger and without any protection whatever to travel in a country which could not be safe for any European at that time ... murdered most cruelly at some distance from Manipur, whilst he was actually employed in the service of Government.

The widow remonstrated that the proposed meagre pension of £100 a year, plus £18 for the education of each of her sons, was hardly 'an adequate remuneration' for the family of a man who was already entitled to the pension of Rs 4,000 a year, and the India Office eventually agreed to an additional compassionate allowance of £50 a year for so long as she remained unmarried.[25] Hilda Brackenbury also wrote an impassioned letter to the India Office stating that she had now lost two sons in service in India, and of her remaining three, two were in America and unable to assist her two daughters who were artists with little income. However, since Mrs Brackenbury was already receiving a pension from the War Office as a widow, she was ineligible for any additional allowance on account of her son's death.[26] The family of Lieutenant Simpson was deemed to be 'in good circumstances' and therefore not recompensed.

Sir James Johnstone lived to see the threat of annexation of Manipur removed, dying in 1895 at his home in Warwickshire as the result of a riding accident.[27] However in the immediate aftermath of the revolt there was an assumption by the press in Britain that Manipur would be absorbed into British India with 'a good deal of acceptance in official circles'. Lansdowne was not prepared to admit that annexation must follow as a matter of course. There were points to be resolved: whether, by annexation, responsibilities would be incurred which would be better avoided; what would be the financial cost of the step; what political effect it would have on other states; and 'whether it was beyond the power of the Government to devise an arrangement which would secure all the advantages of annexation, without its disadvantages'.[28] Lansdowne considered that if the state were not annexed, the government should declare that Manipur had forfeited its independence but that, 'as an act of clemency, we are prepared to restore it, subject to any conditions upon which we may find it desirable to insist'.[29]

The latter route was taken, and in September 1891 a decision was made in council to select as the new ruler of the state Chura Chand, aged five, descended from an obscure line of the royal family.[30] According to the Manipur Court Chronicle, two pundits, after consulting the royal records kept in a sealed safe box, compiled a list of all the Manipuri princes, and

> Maxwell Sahep, after consulting the list for almost twenty days, said that the descendants of Gambhir Singh had wronged the Sarkar (British) and the king of Manipur must be from the lineage of Nara Singh ... To this Sarang Panchi the astrologer replied and said that Nara Singh's eldest son was called Bhuban Sing, who had also been the Jubraj. But (now) he was dead ... Bhuban Sing Jubraj's brother was called up and (Bara Sahep) asked 'How many sons do you have?' He replied and said that he had four sons. To this Sahep asked him to bring to him all their birth

> certificates. All the four horoscopes were brought and presented to the Bara Sahep. Then his youngest son [Chura Chand] born by his wife the Moirangthem maiden, was appointed to be the king by the Bara Sahep.[31]

The selection of a candidate somewhat removed from the now tainted principal royal line was undoubtedly in accordance with Government of India policy. Lansdowne was adamant that it was

> most important to show that we are making an entirely new departure and that the new ruler will owe his position altogether to our favour ... a long minority under the guidance of a careful British officer will be much the best for this purpose.[32]

Michell, following his presidency of the trial of the princes, agreed with the Viceroy that Manipur would be in a more satisfactory position than before with the enforcement of British authority, but confessed that as a result of sifting through the mass of evidence which had come before him he was 'very much struck' with the fairness of the government of Manipur prior to the uprising and 'the extraordinary deference that seemed to be paid to public opinion and the absence of all despotism'. In his view, 'The "Top-guard" was a veritable Governor-General's Council and no one man, Prince or Minister, had any individual power except in times of popular excitement.'[33]

The choice of Chura Chand (with the downgraded title of raja and a salute of 11 guns) was announced in *The Gazette of India* on 21 August 1891. It was declared that

> Her Majesty the Queen, Empress of India, has been pleased to forego her right to annex to Her Indian Dominions the territories of the Manipur State and has graciously assented to the reestablishment of Native rule under such conditions as the Governor-General in Council may consider desirable, and in the person of such ruler as the Governor-General in Council may select. Her Majesty has been moved to this act of clemency by the belief that the punishment inflicted upon the leaders of the revolt, together with the imposition upon the State of suitable conditions of regrant, will afford an adequate vindication of Her authority.[34]

The announcement was 'received with some amazement and disappointment'. Maxwell's 1891/2 Administration Report stated that the Manipuri population were

> all in favour of the country being annexed to the British Empire and never for one instant expected, after the gross act of treachery on 24th March, which ended so fatally for Mr. Quinton and his officers, that the country would be given back to them.

However if the unexpected did occur it was presumed that the government would either permit the return of the ex-maharaja Sur Chandra, who had been conducting his own propaganda war in Calcutta with a view to retrieving the vacant throne, or nominate to the *gadi* his only son, Sura Chandra, a boy of 14 living in Manipur.[35] In fact, the ex-maharaja had written to this effect from Calcutta and told his supporters to 'keep up a brave heart'. To this faction the choice of a member of a collateral branch of the royal family 'came like a bombshell', and the fact that the youngest of four brothers was chosen was even less acceptable.[36]

Maxwell remained confident that:

> The people now realise that the minor Raja's right to the succession rests solely on his selection by the Government of India, and have loyally accepted the decision; and I doubt whether any attempt, even in the distant future, will be made by disappointed partisans to alter the succession.[37]

As it happened the 'disappointed partisans' were soon silenced. In October the ex-maharaja's son died from smallpox in Manipur, and the following month the death of Sur Chandra himself was reported from Calcutta. To remove the possibility of further conspiracy, Kula Chandra and Angao Senna, with the Ayapurel, the Luang Ningthou and several other nobles, were transported across the dreaded 'black water'[38] to the Andaman Islands, and Zillah Singh was exiled to Sylhet with the wives and male children of the Regent and the Senapati. Apart from Zillah Singh, who was considered by the British to be capable of earning his own living immediately, each was given an allowance of Rs 50 per month for three years only. By the end of this time they were supposed to have established themselves sufficiently to support their own needs. The minor raja took up residence in a block of houses to the south east of the *pat* under the guardianship of his mother and grandfather, an honorary magistrate of the Chirap (Chief) Court. Maxwell gave them strict orders to regulate the young ruler's life so that he would 'grow up healthy and strong' but held out little hope that this would be the case while he was still living in Manipur. An allowance of Rs 500 per month was granted to meet the expenditure of the household.[39]

The Times stated confidently that if Chura Chand

> turns out to be the possessor of wisdom befitting his high position, he will undoubtedly regard his long minority, with its unique opportunities for political education, as the most fortunate of circumstances, alike for himself and his people. Until he comes of age Manipur will be administered by a British Resident governing in his name, who will not only offer him invaluable lessons in the art of government, but will at last hand over to him administrative machinery working with perfect smoothness and efficiency.[40]

It was noted that:

> As a stimulus to worthy ambition, the title is made hereditary, descending in direct line so long as each successive Rajah recognizes the paramount authority of the Government of India. The payment of tribute and other well-understood incidents of political dependency will impress the reality of that authority upon the native mind. In this way it may be hoped that no pretender will again be able to delude himself or the people of Manipur with the notion that he can treat as an equal with the Government of India, or can claim belligerent rights in the event of rebellion.[41]

Although it was regretted that not all the material advantages of annexation would be gained, there was

> an opportunity to organise the administration of Manipur upon broad and sound lines, to accustom the people to the just and

> orderly ways of Western government, and, in short, to confer upon Rajah and people alike a political education which they will find invaluable.

Moreover, in the light of increasing rumblings of nationalist feeling it was agreed that objections to annexation could not now be based solely on 'the effacement of all local colour and the introduction of a commonplace uniformity'. As *The Times* declared with feeling,

> The practical question is mainly in what native hands we shall place the powers of which we are gradually divesting ourselves. To destroy native governments and abase the native aristocracy, only to hand over the administration of our swollen provinces to the baboos who anathematize us in native newspapers is not at all a wise policy. Notwithstanding the flood of European claptrap, poured over India by the small minority who imagine themselves to have had an English education, India remains an essentially aristocratic country. An overwhelming majority will, for generations to come, yield a ready allegiance to their hereditary rulers, and it is infinitely better for us in the long run to hold the respect and affection of these rulers than to embark upon the unprofitable and futile task of trying to satisfy the measureless conceit and ambition of the aspiring young men who pervert Burke and Macaulay.[42]

On 29 April 1892, in the presence of 8,000 people, Chura Chand was installed by Major Maxwell. Under the *sanad* of appointment the Raja's right was declared to derive solely from the Government of India, and the recognition of such right to depend upon the loyal fulfilment of his duties as a tributary prince. The British took pains to display their magnanimity. Maxwell's speech announced the abolition of the 'cruel custom' of slavery, the termination of the *lalup* system and in its place the levy of a house tax of Rs 2 per house per annum, and the establishment of a uniform rate of land revenue at Rs 5 per *pari*. Additionally, 15 prisoners were released from the state jail. The band of the 43rd Gurkha Rifles played the Manipuri anthem followed by 'God Save the Queen', during which all the spectators stood, and a salute of 11 guns was fired. For the days before and after the installation sports such as polo, hockey and wrestling took place on the polo ground, and the nights were passed in 'nautches and song'. Maxwell reported that 'several hundreds of the poorer classes were fed daily' and a spectacular firework display brought the celebrations to an end.[43]

Rising to the rank of colonel, Maxwell served as Political Agent in Manipur four times between 1891 and 1905, acting as the 'superintendent' of the state and conducting the administration during the Raja's minority.[44] Soon after his appointment, bizarrely emulating the Grimwoods' close connections with the royal family, he formed a liaison with the youngest daughter of Sur Chandra, a relationship which became the source of some scandal and lasted until her early death in 1906. In his first year in office there was much illness in the state. Following the return of the Manipuris to their villages after the fighting, the cholera which had followed the troops from Cachar broke out among the native population and mortality was very heavy.[45] In September 1891 there was an epidemic of smallpox which continued 'with great virulence' until the following January. The rice harvest of 1890–1 had been satisfactory, however after March the Durbar began to collect large quantities for consumption by the Manipuri troops. Much of this rice was lost in wasteful looting before British soldiers were called in to deal with the situation. For the four months from August to November 1891 at least half the population was living on one meal a day, and many people showed signs of emaciation. As the *Court Chronicle* reported, 'There was a severe famine. The price of one sangbai basket of paddy soared up to two Lakhs of sen ... Cattle were scarce and cattle princes also soared. Many cattle were also stolen. Fish, salt, and anything edible was very costly.'[46] However in the rainy season there were fortunately a great many edible aquatic plants available in the numerous lakes in the valley, and these helped to feed the Manipuris until there were supplies from an excellent harvest in December 1891.[47]

The financial demands placed upon Manipur by the Government of India were not as draconian as had been feared. The Viceroy's Council came to the decision that the ordinary tribute to be levied from the state should for the time be fixed at Rs 50,000, subject to reconsideration when government was transferred to the Raja. The fine to be paid by the Manipuri people as punishment for the outbreak was to be fixed at no more than 2½ *lakhs* altogether, comprising the Rs 186,000 looted from the Government Treasury and an additional Rs 61,000 for 'misconduct in opposing the Paramount Power by arms'. This amount was to be recovered in five years or less through the new house tax, giving an exemption to villages which could be shown to have had no hand in the rebellion. Maxwell reported that 'The Leniency of the Supreme Government in the matter of this fine has struck the Manipuri people with astonishment and will, I hope, tend to foster a spirit of future loyalty among them.'[48]

In his 1891/2 Administration Report Maxwell recorded that following the looting and burning of government buildings after the British retirement on 24 March, a new treasury and post and telegraph office had been erected in the citadel and a dispensary was under construction to the north of the polo ground. A site to the west of the dispensary was set up for a new school house, and a bazaar containing 19 shops had been built to the west of the polo ground. A wing of the 42nd Gurkha Rifles occupied new barracks in the citadel and the lines of the 43rd Gurkha Rifles were situated on the north-eastern face of the *pat* outside the moat. The mess house and the quarters of the officers of the regiment were situated in the Senapati's compound. Taking advantage of the desertion of the capital when British troops reached Manipur, a large area was notified as a British reserve and denuded of houses. There was to be a large open area around the *pat*, replacing the 'crowded and filthy compounds which are the hotbed of disease'. It was proposed to tap a spring near Kunjopkol, 12 miles from Manipur where Johnstone had built a sanitorium, to bring water through pipes into the town, the cost of which would be Rs 5 *lakhs*. If the government were prepared to provide this loan there was little doubt in Maxwell's view that before the Raja came of age the capital would be repaid in full and 'the greatest of boons – a pure water supply' would be given to the large population of Manipur.[49]

Along the Cachar road, the main trade route into Manipur, the rest houses which had been destroyed by the insurgents were rebuilt by the end of 1891 and the road thoroughly cleared of jungle with some rebridging of the rivers. The bridle path from Kohima was used throughout the year for the transport of commissariat supplies, and was repaired from imperial funds. New rest houses were built, and strong suspension bridges erected over two main rivers. The bridle path to Tammu was also well repaired during the year by villagers living near the road. In February 1892, orders were received from the Government of

India sanctioning a police force of 400 Manipuris, to be armed with muzzle-loading carbines. In the meantime unarmed soldiers of the disbanded Manipuri army were placed at the halting stages of the Cachar, Kohima and Tammu routes to assist and 'give confidence' to travellers.[50] The expeditionary arrangements ceased at Manipur on 9 March 1892, almost one year after the anti-British rebellion, when the last of the bullocks not required for the 43rd left Manipur. Supplies at each stage between Manipur and Kohima were collected on the way out of the state, and on 17 March the road was cleared of all government transport.

In May 1896 Maxwell announced that plans had been made for the young raja, Chura Chand, and his half-brother to attend Mayo College in Ajmer, one of the colleges set up under British control to educate Indian royalty and nobility. The boys by no means experienced great hardship in their new environment, taking with them a Manipuri interpreter, a Manipuri guardian, a bearer and two Brahmin cooks, and appeared to flourish at the college, displaying 'industry, obedience and energy' and a fondness for 'manly sports'. Maxwell reported that for some days before the boys left Manipur there was much gossip as to the reason for sending the Raja out of the state; on the morning of their departure the streets were lined by crowds of people, and

> as the elephant on which the boys rode passed by, the men shouted salaams, and the women set up howls of grief. Throughout this somewhat trying ordeal the youthful Raja remained unmoved, and as some old men told me later in the day, they were much pleased at the Raja's behaviour; his heart was in the right place, and he promised to be a man of courage.[51]

However, it appeared that in the twentieth century the local popularity of Chura Chand waned, and the British presence in the state was also viewed in an unfavourable light. In September 1904 the inhabitants of Manipur city rioted against an order issued by the Political Agent, directing them to rebuild a bungalow occupied by his assistant which had been burned down. An official despatch reported that:

> The fire in this, as in two previous cases which had occurred, was attributed to incendiarism. The disturbance was political and was intended as a demonstration against the Raja who had been

> selected by the Government of India for the post in 1891 and who was very unpopular with the people.[52]

Johnstone had accurately predicted the emergence of such a situation as a result of British insensitivity in installing what were effectively puppet rulers in Indian states, declaring that in his opinion

> the machine-like system which we have introduced and are endeavouring to force into every corner of India, till all personal influence is killed out, [is] ill-adapted to the requirements of these Oriental races, and blighting in its effects. Not one native chief has adopted it in its integrity, which is in itself a fair argument that it is distasteful to the native mind; and we may be assured that if we evacuated India to-morrow, personal rule would again make itself felt through the length and breadth of the land and grow stronger every day.[53]

The last word on the uprising was delivered in November 1901 when Lord Curzon paid the first visit in history by a Viceroy to Manipur. Ten years after the hostilities his condemnation of the Government of India was unequivocal, pronouncing scathingly that the Manipuris were 'the most good-natured, harmless, though excitable, people in creation, who were only driven into a revolt against us by a series of blunders almost unparalleled in history'.[54]

CONCLUSION

The 1891 conflict in Manipur was by no means the finest hour of imperial rule in India. For the British at the end of the nineteenth century there was always a tension between intervention and laissez-faire in the princely states, and policies had frequently wavered as to when and how to interfere with Indian rulers in order to secure imperial interests. However the ruling of the paramount power in matters of succession remained a highly sensitive issue for the Government of India, and any perceived challenge to such a ruling – real or imagined – was bound to raise the hackles of senior British officials. At the highest level there appeared to have been no rational strategy emanating from the Viceroy's Council to support the despatch of Quinton to arrest the Senapati. Having reacted late to the abdication of Sur Chandra, an ill-conceived scheme was speedily adopted to make an example of Tikendrajit as a recalcitrant prince whose position of power would not be tolerated under the Raj. Such a scheme, lacking any attempt at diplomatic finesse, appeared all the more extraordinary since to all intents and purposes Manipur was not only an ally of the British but also, in Lansdowne's view, a vital link in the chain of defences ringing Indian borders – and as such meriting preferential treatment to maintain its loyalty. On the part of the Political Department any serious research into the recent history of the state appears to have been minimal; the sinister motives attributed to Tikendrajit in the abdication saga owed much to speculation, and the reputation of the Prince rested on the views of Colonel Johnstone and other earlier political agents, with little regard for bias.

As to the execution of the plan emanating from the knee-jerk reaction of the government, the events leading up to and during March 1891 reveal a woeful lack of judgement throughout the chain of command, from the most senior officials down to Grimwood himself. With an ill-armed escort, despite a history of tribal violence in the area, the Chief Commissioner resorted to a dangerous game of 'cat and mouse' with the Senapati which hardly reflected well on the powerful and open administration upon which the Raj prided itself. Whether or not arresting a man, let alone a prince, at a *durbar* was morally defensible, the bizarre proposition that it was permissible to invade a palace in a princely state supposedly under the protection of the paramount power showed little imaginative thought on the part of British officers. Whether or not the British fired first, the forced entry into the grounds of the fort was a gross violation of property and person. The ensuing violence was the inevitable retaliation to such a violation and, in a particularly volatile situation, the absurd decision, based solely upon Grimwood's blind trust in the royal family, for a party of unarmed British officers to enter a building from which an attack had been made upon the residency throughout the day showed a total absence of forethought and wisdom. In the aftermath the excesses of the elephantine field force sent to assert British supremacy, with the associated expense and suffering, owed more to bolstering the precarious image of the Government of India than to fulfilling a genuine need for a significant number of troops on the ground. Moreover the series of trials conducted with scant regard for acceptable legal procedure singularly failed to provide a convincing picture of an imperial power intent upon the principles of fair, transparent government.

It transpired that after the Manipur uprising the traditional uncritical devotion of Indian subjects to their local ruler was never again to be demonstrated with such force and determination. In the twentieth century, with nationalist feeling seeping gradually over the borders of British India into the princely states, there was increasing adherence to popular movements, as Indian princes were perceived more and more to be lackeys of the British and over-extravagant in their habits. As has been shown, for the subjects of Manipur in 1891 there was no conflict of interest. They proved willing to fight unconditionally to contest British attempts to usurp members of the royal family, a contingency which the British ignored to their huge cost. One of the last gasps of centuries of traditional rule in India proved to be a catastrophic event for the Government of India and its officers in the field.

GLOSSARY

ahing	after midnight
atta	flour used to make most South Asian flatbreads
ayah	native maid or nanny employed by Europeans in India
babu	term of respect attached to a name
banian	undershirt, originally of muslin
betel	leaf of evergreen plant *Piper Betle*, chewed with the areca nut
chong	large white umbrella with decorated fringes used in religious processions
chowkidar	watchman or gatekeeper
cooly	hired unskilled labourer
dal	kind of pulse
dana, dhan	grain
dao, dhao	hill knife used for cutting jungle, sword
dhoti	long loincloth
dooly	covered litter
durbar	formal assembly, the court of an Indian prince
fakir	Muslim or Hindi religious ascetic who lives solely on alms
gaddi/gadi	throne
ghee, ghi	clarified butter
havildar	non-commissioned officer in the Indian army
Holi	Hindu spring festival
jeel/jheel	mere or lagoon
jemadar	second rank of native officer in company of sepoys

jubraj	crown prince
kahar	one who carries loads on his shoulders
kheda, khedda	an enclosure into which wild elephants are driven to be captured
kookai, kookry	weapon peculiar to the Gurkhas, literally 'a twisted skein of thread'
lakh	a hundred thousand (unless otherwise specified, rupees)
lalup	forced labour
lam	approximately six feet
lascar	a sailor from India or South-East Asia
macharn	raised platform
mahout	elephant driver or keeper
mali	gardener
nala, nullah	stream or drain
nautch	traditional dance performed by professional dancing girls
nongangpung	daybreak
nongyaipung	midnight
numidang	before midnight
numityungba	midday
pagri	turban
pari	2½ acres
pat	enclosure
pice	former Indian coin, worth one sixty-fourth of a rupee
pukka	solidly built
punkah	portable fan made from palm leaves or cloth
raja/maharaja	Hindu king
rajmantri	prime minister
rani/maharani	Hindu queen
reduit	fortified structure into which defending troops can retreat when outer defences are breached
salaams	salutations
sanad	grant or deed conferring rights or title
sen	fractional monetary unit
shikari	sportsman who either brings in game or accompanies European sportsmen
subadar	chief native officer of a company of sepoys
syce	groom
terreplein	top surface of a rampart on which cannon are placed

thakpa	drink
thana	police station
thanadar	chief of a police station
yachangpung	nightfall
yu	rice beer
yumang	morning
yuthak	'drink time'
yutung	afternoon
zemindar	owner of an agricultural estate

NOTES

Chapter 1 The Road to Manipur

1. Despite the grandeur of the architecture, Rudyard Kipling considered Calcutta to be a city of squalor, permeated throughout by the stench of drains, 'the big Calcutta stink . . . sickly . . . indescribable'. Quoted Charles Allen, *Kipling Sahib* (London: Little, Brown and Co., 2007), p. 256. However this picture is undoubtedly an exaggeration. A Calcutta Municipal Corporation was established in about 1864 and made huge improvements by installing a sewerage system, re-siting meat markets, installing gas lighting and collecting land tax from houses which paid for street *chowkidars*.
2. George M. Barker, *A Tea Planter's Life in Assam* (London: Thacker Spink & Co., 1884), p. 39.
3. Barker, *A Tea Planter's Life*, p. 41.
4. Ibid., p. 44.
5. Ibid., p. 48.
6. Ibid., p. 61.
7. James Alban Wilson, *Sport and Service in Assam and Elsewhere* (London: Hutchinson & Co., 1924), p. 33.
8. The British adopted the term 'Naga' to refer to a number of tribes in north-eastern India, based on loose linguistic and cultural associations. One of the major tribes in the Manipur area, the Angami Nagas, were described as hardy and active, the men averaging 5 feet 8 inches to 6 feet in height with 'a manly independent bearing, and . . . bred up to war from their earliest years'. As republicans, their chiefs were elected and were in theory *primus inter pares*. An Angami in full war paint was 'a very formidable-looking individual', and several clans often inhabited one village 'in deadly feud with each other'. No Angami would assume the 'toga virilis' of a kilt decorated with cowrie shells until he had slain an enemy, and 'Life for life' was the rule. Major General

Sir James Johnstone, *My Experiences in Manipur and the Naga Hills* (London: Sampson Low, 1896), pp. 27–30.

9. The Kukis consisted of several tribes who worked their way north to Manipur in the middle of the nineteenth century, pouring into the hill tracts of the state where they drove out many of the established inhabitants. They were strictly monarchical and their 'absolutely despotic' chiefs murdered or sold their subjects into slavery without question. The Political Agent at that time, Lieutenant McCulloch, advanced the tribesmen large sums of money from his own pocket, assigning different duties to each chief's followers and planting Kuki settlements on exposed frontiers. 'So great was his influence, that he had only to send round his silver mounted *dao* [Burmese sword] as a kind of fiery cross, when all able-bodied men at once assembled at his summons'. Johnstone, *My Experiences in Manipur*, pp. 26–7.
10. Ethel Grimwood described the suspension bridges as 'curiosities' made of wire twisted into thick ropes which were stretched from trees on either side of the river at different heights. Bamboo was hung on to the wires to form a sort of railing on each side, and these were fastened with cane to the floor of the bridge, which was also of bamboo, woven into a coarse matting. Despite appearing 'most flimsy and airy erections', the bridges were remarkably strong, capable of carrying a number of men and animals on them at the same time. Ethel Grimwood, *My Three Years in Manipur and Escape from the Recent Mutiny* (London: Richard Bentley and Son, 1891), pp. 18–19.
11. L/MIL/17/19/33, p. 1.
12. Senior Papers D507, p. 1.
13. Although rigid Hindus outwardly, it was possible in Manipur for a man of low caste marrying a high-caste woman to be adopted into her tribe – the exact reverse of the situation in India, where a woman of high-caste marrying a low-caste man was 'hopelessly degraded and her children outcasts'. Johnson, *My Experiences in Manipur*, p. 98.
14. L/MIL/17/19/33, p. 2. There was also a small Muslim population of about 5,000, descended from early immigrants from India who had taken Manipuri wives.
15. Colonel, later Sir, James Johnstone was posted as ensign to the Bengal Native Infantry in 1858 and served in the latter stages of the Indian Mutiny. From 1868 to 1874, he was placed in charge of the elephant *kheddas* in Orissa and joined the Political Service in 1874. After his time in Manipur and the Naga Hills, Johnstone served as Commissioner on the Burmese Frontier and was the Deputy Commissioner of Assam from 1884 until 1888, when he retired.
16. Johnstone, *My Experiences in Manipur*, pp. 97–8.
17. Senior Papers D507, p. 2.
18. Ibid.
19. Maxwell to Secretary to Chief Commissioner Assam 13 May 1892, L/PS/7/370.
20. Johnstone, *My Experiences in Manipur*, p. 115.

Chapter 2 Manipur in the Nineteenth Century

1. Colonel Johnstone described in disgust the manner in which the Government of India, 'being generally officers brought up in the Secretariat, and with little knowledge of Asiatics' failed to follow a 'manly course' and deprived 'a gallant and loyal ally of part of his territories'. Johnstone, *My Experiences in Manipur*, p. 87.
2. Senior Papers D507, p. 4.
3. At times British relations with the Manipur durbar were decidedly strained. Colonel Johnstone's predecessor, Captain Durand, drew a damning picture in his official report of 1877 of Chandra Kirtee Singh's misgovernment and the most unpleasant position of the political agent, whom he described as 'in fact a British officer under Manipur surveillance ... He is surrounded by spies ... If the Maharaja is not pleased with the Political Agent – he is ostracised'. Johnstone, *My Experiences in Manipur*, p. xxvii.
4. Johnstone, *My Experiences in Manipur*, p. 70.
5. Johnstone, *My Experiences in Manipur*, p. xxvii.
6. The first British encounter with the Naga tribes began in 1832, when two British officers, Captain Jenkins and Lieutenant Pemberton, escorted by Gambhir Singh's Manipuri troops, forced a passage through the hills in search of a practicable route into Assam. Several Naga villages, including the largest, Kohima, were forced into allegiance to Gambhir Singh, and even up to the Naga Hills Campaign of 1879–80 the Nagas regarded Manipur as a greater power than Britain: 'One British subject after another might be murdered with impunity, but woe betide the village that murdered a subject of Manipur. A force of Manipuris was instantly despatched, the village was attacked, destroyed, and ample compensation exacted.' Johnstone, *My Experiences in Manipur*, p. 23.
7. Ibid., pp. 272–4.
8. Ibid., pp. 276–7.
9. Secretary to Chief Commissioner Assam to Secretary to Government of India, 23 May 1888, L/MIL/7/15107, p. 63.
10. Residencies were British political offices, each managed by a resident or political agent, which dealt with relations between British India and the state in which they were situated.
11. Secretary to Chief Commissioner Assam to Secretary to Government of India, 23 May 1888, L/MIL/7/15107, p. 63.
12. Johnstone, *My Experiences in Manipur*, p. 277. Johnstone was convinced that 'as a race we are a little careless of the feelings of others'. He was of the opinion that the position of the British in Manipur had deteriorated towards the end of the nineteenth century and the arrival of European officers in Manipur following the Burmese War was a great 'source of annoyance to the high officials of Manipur, who would always suspect them of making enquiries with a view to an unfavourable report to Government. All natives of India are suspicious, and this

remark applies with tenfold force to Manipuris.' Johnstone, *My Experiences in Manipur*, p. 276.

Chapter 3 Cast of Characters

1. The Warden of Merton at the time was Robert Bullock Marsham. Having been elected in 1827, by the time Grimwood came up Marsham had been Warden for over 40 years, which may have contributed to the college's complacency.
2. The comparison with Hurlingham is interesting, since from a contemporary description Manipuri polo appears to have been a most unstructured affair. It is said to have started in the state in about AD 1600, and was played on 11- or 12-hand ponies specially equipped with a saddle with a high peak in front and behind, and an enormous leather flap on either side under the stirrup leathers, which curved around in front and behind the rider's bare legs to protect them from the blows of a stick or ball. There appear to have been no rules other than the fact that the width of the ground at either end formed the goals, and that the ball had to be got there in any way possible. There was no offside, and no objection to fouling, crossing or hooking sticks. Play was at full speed the entire time, and if a player or pony was injured or tired a fresh one took his place. The only pause occurred when a goal was hit or the ball went off the ground. Wilson, *Sport and Service in Assam*, p. 128.
3. Ibid., pp. 18–19.
4. Ibid., p. 19.
5. Ibid., p. 24.
6. Ibid., p. 25.
7. Ibid., p. 26.
8. Anglo-Indians were originally British persons in India, but later specifically those of mixed blood.
9. Grimwood, *My Three Years in Manipur*, pp. 29–30.
10. The boat races described by Johnstone formed the great event of the year, and generally took place in September when the moat was full: 'Close to the palace gateway a grandstand was erected, from which the Rajah and his relations, including the Ranis and other female relations as in Manipur there was no concealment of women, could watch the events, while on the other side the road was thronged with spectators. The boatmen had a handsome dress peculiar to the occasion and the boats were canoes hewn out of huge single trees, decorated with colour and carving.' Johnstone, *My Experiences in Manipur*, p. 109.
11. Ibid., pp. 105–7.
12. Grimwood, *My Three Years in Manipur*, pp. 29–30.
13. Johnstone, *My Experiences in Manipur*, p. 92.
14. Grimwood, *My Three Years in Manipur*, p. 50.
15. Ibid., p. 31.
16. Ibid., p. 33.

17. In Gambhir Singh's reign a new palace was built at Langthobal, but deserted in 1844 and in Johnstone's time the buildings were 'picturesque ruins', partially destroyed by the earthquakes of 1869 and 1880. Johnstone, *My Experiences in Manipur*, p. 88.
18. Grimwood, *My Three Years in Manipur*, p. 32.
19. Johnstone, *My Experiences in Manipur*, p. 71.
20. N. Khelchandra Singh, *Documents of Anglo-Manipur War 1891* (Imphal: N. Debendra Singh, 1984), p. 13: Sur Chandra to Quinton, 14 November 1890.
21. Johnstone, *My Experiences in Manipur*, p. 71.
22. Senior Papers D507, p. 5.
23. *Manipur: compiled from the columns of The Pioneer* (Allahabad: Pioneer Press, 1891), p. 80.
24. Johnstone, *My Experiences in Manipur*, p. 72.
25. Grimwood, *My Three Years in Manipur*, p. 27.
26. Betel (areca) nuts, chewed for their mild stimulant.
27. Undated report by Signaller C. Williams, L/MIL/17/18/22.
28. Senior Papers D507, p. 5.
29. During his tenure as political agent, Johnstone reported in 1881 that the Senapati had been sentenced by Maharaja Chandra Kirtee to a year's banishment to an island on the Logtak Lake, and temporary degradation of caste for the severe beatings of three men, one of whom died. Johnstone, *My Experiences in Manipur*, p. 205.
30. Ibid., p. 72. Tikendrajit's mother had been unfaithful to Chandra Kirtee, who used to say that the son was worthy of her.
31. Grimwood, *My Three Years in Manipur*, p. 34.
32. Ibid., p. 39.
33. A short, open-fronted style similar to the uniform worn by the Zouaves, French light-infantry regiments serving normally in French North Africa.
34. Grimwood, *My Three Years in Manipur*, pp. 39–40.
35. Senior Papers D507, p. 6.
36. The name means chief of elephants, Samoo being the Manipuri name for an elephant and Hengeba head or chief.
37. A *dooly* was a sort of palanquin, made of cane, in which dignitaries were carried.
38. Grimwood, *My Three Years in Manipur*, pp. 133–4.
39. Ibid., p. 135.
40. Grimwood, *My Three Years in Manipur*, p. 40.
41. Originally, different groups had settled in Manipur, each with its own *ningthou*, or king, who in 1891 continued to maintain wide-ranging powers within the state. Other important positions were those of the Ayapurel, the officer responsible for the security of the area between the capital and the Burmese border, and the Wangkheirakpa, the second in command to the Senapati. These men, together with the princes, were members of the Top Guard, as were high-ranking military officers. John Parratt and Saroj Nalini Parratt, *Queen Empress vs*

Tikendrajit, Prince of Manipur (New Delhi: Har-Anand Publications/Vikas House, 1992), p. 17.

42. Senior Papers D507, p. 6.
43. Johnstone, *My Experiences in Manipur*, pp. 75–6.
44. Grimwood, *My Three Years in Manipur*, pp. 85–6.
45. Ibid., pp. 86–7.
46. Johnstone, *My Experiences in Manipur*, p. 279.

Chapter 4 The Abdication of Sur Chandra Singh

1. Grimwood, *My Three Years in Manipur*, p. 98.
2. Ibid., pp. 118–19.
3. Ibid., p. 131.
4. It was by no means *infra dig* for Manipuri girls to perform in *nautches*, or dancing displays. Some were daughters of men of the highest caste.
5. Grimwood, *My Three Years in Manipur*, p. 132.
6. Mano Mahun Ghose, *Did the Manipur Princes Obtain a Fair Trial?* (London: William Hutchison and Co., 1891), pp. 114–15.
7. Ghose, *Did the Manipur Princes*, p. 115.
8. Singh, *Documents of Anglo-Manipur War*, p. 16: Sur Chandra to Chief Commissioner of Assam, 14 November 1890.
9. *Pung* literally means 'drum', suggesting that the 'hours' were originally marked by a drumbeat. In Meetei reckoning the 24 hours of the day were divided into eight *yuthaks*: *nongangpung* – daybreak; *yumang* – morning; *numityungba* – midday; *yutung* – afternoon; *yachangpung* – nightfall; *numidang* – before midnight; *nongyaipung* – midnight; *ahing* – after midnight. *Yuthak* is literally 'drink time' – *yu* is rice beer, *thakpa* to drink.
10. Saroj Nalini Parratt, *The Court Chronicle of the Kings of Manipur: the Cheitharon Kumpapa, Vol. 3, 1843–1892* (New Delhi: Foundation Books (CUP India), 2012), p. 261.
11. Singh, *Documents of Anglo-Manipur War*, p. 21: Sur Chandra to Chief Commissioner of Assam, 14 November 1890.
12. Quinton, the son of an Enniskillen wine merchant, was born in 1834 and educated at Trinity College, Dublin. He was appointed to the Bengal Civil Service in 1856 and served in the North-Western Provinces and Oudh until 1875, when he officiated for two years as judicial commissioner in Burma. In 1877 he returned to the North-Western Provinces, where he was appointed Magistrate and Collector of Allahabad District and became an officiating civil and sessions judge in 1878. He later served as commissioner in the Jhansi and Lucknow divisions and in February 1883 was appointed an additional member of the Governor-General's Council, an office which he held in 1884, and again in 1886 and 1889. In October 1889 he was appointed Chief Commissioner of Assam. He was an ardent supporter of the policy of associating Indians more closely with the administration, which was proposed by the Liberal viceroy,

Lord Ripon, and of which the majority of Anglo-Indians strongly disapproved. Katherine Prior, *Oxford Dictionary of National Biography* (Oxford: Oxford University Press, 2004).

13. 'The Manipur Expedition', L/MIL/17/19/33, p. 7.
14. Grimwood, *My Three Years in Manipur*, pp. 140–1.
15. 'The Manipur Expedition', L/MIL/17/19/33, p. 7.
16. Grimwood, *My Three Years in Manipur*, pp. 143–4.
17. Undated memorandum, Sir John Gorst, Under Secretary of State for India, to Lord Cross, Secretary of State for India, L/PS/18/B56.
18. Ghose, *Did the Manipur Princes*, p. 115.
19. Grimwood to Quinton, 25 September 1890, L/MIL/7/15107.
20. S. Parratt, *The Court Chronicle of the Kings of Manipur*, p. 262.
21. Undated memorandum Gorst to Cross, L/PS/18/B56.
22. Ghose, *Did the Manipur Princes*, p. 115.
23. 'The Manipur Expedition', LMIL/17/19/33, p. 8.
24. Singh, *Documents of Anglo-Manipur War*, p. 21: Sur Chandra to Chief Commissioner of Assam, 14 November 1890.
25. 'The Manipur Expedition', LMIL/17/19/33, p. 8.

Chapter 5 The Government of India

1. 'The Manipur Expedition', L/MIL/17/19/33, p. 8.
2. Ibid.
3. Chief Commissioner of Assam to Government of India, 24 September 1890, L/PS/18/B56.
4. Ibid.
5. Grimwood, *My Three Years in Manipur*, pp. 148–9.
6. 'The Manipur Expedition', L/MIL/17/19/33, pp. 8–9.
7. Ibid., p. 9.
8. Chief Commissioner of Assam to Government of India, 9 February 1891, L/PS/18/B56.
9. 'The Manipur Expedition', L/MIL/17/19/33, p. 9.
10. Ibid.
11. Ibid.
12. Lansdowne to Cross, 25 February 1891, Cross Papers E243/30.
13. Lansdowne's less than glittering viceroyalty by no means represented his total public life, which over 50 years included the posts of Under-Secretary for War, Under-Secretary for India, Governor-General of Canada, Secretary of State for War and Foreign Secretary. David Gilmour, *The Ruling Caste: Imperial Lives in the Victorian Raj* (London: John Murray, 2005), p. 63.
14. However Lansdowne did become something of a hero to Congress at the start of his term of office by repudiating an order by the Government of Bengal prohibiting officials from attending its 1890 session. This adulation rapidly disappeared when he took steps to curb sedition in the press and proposed to

dispense with juries in murder trials in Bengal, a move which produced liberal outrage in England and a sharp rebuke from the Secretary of State for India.

15. When entertained by the Indian princes, he felt disgusted at being 'garlanded and smeared with their horrible attar of roses some half dozen times'. Quoted Mark Bence-Jones, *The Viceroys of India* (London: Constable and Co., 1982), p. 15.
16. Cross first came to prominence as home secretary in Disraeli's second government (1874–80), after which in 1903 he caused some consternation by circulating an account of Disraeli's cabinets in an effort to reveal the alleged shallow nature of that prime minister's political vision. Cross may well have found the lack of transparency on the part of the Government of India in the Manipur affair equally distasteful.
17. Cross to Lansdowne, 28 May 1891, Lansdowne Papers D558/4.
18. Ibid.
19. Government of India to Chief Commissioner of Assam, 21 February 1891, L/PS/18/B55.
20. 'The Manipur Expedition', L/MIL/17/19/33, p. 9.
21. Undated memorandum from Gorst to Cross, L/PS/18/B56.

Chapter 6 The Chief Commissioner's Escort

1. Grimwood, *My Three Years in Manipur*, p. 162.
2. Political Agent to Secretary to Chief Commissioner of Assam, 25 September 1890, L/MIL/7/15107.
3. Sur Chandra to Officiating Secretary to Government of India, 9 February 1891, L/MIL/7/15107.
4. Singh, *Documents of Anglo-Manipur War*, p. 21: Sur Chandra to Chief Commissioner of Assam, 14 November 1890.
5. As Tikendrajit, the Senapati, became crown prince when Kula Chandra was recognised as maharaja, the Grimwoods referred to him as the Jubraj. Most other British observers continued to call him the Senapati, and I have therefore used this title throughout the book.
6. Grimwood, *My Three Years in Manipur*, p. 163.
7. Ibid., pp. 160–1. Due to his height, Manipuris apparently called Simpson 'the long sahib'.
8. Grimwood, *My Three Years in Manipur*, p. 166.
9. Sir Henry Collett, born in 1836, was educated at Tonbridge School and Addiscombe Military Seminary. He entered the Bengal Army in 1855, rising through the ranks to become a lieutenant colonel in 1879. In the Second Anglo-Afghan War (1878–80) he acted as quartermaster-general on the staff of Sir Frederick Roberts. He was promoted to colonel in 1884, made a Knight Commander of the Bath in 1891, and from 1892 he commanded the Peshawar district with the rank of major-general. He retired from the army in 1893.

Collett was a keen botanist and at the time of his death in 1901 was working on a book on the flora of Simla.

10. Lieutenant Gurdon was formerly of the Devon Rifles, before joining the Assam Civil Service.
11. Chief Commissioner of Assam to Brigadier-General H. Collett, 8 March 1891, L/MIL/17/18/22.
12. Telegram Collett to Chief Commissioner of Assam, 14 February 1891, L/MIL/17/18/22.
13. Sir George Tomkyns Chesney, born in 1830, was educated at Blundell's School, Tiverton, and Addiscombe, and entered the Bengal Engineers as second lieutenant in 1848. At the outbreak of the Indian Mutiny he joined the Ambala column and was brigade-major of engineers during the siege of Delhi, where he was severely wounded. The originator of the Royal Indian Civil Engineering College at Coopers Hill, Egham, he was also its first president (1871–80). In 1871, he contributed a highly influential story to *Blackwoods Magazine*, 'The Battle of Dorking', a vivid account of a supposed invasion of England by the Germans after their victory over France. From 1881 to 1886, he was Secretary to the Military Department of the Government of India, and Military Member of the Viceroy's Council from 1886 to 1892. He was made a Knight Commander of the Bath in 1890, and left India in 1892. In the same year he was elected to parliament as the Conservative member for Oxford. Sir George died in 1895.
14. Lieutenant Colonel Charles McDowall Skene, was born in about 1844 in Aberdeenshire, a kinsman of the Duke of Fife. He was educated at Addiscombe and joined the 43rd Gurkha Rifles, serving in the North-West Frontier Campaign in 1863. He was present at the forcing of the Ambala Pass in 1874, and joined the Akka Expedition of 1873–4 and the Burmese Expedition of 1886–9. Mentioned in despatches, he was created a Companion of the Distinguished Service Order in 1887 and commanded the Northern Column in the Chin-Lushai Expedition. In March 1891, aged 47, he had just been transferred to the 42nd Gurkha Rifles as commanding officer.
15. Collett to Adjutant-General in India, 31 March 1891, L/MIL/17/18/22.
16. Sir Frederick Roberts, Commander in Chief in India, to General Sir Donald Martin Stewart, 29 April 1891, Roberts Papers A164.
17. Collett to Adjutant-General in India, 31 March 1891, L/MIL/17/18/22.
18. Babu Rassik Lal Kundu to Secretary to Chief Commissioner of Assam, 4 April 1891, L/MIL/17/18/22.
19. 'The Manipur Expedition', L/MIL/17/19/33, pp. 11–12.
20. Ibid., p. 10.
21. *The Times*, 15 December 1891, Reid Papers E278/20.
22. Ibid.
23. Ibid.
24. Gurdon to F. C. Dankes, Secretary to Chief Commissioner of Assam, 9 May 1891, Cross Papers E243/30.
25. *The Times*, 15 December 1891, Reid Papers, E278/20.

26. Ibid.
27. Grimwood, *My Three Years in Manipur*, p. 174.

Chapter 7 The Arrival of the Chief Commissioner

1. Lieutenant C. S. Williams, 12 March 1891, L/MIL/7/15114.
2. *Manipur: compiled from the columns of The Pioneer*, pp. 4–5.
3. Ghose, *Did the Manipur Princes*, p. 117.
4. Report by Butcher, 1 May 1891, L/MIL/17/18/22.
5. Grimwood, *My Three Years in Manipur*, p. 175.
6. S. Parratt, *The Court Chronicle of the Kings of Manipur*, pp. 264. This manner of welcome was the highest honour in the tradition of the Meeteis, the principal ethnic group of Manipur.
7. Grimwood, *My Three Years in Manipur*, p. 179.
8. *Manipur: compiled from the columns of The Pioneer*, p. 7.
9. Grimwood, *My Three Years in Manipur*, p. 182.
10. Ibid., p. 183.
11. Ibid., p. 184.
12. Ghose, *Did the Manipur Princes*, p. 117.
13. Report by Rassik Lal Kundu, 4 April 1891, L/MIL/17/18/22.
14. Regent to Lansdowne, 25 March 1891, L/MIL/17/18/22.
15. Grimwood, *My Three Years in Manipur*, p. 184.
16. Evidence of Boileau, Court of Enquiry, L/MIL/7/15114, p. 13.
17. Report by Lugard, 1 May 1891, L/MIL/17/18/22.
18. Grimwood, *My Three Years in Manipur*, p. 185. The maharaja's band was composed of Nagas, who apparently found English music easy to learn – especially waltzes and other dances.
19. Report by Butcher, 1 May 1891, L/MIL/17/18/22.
20. Grimwood, *My Three Years in Manipur*, p. 187.
21. Regent to Lansdowne, 25 March 1891, L/MIL/17/18/22.
22. Evidence of Rassik Lal Kundu, Court of Enquiry, L/MIL/7/15114, p. 32.
23. Grimwood, *My Three Years in Manipur*, pp. 187–8.
24. Report by Gurdon, 10 April 1891, L/MIL/17/18/22.
25. Evidence of Chatterton, Court of Enquiry, L/MIL/7/15114, p. 23.
26. Grimwood, *My Three Years in Manipur*, pp. 190–1.
27. Report by Boileau, 8 April 1891, L/MIL/17/18/22.
28. Grimwood, *My Three Years in Manipur*, p. 193.
29. 'The Manipur Expedition', L/MIL/17/19/33, p. 12.
30. Ibid., p. 13.
31. The statues bore a remarkable likeness to the Burmese *chinthe*, mythical creatures guarding Buddhist pagodas. J. and S. Parratt, *Queen Empress vs Tikendrajit*, p. 44.
32. 'The Manipur Expedition', L/MIL/17/19/33, p. 13.
33. Report by Lugard, 1 May 1891, L/MIL/17/18/22.

Chapter 8 Hostilities

1. Actual strength: two native officers, two buglers and 100 sepoys, 'The Manipur Expedition', L/MIL/17/19/33, p. 10.
2. Report by Butcher, 1 May 1891, L/MIL/17/18/22.
3. Grimwood, *My Three Years in Manipur*, p. 198.
4. Report of Rassik Lal Kundu, 4 April 1891, L/MIL/17/18/22.
5. Undated report by Calvert, L/MIL/17/18/22. The temple in question was one of a number in the Manipur capital of which James Johnstone had made models to be displayed at the Indian and Colonial Exhibition in South Kensington in 1886.
6. Undated report by Calvert, L/MIL/17/18/22.
7. Evidence of Calvert, Court of Enquiry, L/MIL/7/15114, p. 22.
8. Report by Boileau, 8 April 1891, L/MIL/17/18/22.
9. Singh, *Documents of Anglo-Manipur War*, p. 68.
10. Ibid., p. 69.
11. Ibid., p. 71.
12. Evidence of Chatterton, Court of Enquiry, Gimson Papers E325/9, pp. 37–9.
13. Regent to viceroy, 25 March 1891, L/MIL/17/18/22.
14. Secretary to Chief Commissioner of Assam to Secretary to Government of India, Foreign Dept., 14 May 1891, Gimson Papers, E325/7.
15. Grimwood, *My Three Years in Manipur*, p. 206.
16. Report by Lugard, 1 May 1891, L/MIL/17/18/22.
17. Undated report by Chatterton, L/MIL/17/18/22.
18. Adjutant-General to Secretary to Government of India, Military Dept., 24 June 1891, L/MIL/7/15107.
19. Report by Boileau, 8 April 1891, L/MIL/17/18/22.
20. Report by Gurdon, 10 April 1891, L/MIL/17/18/22.
21. Undated report by Calvert, L/MIL/17/18/22.
22. Evidence by Calvert, Court of Enquiry, Gimson Papers E325/9, p. 32.
23. Adjutant-General to Secretary to Government of India, Military Dept., 24 June 1891, L/MIL/7/15107.
24. Report by Gurdon, 10 April 1891, L/MIL/17/18/22.
25. Senior Papers, D507, p. 12.
26. Evidence of Naick Purun Thapa, Court of Enquiry, Gimson Papers, E325/9.
27. *The Times*, 29 April 1891, Reid Papers, E278/20.
28. Undated report by Calvert, L/MIL/17/18/22.
29. Report by Gurdon, 10 April 1891, L/MIL/17/18/22.
30. Statement of Chatterton at trial of Senapati, Gimson Papers, E325/11.
31. Report by Gurdon, 10 April 1891, L/MIL/17/18/22.
32. Senior Papers, D507, p. 13.
33. Report by Gurdon, 10 April 1891, L/MIL/17/18/22.
34. Adjutant-General to Secretary to Government of India, Military Dept., 24 June 1891, L/MIL/7/15107.
35. Report by Gurdon, 10 April 1891, L/MIL/17/18/22.

Chapter 9 The Retreat

1. Boileau to Officer Commanding 44th Gurkha Rifles, 14 July 1891, L/MIL/17/18/22.
2. Butcher to Officer Commanding 42nd Gurkha Rifles, 3 August 1891, L/MIL/17/18/22.
3. *The Times*, 29 April 1891, Reid Papers, E278/20.
4. Butcher to Officer Commanding 42nd Gurkha Rifles, 3 August 1891, L/MIL/17/18/22.
5. Boileau to Officer Commanding 44nd Gurkha Rifles, 14 July 1891, L/MIL/17/18/22.
6. *The Times*, 29 April 1891, Reid Papers, E278/20. However Chatterton in a telegram to the Adjutant-General in India dated 4 May 1891 stated that 'The enemy did not pursue nor molest us en route.' L/MIL/17/18/22.
7. Report by Gurdon, 10 April 1891, L/MIL/17/18/22.
8. Butcher to Officer Commanding 42nd Gurkha Rifles, 3 August 1891, L/MIL/17/18/22.
9. The local and temporary rank of major-general was conferred upon Brigadier-General Collett during the operations in Manipur. L/MIL/7/15109.
10. Collett to Adjutant-General in India, 3 May 1891, L/MIL/7/15107, p. 183.
11. Grimwood, *My Three Years in Manipur*, p. 241.
12. It was recorded after the revolt that when the alcohol ran out in the citadel the Kukis deserted the royal family. A British officer reported that 'without a skinful [sic] of liquor, the Kukis say, no man can fight'. Assam Administration Report, V/10/99, p. 11.
13. Report by Gurdon, 10 April 1891, L/MIL/17/18/22.
14. Report by Boileau, 8 April 1891, L/MIL/17/18/22.
15. Grimwood, *My Three Years in Manipur*, p. 245.
16. Report by Lugard, 1 May 1891, L/MIL/17/18/22.
17. *The Times*, 29 April 1891, Reid Papers, E278/20.
18. Report by Boileau, 8 April 1891, L/MIL/17/18/22.
19. Grimwood, *My Three Years in Manipur*, p. 243.
20. Report by Lugard, 1 May 1891, L/MIL/17/18/22.
21. Ibid.
22. Report by Boileau, 8 April 1891, L/MIL/17/18/22.
23. Grimwood, *My Three Years in Manipur*, pp. 261–2.
24. Report by Gurdon, 10 April 1891, L/MIL/17/18/22.
25. Report by Cowley, 5 April 1891, L/MIL/17/18/22.
26. Ibid.
27. Collett to Adjutant-General in India, 15 April 1891, L/MIL/17/18/22.
28. Report by Boileau, 8 April 1891, L/MIL/17/18/22.
29. J. and S. Parratt, *Queen Empress vs Tikendrajit*, p. 78.
30. Wright Papers, F174/2287, p. 143.
31. Ibid., p. 146.

32. Ibid., p. 151.
33. Grimwood, *My Three Years in Manipur*, p. 268.

Chapter 10 The Soldier's Account: Lieutenant Charles Grant

1. Grimwood, *My Three Years in Manipur*, p. 159.
2. 'The Manipur Expedition', L/MIL/17/19/33, p. 18.
3. Senior Papers, D507, p. 17.
4. Evidence of Birbal Nagarkoti, Court of Enquiry, L/MIL/7/15114, p. 31.
5. Senior Papers, D507, p. 17.
6. Grimwood, *My Three Years in Manipur*, p. 285.
7. Ibid., p. 287.
8. Report by Grant, 13 April 1891, L/MIL/17/18/22.
9. Grant declared that 'A great reason of our success was the fact of the enemy wearing white coats. Every movement could be seen from afar and anticipated. Their musketry is of course contemptible.' Report by Grant, 13 April 1891, L/MIL/17/18/22.
10. Grimwood, *My Three Years in Manipur*, p. 288.
11. Grant to Civil Officer, Tammu, 3 April 1891, P/4167.
12. Grimwood, *My Three Years in Manipur*, pp. 290–1.
13. Ibid., p. 291.
14. Ibid., p. 293.
15. Ibid., p. 294.
16. Ibid., p. 295.
17. Report by Grant, 13 April 1891, L/MIL/17/18/22.
18. S. Parratt, *The Court Chronicle of the Kings of Manipur*, p. 269.
19. Report by Grant, 13 April 1891, L/MIL/17/18/22.
20. Grimwood, *My Three Years in Manipur*, p. 299.
21. Ibid.
22. Grimwood, *My Three Years in Manipur*, p. 300.
23. Ibid., p. 303.
24. Telegram, Government of India to Graham, 21 April 1891, Lansdowne Papers, D558/32.
25. Sur Chandra to Government of India, Foreign Dept., 20 April 1891, Gimson Papers, E325/7.
26. Telegram, Government of India to Graham, 21 April 1891, Lansdowne Papers, D558/32.
27. S. Parratt, *The Court Chronicle of the Kings of Manipur*, p. 271. 'Nake' means literally 'I will attack'.
28. S. Parratt, *The Court Chronicle of the Kings of Manipur*, p. 272.
29. Grimwood, *My Three Years in Manipur*, p. 306.
30. Singh, *Documents of Anglo-Manipur War*, p. 115.
31. Ibid., p. 116.

32. Grimwood, *My Three Years in Manipur*, p. 307.
33. Ibid., p. 308. This encounter was known as the Battle of Khongjom. Each year, 23 April is still observed in Manipur as Khongjom Day in memory of the courage of the Manipuri forces.
34. *The Times*, 15 August 1891, Reid Papers, E278/20.
35. *The Times*, 11 May 1891, Reid Papers, E278/20.

Chapter 11 The Civilian's Account: Signaller C. Williams

1. Undated report by Williams, L/MIL/17/18/22, p. 1.
2. Ibid., p. 2.
3. Ibid.
4. Ethel recalled the unease felt by the Grimwoods as they watched Melville leave the residency on the afternoon of 23 March, and regretted his insistence upon travelling alone without a guard as in his opinion he was 'not important enough to be captured by the Manipuris'. Grimwood, *My Three Years in Manipur*, p. 189.
5. *The Pioneer*, 15 May 1891. In December 1891, while Major Maxwell, the Political Agent, was on tour, Melville's hands and feet were discovered at Myangkhang and placed with his remains.
6. Political Agent Manipur to Foreign Secretary Simla, 19 July 1891, L/PS/7/369.
7. Undated report by Williams, L/MIL/17/18/22, p. 3.
8. Ibid., pp. 3–4.
9. Ibid., p. 4.
10. Probably the taro, a tropical plant primarily grown as a root vegetable for its edible starchy corm, and also as a leaf vegetable.
11. Undated report by Williams, L/MIL/17/18/22, p. 5.
12. Ibid.
13. Ibid.
14. Ibid., p. 6.
15. Ibid.
16. Ibid.
17. Ibid., pp. 6–7.

Chapter 12 The Three Columns

1. Viceroy to Secretary of State for India, 9 April 1891, L/MIL/7/15107.
2. Senior Papers D507, p. 17.
3. Rassick Lal Kundu to Secretary to Chief Commissioner of Assam, 4 April 1891, L/MIL/17/18/22.
4. Acting Chief Commissioner of Assam to Government of India, Foreign Dept., 21 April 1891, L/MIL/17/18/22.

5. Great mortality occurred among the working elephants for no apparent reason; plenty of natural fodder existed and the animals were not heavily worked.
6. Commissariat, Supply and Transport Report, L/MIL/17/5/1857.
7. *Manipur: compiled from the columns of The Pioneer*, p. 62.
8. Commissariat Transport Arrangements for Manipur Field Force, L/MIL/7/15120.
9. *Manipur: compiled from the columns of The Pioneer*, p. 63.
10. *The Pioneer*, 26 April 1891.
11. Major-General H. Collett to Adjutant-General in India, 2 May 1891, L/MIL/7/15107.
12. Lansdowne to Cross, 8 and 22 April 1891, Cross Papers E243/30.
13. Lt.-Col. R. H. F. Rennick to Quartermaster General, 19 April 1891, L/MIL17/18/22.
14. Commissariat Transport Arrangements for Manipur Field Force, L/MIL/7/15120.
15. Lt.-Col. R. H. F. Rennick to Assistant Adjutant-General, Manipur Field Force, 3 May 1891, L/MIL/7/15107.
16. Maxwell had been born in 1850 in Chittagong.
17. Lansdowne to Cross, 25 October 1891, Cross Papers E243/30.
18. *The Pioneer*, 6 May 1891. The trader, given the title of 'Lionhearted', was subsequently rewarded by a payment of Rs 100, 12 plough cattle, and a grant of 20 acres of land in Manipur rent free for life. Assam Administration Report 1891/2, V/10/99.
19. S. Parratt, *The Court Chronicle of the Kings of Manipur*, p. 274.
20. Evidence of Jatra Sing, Proceedings of Manipur Commission, Gimson Papers E325/11.
21. Lansdowne to Cross, 18 April 1891, Cross Papers E243/30.
22. *The Times*, 29 April 1891, Reid Papers E278/20.
23. Telegram Queen to Lansdowne, 18 April 1891, Cross Papers E243/30.
24. Roberts to Lansdowne, 24 April 1891, Cross Papers E243/30. The desire to avoid the undue suffering of both civilians and troops was demonstrated throughout Roberts' military career. Following his appointment as Colonel-in-Chief of the Empire Troops in France, he discovered on a visit to Ypres that the Indian sepoys lacked winter greatcoats, declined to wear his own, contracted pneumonia and died in St Omer on 14 November 1914.
25. Sir James Willcocks, *The Romance of Soldiering and Sport* (London: Cassell and Co., 1925), p. 78.
26. Secretary to Chief Commissioner of Assam to Secretary to Government of India, Foreign Dept., 3 May 1891, L/MIL/7/15107.
27. Willcocks, *The Romance of Soldiering and Sport*, p. 78.
28. Collett to Adjutant-General, 2 May 1891, L/MIL/7/15107.
29. Maxwell to Collett, 3 July 1891, L/MIL/7/15107. Maxwell stated that he had a Manipuri in his employment who 'thinks picking a Chubb lock an easy matter'.
30. Telegram from Assam, Shillong to Government of India, Foreign Dept., Simla, 11 April 1891, L/MIL/7/15107.

31. Government of India, Foreign Dept., to General Graham, 13 April 1891, L/MIL/7/15107.
32. Ibid.
33. Secretary to Chief Commissioner of Assam to Secretary to Government of India, Foreign Dept., 15 April 1891, L/MIL/7/15107.
34. A hill knife, blade about 18 inches long, narrow at the haft, and square and broad at the tip; pointless and sharpened on one side only, and set in a handle of wood. The fighting *dhao* is differently shaped. It is a long pointless sword, set in a wooden or ebony handle. It is very heavy and a blow of huge power can be given by one of these weapons. Henry Yule and A. C. Burnell, *Hobson–Jobson: A glossary of Anglo-Indian colloquial words and phrases* (London: Routledge and Kegan Paul, 1968), p. 326.
35. *Manipur: compiled from the columns of The Pioneer*, p. 28.
36. Collett to Adjutant-General, 11 May 1891, L/MIL/7/15107.
37. Proceedings of Special Committee assembled at Manipur by order of Collett, L/MIL/17/18/22.
38. Collett to Adjutant-General, 30 April 1891, L/MIL/17/18/22.
39. Addis to Mills, 2 November 1891, Addis Papers SOAS PP MS 14/66.
40. Collett to Adjutant-General, 28 April 1891, L/MIL/17/18/22.
41. The arrest of the Regent was carried out by Angom Nongthou Giridhani, who received a reward of Rs 4,900.
42. *Manipur: compiled from the columns of The Pioneer*, p. 80.
43. Tikendrajit was arrested by Subadar Khelandra Singh, who received a reward of Rs 4,000, and Sipahi Amu Singh, who was given Rs 1,000.
44. Telegram Collett to Secretary to Government of India, Foreign Dept., 24 May 1891, Lansdowne Papers D558/32.
45. Lansdowne to Cross, 10 May 1891, L/MIL/7/15107.
46. The issue recommended by the Principal Medical Officer for 50 British troops, 1,800 native troops and 400 followers was 634 gallons of lime juice, 25,313 lbs preserved potatoes, 12,657 lbs of compressed vegetables and 20,250 lbs of condensed milk. However these rations were deemed unnecessary due to the abundance of local fresh produce available in Manipur. Commissariat General-in-Chief to Secretary to Government of India, Military Dept., 9 May 1891, L/MIL/7/15110.
47. S. Parratt, *The Court Chronicle of the Kings of Manipur*, p. 276.
48. *The Pioneer*, 25 May 1891.
49. Commissariat Transport Arrangements for Manipur Field Force, L/MIL/7/15120.
50. The Meeteis were the majority ethnic group of Manipur.
51. S. Parratt, *The Court Chronicle of the Kings of Manipur*, pp. 274–5.
52. This suggestion was later overruled by the Government of India.
53. Report by Capt. R. F. Allen RE, 22 May 1891, L/MIL/7/15107.
54. Johnstone, *My Experiences in Manipur*, p. 281.

Chapter 13 The Court of Enquiry

1. *The Statesman*, 3 June 1891.
2. J. and S. Parratt, *Queen Empress vs Tikendrajit*, p. 105.
3. Telegram Cross to Lansdowne, 9 May 1891, Lansdowne Papers D558/8.
4. Adjutant-General to Secretary to Government of India, Military Dept., 24 June 1891, L/MIL/7/15107.
5. Ibid.
6. Ibid.
7. *Manipur: compiled from the columns of The Pioneer*, p. 83.
8. Adjutant-General to Secretary to Government of India, Military Dept., 24 June 1891, L/MIL/7/15107.
9. Ibid.
10. Evidence of Native Troops, Court of Enquiry, P/4167, pp. 450–9.
11. Evidence of Chatterton, Court of Enquiry, Gimson Papers E325/9, pp. 37–9.
12. Evidence of Lugard, Court of Enquiry, Gimson Papers E325/9, p. 30.
13. Telegram from Adjutant-General in India to General Officer Commanding Manipur Field Force, 11 July 1891, L/MIL/17/18/22.
14. Despatch from Military Dept., 19 November 1891, L/MIL/7/15114.
15. Secretary to Government of India, Military Dept., to Adjutant-General in India, 11 August 1891, L/MIL/17/18/22.
16. Boileau to Officer Commanding 44th Gurkha Rifles, 14 July 1891, L/MIL/17/18/22.
17. Secretary of State for India to Viceroy, 19 November 1891, L/MIL/7/15114.
18. India Office to Boileau, 7 December 1921, L/MIL/7/15114.
19. Col. D. W. Boileau to Sir Robert Reid, 6 July 1962, Reid Papers E278/20.
20. Adjutant-General Manipur Field Force to Officer Commanding 42nd Gurkha Rifles, 11 July 1891, L/MIL/17/18/22.
21. Evidence of Butcher, Court of Enquiry, Gimson Papers E325/9, p. 24.
22. Butcher to Officer Commanding 42nd Gurkha Rifles, 3 August 1891, L/MIL/17/18/22.
23. Lansdowne to Cross, 25 August 1891, L/MIL/17/18/22.
24. Secretary of State for India to Viceroy, 19 November 1891, L/MIL/7/15114.
25. Adjutant-General in India to Secretary to Government of India, Military Dept., 10 October 1891, L/MIL/7/15119.
26. Undated Butcher to Secretary of State for India, L/MIL/7/15119.
27. War Office to Government of India, 15 February 1894, L/MIL/7/15119.
28. Lugard died in 1957 aged 91. He served in the Boer War, retired from the army and became political assistant to the High Commissioner of Northern Nigeria. He was recalled to Europe in 1915, and after a year with the Machine Gun Corps served in a Naval Intelligence Unit. Obituary, *The Times*, 5 January 1957.
29. Adjutant-General in India to Secretary to Government of India, Military Dept., 15 August 1891, L/MIL/17/18/22.
30. *The Bengalee*, 20 June 1891.

Chapter 14 Reaction at Home

1. *The Times*, 6 April 1891, Reid Papers E278/20.
2. Letter from Sir James Johnstone, *The Times*, 6 April 1891, Reid Papers E278/20. Johnstone remained firm in the conviction that 'he who retreats before an Asiatic is doomed'.
3. *The Times*, 6 April 1891, Reid Papers E278/20.
4. Letter from Sir James Johnstone, *The Times*, 10 April 1891, Reid Papers E278/20.
5. Ibid.
6. Ibid.
7. Ibid. Johnstone made an offer to return to Manipur in 1891 as political agent, however this was not rapturously received. The Viceroy's Council expressed the opinion that it was 'not favourably inclined to consider the suggestion of selecting a retired officer to manage the matter'. S. C. Bayley to Cross, 12 August 1891, L/PS/8/12.
8. Letter from Sir George Campbell, *The Times*, 11 April 1891, Reid Papers E278/20.
9. Telegrams Cross to Lansdowne, Lansdowne to Cross, 8/9 May 1891, Lansdowne Papers D558/8.
10. *The Times*, 29 April 1891, Reid Papers E278/20.
11. Letter, 2 April 1891, from Ethel Grimwood, *The Times*, 29 April 1891, Reid Papers E278/20.
12. Cross to Lansdowne, 1 May 1891, Lansdowne Papers D558/4.
13. Sir William Hunter (1840–1900), a member of the Indian Civil Service, was an historian and statistician who in 1869 was asked by the viceroy, Lord Mayo, to submit a scheme for a comprehensive statistical survey of British India. This gigantic project resulted in the publication of *The Imperial Gazetteer of India* in nine volumes in 1881. In 1882, as a member of the Governor-General's Council, Hunter presided over the Commission on Indian Education, and in 1886 was elected vice-chancellor of the University of Calcutta. In the course of his retirement he became vice-president of the Royal Asiatic Society.
14. Letter from Sir William Hunter, *The Times*, 5 May 1891, Reid Papers E278/20.
15. *The Times*, 16 May 1891, Reid Papers E278/20.
16. Roberts to General Sir Donald Martin Stewart, 3 May 1891, Roberts Papers A164.
17. Sir Richard Temple was lieutenant-governor of Bengal 1874–6 and governor of Bombay 1877–80.
18. Sir Richard Temple, speech in House of Commons, 16 June 1891, Temple Papers F86/289.
19. Lansdowne to Cross, 23 June 1891, Cross Papers E243/30.
20. The case of the prince of the Punjab, Duleep Singh, deposed by the British following the second Sikh War in 1849, was observed with some sympathy, as was that of Malharro, gaekwar of Baroda, who was removed in 1875 on somewhat dubious grounds following the inconclusive evidence of a British-

based commission set up to assess the ruler's involvement in attempts to poison the Baroda Resident.

21. *The Times*, 19 May 1891, Reid Papers E278/20.
22. *The Times*, 17 June 1891, Reid Papers, E278/20.
23. Gorst was apparently suffering from an attack of gout at the time.
24. Letter from Sir George Chesney, *The Times*, 20 June 1891, Reid Papers E278/20.
25. Nana Sahib, born in 1824, was one of the Indian leaders of the 1857 Mutiny, and allegedly responsible for anti-British atrocities. As the adopted son of the Maratha Peshwa Baji Rao II, his goal was to restore the Maratha Confederacy.
26. Letter from Sir George Chesney, *The Times*, 20 June 1891, Reid Papers, E278/20.
27. *The Times*, 23 June 1891, Reid Papers E278/20.
28. G. E. Buckle, ed., *Letters of Queen Victoria 3rd Series, Vol. 2* (London: John Murray, 1931): telegrams Queen to Lansdowne, 8 and 20 April 1891.
29. Buckle, *Letters of Queen Victoria*: memorandum by Queen, 2 May 1891.
30. Cross to Lansdowne, 15 October 1891, Lansdowne Papers D558/4.
31. In October 1896 the Munshi wrote a minute declaring that 'There is well known a great amount of unhappiness among the Princes of the Native States of India arising from their being so subject to and under the control of Political Agents. These agents have raised themselves to such a height of power that they act as if they themselves were the head of the States ... and as if nothing could be done privately or publicly unless it was sanctioned and approved by them ... Thus it is that the agents are more comfortably and richly placed than "the" Princes themselves.' Minute by Munshi Abdul Karim, October 1896, L/PS/8/61.
32. Cross to Lansdowne, 15 October 1891, Lansdowne Papers D558/4.
33. Buckle, *Letters of Queen Victoria*: Lansdowne to Queen, 16 April 1891. James Johnstone was particularly scathing of the casual system of appointing political officers in Manipur, declaring that 'no pains seem to have been at any time taken to find a suitable man; if one happened to be appointed, it was a matter of chance, and the post seems generally to have been put up to a kind of Dutch auction.' Johnstone, *My Experiences in Manipur*, p. 273. There was also considerable criticism of the current habit of employing civilian rather than military officers on Indian frontiers where a forceful presence was required. See letter from Thomas H. Lewin, retired deputy-commissioner of the Chittagong Hill Tracts, to *The Times*, 2 April 1891.
34. Buckle, *Letters of Queen Victoria*: Lansdowne to Queen, 13 May 1891.
35. Buckle, *Letters of Queen Victoria*: Lansdowne to Queen, 22 June 1891.
36. Buckle, *Letters of Queen Victoria*: Queen to Lansdowne, 27 May 1891.
37. Buckle, *Letters of Queen Victoria*: Lansdowne to Queen, 22 June 1891.
38. Buckle, *Letters of Queen Victoria*: Cross to Queen, 30 May 1891.
39. Buckle, *Letters of Queen Victoria*: Queen's Journal, 1 July 1891.
40. Buckle, *Letters of Queen Victoria*: Telegram Queen to Cross, 16 June 1891.

Chapter 15 The Trial of the Princes

1. Niranjan, formerly of the 34th Gurkhas, worked as a guard attached to the British Residency in Manipur for some time, but later joined the Manipur army after being appointed a *subadar* by Tikendrajit.
2. Senior Papers D507, p. 15.
3. Trial of Thangal General, Gimson Papers E325/10.
4. Ibid.
5. James Johnstone to the end was convinced that Thangal General was 'in no way a willing accessory to the rebellion, that he in no way connived at the invitation to our officers to enter the palace at night, and further that he never suggested or consented to their murder!' The Senapati in his opinion was the '*fons et origo*' of the rebellion. Johnstone, *My Experiences in Manipur*, p. 280.
6. Michell, said to be 'decidedly good looking', was apparently 'a great favourite with the ladies to whom, however, he is rather sparing of his favours'. Sir Charles Stewart Addis to Dudley Mills, 2 November 1891, Addis Papers SOAS PP MS 14/66.
7. Lt. Col. St John Michell to Sir H. M. Durand, 14 August 1891, Ardagh Papers NA PRO 30/40/12/3.
8. Ghose, *Did the Manipur Princes*: Evidence of 3rd Witness for Prosecution, Girdhari Sing, pp. 11–12.
9. Ghose, *Did the Manipur Princes*: Summary of Facts, p. 12.
10. Ibid.: Evidence of 6th Witness for Prosecution, p. 12.
11. Ibid.: Summary of Facts, pp. 12–13.
12. The witnesses called by the defence stated that Tikendrajit opposed the suggestion made by Thangal General until, unwell, he went to sleep.
13. Ghose, *Did the Manipur Princes*: Summary of Facts, p. 13.
14. Ghose, the first Indian barrister to practise in the Calcutta High Court, was notable for his contribution towards women's education. Despite his espousal of nationalism, his anglicised habits often made him a target of ridicule in Calcutta. David Kopf, *The Brahmo Samaj and the Shaping of the Modern Indian Mind* (Princeton: Princeton University Press, 1979), pp. 96–7.
15. Cross assured the Queen that the Indian Penal Code was not used as it was more severe on the question of aiding and abetting murder than English law. Cross to Lansdowne, 1 August 1891, Cross Papers E243/37. However, Lansdowne revealed a healthy disregard for either English or Indian legal procedure, declaring that 'the only question we have to decide on is whether, beyond all reasonable doubt, he [the Senapati] was responsible for the murders without reference to the technical definition of abetment to be found either in Indian or English law'. Lansdowne to Cross, 3 September 1891, Cross Papers E243/37.
16. Ghose, *Did the Manipur Princes*: Memorandum of Arguments, pp. 3–5.
17. The method of trial was peculiar in that the court first heard the evidence for the prosecution before stating the charges against the prisoner and receiving his plea. J. and S. Parratt, *Queen Empress vs Tikendrajit*, p. 134.
18. Ghose, *Did the Manipur Princes*: Memorandum of Arguments, pp. 3–5.

19. Ibid.: The Defence of Tikendrajit Sing, pp. 113–14.
20. Ibid.
21. Ibid.: Result of the Evidence, p. 39.
22. Ibid.: Written Statement of the Accused in the English Language, pp. 53–5.
23. Ibid.: Result of the Evidence, pp. 39–40.
24. Ibid.: Omissions on the Part of the Accused, p. 47.
25. Ibid.: The Defence of Tikendrajit Sing, p. 113.
26. Ibid.: The Defence of Tikendrajit Sing, p. 115.
27. Ibid.: Illness of the Accused, pp. 49–50.
28. Ibid.: The Actual Offenders not Punished, p. 51.
29. Ibid.: Conclusion, p. 58.
30. Lansdowne to Cross, 14 July 1891, Cross Papers E243/30.
31. However, the evidence of Butcher and Chatterton appears to confirm that the British did not fire first. Both men testified to the strict orders given to the officers in command that British troops were not to fire unless fired upon.
32. Ghose, *Did the Manipur Princes*: Evidence of Manipur Being an Asiatic Power in Alliance, pp. 21–4. A resolution by the Government of India published in the *Gazette of India* made it crystal clear that 'The principles of international law have no bearing upon the relations between the Government of India as representing the Queen-Empress on the one hand and the native States under the suzerainty of Her Majesty on the other. The paramount supremacy of the former presupposes and implies subordination of the latter in the exercise of their high prerogative.' Quoted *The Times*, 18 September 1891.
33. Trial of Kula Chandra, Gimson Papers E325/12.
34. Ibid.
35. Lt. Col. Alban Wilson of the 44th Gurkhas, who had travelled up the Brahmaputra to Nigriting as a member of the relief force, reported that a young Irish doctor, who went to attend the regent for a pain in the toe, prescribed 'a good dose of Epsom salts or a "number nine" pill which his patient refused to take, believing that it was poison. On this the doctor gave him a cuff on the head and came away. It is not often a king gets his ears boxed for refusing to take a purgative.' Wilson, *Sport and Service in Assam*, p. 39.
36. Telegram Secretary to Government of India, Foreign Dept., to Major-General H. Collett, 10 August 1891, L/MIL/7/15107, p. 51.
37. Buckle, *Letters of Queen Victoria*: telegram Queen to Cross, 1 August 1891.
38. Ibid.: Queen to Sir Henry Ponsonby, 8 August 1891.
39. In a letter of 14 July 1891 to Cross, Lansdowne had made it patently clear that were the sentence of death in this case to be overruled by the Home Government, suggesting injustice on the part of the Government of India, it would have a catastrophic effect on the 'public mind' in India. Lansdowne to Cross, 14 July 1891, Cross Papers E243/30.
40. Buckle, *Letters of Queen Victoria*: Cross to Queen, 9 August 1891.
41. Ibid.: Queen to Cross, 11 August 1891.
42. Ibid.: Telegram Lansdowne to Queen, 12 August 1891.

43. Ibid.: Lansdowne to Queen, 18 August 1891.
44. *Amrita Bazar Patrika*, 19 August 1891.
45. The *Manipur Court Chronicle* reported that a meteorite fell on the day of the executions.
46. Wilson, *Sport and Service in Assam*, pp. 40–1.

Chapter 16 The Aftermath

1. *The Times*, 27 May 1891, Reid Papers E278/20.
2. Report of Proceedings by Secretary to Government of India, Military Dept., 7 July 1891, L/MIL/7/15111.
3. *The Times*, 4 June 1892, Reid Papers E278/20.
4. The historian John William Kaye declared that 'the countries to the East of the Bay of Bengal, were the grave of fame', and James Johnstone bemoaned the fact that not even a clasp, let alone a medal, was given to those who participated in the Naga Hills Campaign of 1879–80. Johnstone, *My Experiences in Manipur*, p. 181.
5. Lord Stanhope, Secretary of State for War, considered it 'extremely inadvisable' to grant a medal for the Manipur operations, as it had 'never been the practice of the English army to commemorate a disaster'. War Office to Under-Secretary of State for India, 2 November 1891, L/MIL/7/15117.
6. Viceroy's Council to Cross, 27 January 1892, L/MIL/7/15117.
7. Lansdowne to Cross, 30 December 1891, Cross Papers E243/30.
8. Cross to Lansdowne, 2 July 1891, L/MIL/7/10945. Ethel was given £330 from the Bengal Civil Fund in compensation for loss of property. In Manipur, Maxwell assessed the belongings of the Grimwoods which had not been destroyed, including five horses, diamonds, silverware, guns and photographic equipment. He auctioned what he could recover and sent the proceeds to be added to the insurance payment.
9. Lansdowne to Cross, 14 July 1891, Cross Papers E243/30.
10. Prince Bhairabjit Sing alias Pecca Sing to Sir H. Mortimer Durand, secretary to Government of India, Foreign Dept., June 1891, Ardagh Papers NA PRO 30/40/12/3.
11. Petition from relatives, servants and subjects of Maharaj Kula Chandra Dhwaja Singh and Jubaraj Tekendrajit Bir Singh of Manipur to Viceroy, 26 June 1891, Ardagh Papers NA PRO 30/40/12/3.
12. It was suggested that a scandal was caused in Shillong by Ethel's relations with her half-brother, Captain Boisragon of the Royal Irish Regiment. Undated secret memorandum by Col. J. C. Ardagh, 'Mrs. Grimwood and Manipur', Ardagh Papers NA PRO 30/40/12/3.
13. Petition from relatives, servants and subjects of Maharaj Kula Chandra Dhwaja Singh and Jubaraj Tekendrajit Bir Singh of Manipur to Viceroy, 26 June 1891, Ardagh Papers NA PRO 30/40/12/3.

14. Undated secret memorandum by Col. J. C. Ardagh, 'Mrs. Grimwood and Manipur', Ardagh Papers NA PRO 30/40/12/3.
15. Lansdowne to Cross, 30 June 1891, Cross Papers E243/30.
16. Elliott to Lansdowne, 11 May 1891, Cross Papers E243/30.
17. Undated secret memorandum by Col. J. C. Ardagh, 'Mrs. Grimwood and Manipur', Ardagh Papers NA PRO 30/40/12/3.
18. It was never established whether or not Ethel alerted the Senapati to the British plan to arrest him.
19. Lansdowne to Cross, 1 September 1891, Cross Papers E243/30.
20. For a more detailed account of Ethel's life, see Belinda Morse, *Calamity and Courage: A Heroine of the Raj* (Brighton: Book Guild Publishing, 2008).
21. *The Wykehamist*, July 1891,Winchester College Archives.
22. See L/MIL/7/12266.
23. Cross to Lansdowne, 2 July 1891, L/MIL/7/10945.
24. *The Times* obituary of 13 April 1891 stated that Melville was 'a most capable official, zealous and untiring in his work'. He had just completed an absence of five years, and was intending to spend the following summer in Scotland.
25. Mrs Melville to Cross, 6 July 1891, and Godley (under-secretary of state for India, 1883–1909) to Mrs Melville, 28 January 1892, L/MIL/7/10945.
26. Cross to Lansdowne, 5 November 1891, L/MIL/7/10946.
27. Obituary in *The Times*, 15 June 1895.
28. Lansdowne to Cross, 15 April 1891, Cross Papers E243/30.
29. Lansdowne to Cross, 30 June 1891, Cross Papers, E243/30.
30. Johnstone much regretted that the main line of succession in Manipur had been severed after three generations of rulers loyal to Britain. Johnstone, *My Experiences in Manipur*, p. 282.
31. S. Parratt, *The Court Chronicle of the Kings of Manipur*, p. 278.
32. Lansdowne to Cross, 15 September 1891, Cross Papers E243/30.
33. Michell to Sir H. M. Durand, 14 August 1891, Ardagh Papers NA PRO 30/40/12/3.
34. *The Gazette of India*, 22 August 1891, Cross Papers E243/30.
35. A secret Government of India memorandum of November 1891 expressed the predictable view that Sur Chandra's son was 'too near his majority' and too much 'under the influence of old tradition', such as Pucca Senna, to be a great asset to the British. Government of India Secret Memorandum, 13 November 1891, L/PS/7/361.
36. Assam Administration Report, V/10/99, p. 9.
37. Ibid.
38. The 'black water' was the open sea, across which a Hindu would risk defilement through contact with foreigners.
39. Assam Administration Report 1891/92, V/10/99, p. 10.
40. *The Times*, 14 September 1891, Reid Papers E278/20.
41. Ibid
42. Ibid.

43. Maxwell to Secretary to Chief Commissioner of Assam, 13 May 1892, L/PS/7/370.
44. Maxwell was appointed Companion of the Star of India in 1892, and died in 1928.
45. Michell, president of the court during the trial of the princes, was particularly upset by the fact that 'We entered a healthy happy country and in our train followed the cholera. Whole villages were swept by it.' Addis to Mills, 2 November 1891, Addis Papers SOAS PP MS 14/66.
46. S. Parratt, *The Court Chronicle of the Kings of Manipur*, p. 277.
47. Assam Administration Report 1891/2, V/10/99, p. 8.
48. Maxwell to Chief Commissioner of Assam, September 1892, L/PS/7/370.
49. Assam Administration Report 1891/2, V/10/99, p. 10.
50. Assam Administration Report 1891/2, V/10/99, p. 11.
51. Manipur Administration Report 1895/6, V/10/1577.
52. Summary of viceroyalty of Lord Curzon, V/27/230/54.
53. Johnstone, *My Experiences in Manipur*, p. vii.
54. Curzon to Hamilton, 21 November 1901, Curzon Papers, F111, Vol. 160.

BIBLIOGRAPHY

PRIMARY SOURCES

A. UNPUBLISHED SOURCES

1. PRIVATE PAPERS

BRITISH LIBRARY ASIAN AND AFRICAN STUDIES

Cross Papers	MSS Eur E243
Curzon Papers	MSS Eur F111
Gimson Papers	MSS Eur E325
Lansdowne Papers	MSS Eur D558
Reid Papers	MSS Eur E278
Roberts Papers	MSS Eur A164
Senior Papers	MSS Eur D507
Temple Papers	MSS Eur F86
Wright Papers	MSS Eur F174/2287

SCHOOL OF ORIENTAL AND AFRICAN STUDIES

Addis Papers	PP MS 14/66

NATIONAL ARCHIVES

Ardagh Papers	PRO 30/40/12/3

2. *OFFICIAL PAPERS*
BRITISH LIBRARY ASIAN AND AFRICAN STUDIES

Military Department

L/MIL/17/5/1 – L/MIL/17/5/2420
L/MIL/17/6 – L/MIL/17/20
L/MIL/7/9717 – L/MIL/7/13089
L/MIL/7/13206 – L/MIL/7/16623

Proceedings and Consultations of the Government of India

P/0191/22 – Z/P/1748

Political and Secret Department

L/PS/7 – L/PS/10
L/PS/16 – L/PS/19

Crown Representative Records

R/1/2 – R/1/36

B. PUBLISHED SOURCES

BRITISH LIBRARY ASIAN AND AFRICAN STUDIES

Newspapers

The Pioneer (Allahabad) 1874–1931 Microfilm MC 1101
The Statesman (Calcutta) Microfilm MC 1136

Official Publications

V/10/1 – V/10/2154
V/27/213 – V/27/311

SECONDARY SOURCES

Books

Aitchison, C.U., *A Collection of Treaties, Engagements and Sanads, relating to India and neighbouring countries* (Calcutta: Superintendent of Government Printing, 1909).
Allen, Charles, *Kipling Sahib* (London: Little, Brown and Co., 2007).
Barker, George M., *A Tea Planter's Life in Assam* (London: Thacker Spink & Co., 1884).
Bence-Jones, Mark, *The Viceroys of India* (London: Constable and Co., 1982).
Buckle, G.E. (ed.), *Letters of Queen Victoria, 3rd Series, Vol. 2* (London: John Murray, 1931).

Cotton, Sir Henry, *Indian and Home Memories* (London: T. Fisher Unwin, 1911).
Creagh Coen, T., *The Indian Political Service: A Study in Indirect Rule* (London: Chatto and Windus, 1971).
Dena, Lal, *British Policy towards Manipur* (Imphal: Author, 1984).
Dun, E. W., *Gazeteer of Manipur* (New Delhi: Vivek Publishing House, 1975).
Forrest, G.W., *The Administration of the Marquess of Lansdowne as Viceroy and Governor-General of India, 1888–1894* (Calcutta: Superintendent of Government Printing, 1894).
Ghose, Mano Mahun, *Did the Manipur Princes Obtain a Fair Trial?* (London: William Hutchison and Co., 1891).
Gilmour, David, *The Ruling Caste: Imperial Lives in the Victorian Raj* (London: John Murray, 2005).
Grimwood, Ethel, *My Three Years in Manipur and Escape from the Recent Mutiny* (London: Richard Bentley and Son, 1891).
Hartley, J.H. (ed.), *Three Years in Cachar* (London: S.W. Partridge & Co., 1895).
Hodson, Thomas Callan, *The Naga Tribes of Manipur* (London: Macmillan and Co., 1911).
James, Lawrence, *Raj: The Making and Unmaking of British India* (London: Little, Brown and Co., 1997).
Johnstone, Major-General Sir James, *My Experiences in Manipur and the Naga Hills* (London: Sampson Low, 1896).
Jyotirmoy, Roy, *History of Manipur* (Calcutta: Firma KLM, 1999).
Kabui, Gangmumei, *History of Manipur* (New Delhi: National Publishing House, 1991).
Kingdon-Ward, F., *Plant Hunter in Manipur* (London: Jonathan Cape, 1952).
Kopf, David, *The Brahmo Samaj and the Shaping of the Modern Indian Mind* (Princeton: Princeton University Press, 1979).
List of Ruling Princes, Chiefs and Leading Personages (Delhi: Manager of Publications, 1934).
Manipur: compiled from the columns of The Pioneer (Allahabad: Pioneer Press, 1891).
Misra, J.P., *The Administration of India under Lord Lansdowne (1888–1894)* (New Delhi: Sterling, 1975).
Morse, Belinda, *Calamity and Courage: A Heroine of the Raj* (Brighton: Book Guild Publishing, 2008).
Parratt, John and Saroj Nalini Parratt, *Queen Empress vs Tikendrajit, Prince of Manipur* (New Delhi: Har-Anand Publications/Vikas House, 1992).
Parratt, Saroj Nalini, *The Religion of Manipur* (Calcutta: Firma KLM, 1980).
———, *The Pleasing of the Gods* (New Delhi: Vikas, 1997).
———, *The Court Chronicle of the Kings of Manipur: the Cheitharon Kumpapa, Vol. 3, 1843–1892* (New Delhi: Foundation Books (CUP India), 2012).
Reid, Sir Robert, *History of the Frontier Areas bordering on Assam 1883–1941* (Shillong: Assam Government Press, 1942).
Riddick, John F., *Who was who in British India* (London: Greenwood Press, 1998).
Roberts, of Kandahar, Lord, *Forty-one Years in India* (London: Richard Bentley, 1897).
Singh, N. Khelchandra, *The Battle of Khongjom* (Imphal: Author, 1984).
———, *Documents of Anglo-Manipur War 1891* (Imphal: N. Debendra Singh, 1984).

Willcocks, Sir James, *The Romance of Soldiering and Sport* (London: Cassell and Co., 1925).

Wilson, James Alban, *Sport and Service in Assam and Elsewhere* (London: Hutchinson & Co., 1924).

Yule, Henry and A.C. Burnell, *Hobson–Jobson: A glossary of Anglo-Indian colloquial words and phrases* (London: Routledge and Kegan Paul, 1968).

INDEX